LEARNING FROM THE CHILDREN

New Directions in Anthropology

General Editor: **Jacqueline Waldren**, *Institute of Social Anthropology, University of Oxford*

Volume 1 *Coping with Tourists: European Reactions to Mass Tourism*
Edited by Jeremy Boissevain

Volume 2 *A Sentimental Economy: Commodity and Community in Rural Ireland*
Carles Salazar

Volume 3 *Insiders and Outsiders: Paradise and Reality in Mallorca*
Jacqueline Waldren

Volume 4 *The Hegemonic Male: Masculinity in a Portuguese Town*
Miguel Vale de Almeida

Volume 5 *Communities of Faith: Sectarianism, Identity, and Social Change on a Danish Island*
Andrew S. Buckser

Volume 6 *After Socialism: Land Reform and Rural Social Change in Eastern Europe*
Edited by Ray Abrahams

Volume 7 *Immigrants and Bureaucrats: Ethiopians in an Israeli Absorption Center*
Esther Hertzog

Volume 8 *A Venetian Island: Environment, History and Change in Burano*
Lidia Sciama

Volume 9 *Recalling the Belgian Congo: Conversations and Introspection*
Marie-Bénédicte Dembour

Volume 10 *Mastering Soldiers: Conflict, Emotions, and the Enemy in an Israeli Military Unit*
Eyal Ben-Ari

Volume 11 *The Great Immigration: Russian Jews in Israel*
Dina Siegel

Volume 12 *Morals of Legitimacy: Between Agency and System*
Edited by Italo Pardo

Volume 13 *Academic Anthropology and the Museum: Back to the Future*
Edited by Mary Bouquet

Volume 14 *Simulated Dreams: Israeli Youth and Virtual Zionism*
Haim Hazan

Volume 15 *Defiance and Compliance: Negotiating Gender in Low-Income Cairo*
Heba Aziz Morsi El-Kholy

Volume 16 *Troubles with Turtles: Cultural Understandings of the Environment on a Greek Island*
Dimitrios Theodossopoulos

Volume 17 *Rebordering the Mediterranean: Boundaries and Citizenship in Southern Europe*
Liliana Suarez-Navaz

Volume 18 *The Bounded Field: Localism and Local Identity in an Italian Alpine Valley*
Jaro Stacul

Volume 19 *Foundations of National Identity: From Catalonia to Europe*
Josep Llobera

Volume 20 *Bodies of Evidence: Burial, Memory and the Recovery of Missing Persons in Cyprus*
Paul Sant Cassia

Volume 21 *Who Owns the Past? The Politics of Time in a 'Model' Bulgarian Village*
Deema Kaneff

Volume 22 *An Earth-Colored Sea: 'Race,' Culture and the Politics of Identity in the Postcolonial Portuguese-Speaking World*
Miguel Vale De Almeida

Volume 23 *Science, Magic and Religion: The Ritual Process of Museum Magic*
Edited by Mary Bouquet and Nuno Porto

Volume 24 *Crossing European Boundaries: Beyond Conventional Geographical Categories*
Edited by Jaro Stacul, Christina Moutsou and Helen Kopnina

Volume 25 *Documenting Transnational Migration: Jordanian Men Working and Studying in Europe, Asia and North America*
Richard Antoum

Volume 26 *Le Malaise Créole: Ethnic Identity in Mauritius*
Rosabelle Boswell

Volume 27 *Nursing Stories: Life and Death in a German Hospice*
Nicholas Eschenbruch

Volume 28 *Inclusionary Rhetoric/Exclusionary Practices: Left-wing Politics and Migrants in Italy*
Davide Però

Volume 29 *The Nomads of Mykonos: Performing Liminalities in a 'Queer' Space*
Pola Bousiou

Volume 30 *Transnational Families, Migration and Gender: Moroccan and Filipino Women in Bologna and Barcelona*
Elisabetta Zontini

Volume 31 *Envisioning Eden: Mobilizing Imaginaries in Tourism and Beyond*
Noel B. Salazar

Volume 32 *Tourism, Magic and Modernity: Cultivating the Human Garden*
David Picard

Volume 33 *Diasporic Generations: Memory, Politics, and Nation among Cubans in Spain*
Mette Louise Berg

Volume 34 *Great Expectations: Imagination, Anticipation and Enchantment in Tourism*
Jonathan Skinner and Dimitrios Theodossopoulos

Volume 35 *Learning from the Children: Childhood, Culture and Identity in a Changing World*
Jacqueline Waldren and Ignacy-Marek Kaminski

LEARNING FROM THE CHILDREN

Childhood, Culture and Identity in a Changing World

Edited by
Jacqueline Waldren and Ignacy-Marek Kaminski

Berghahn Books
New York • Oxford

First published in 2012 by
Berghahn Books
www.berghahnbooks.com

Library of Congress Cataloging-in-Publication Data

Learning from the children : childhood, culture and identity in a changing world / edited by
Jacqueline Waldren and Ignacy-Marek Kaminski. – 1st ed.
   p. cm. Includes bibliographical references and index.
   ISBN 978-0-85745-325-9 (hardback : alk. paper) – ISBN 978-0-85745-326-6 (ebook)
   1. Childhood–Cross-cultural studies. 2. Child psychology–Cross-cultural studies. 3.
Child development–Cross-cultural studies. 4. Parenting–Cross-cultural studies. I. Waldren,
Jacqueline, 1937– II. Kaminski, Ignacy-Marek.
   GN482.L43 2012 305.23–dc23

                                                                                    2011046667

British Library Cataloguing in Publication Data

A catalogue record for this book is available from the British Library

Printed in the United States on acid-free paper.

ISBN 978-0-85745-325-9 (hardback)
ISBN 978-0-85745-326-6 (ebook)

Contents

❧

List of Illustrations   vii

Acknowledgements   ix

Preface   xi

Introduction   1
 Jacqueline Waldren and Ignacy-Marek Kaminski

Part I. CHANGING NORMS

1. Invisible Routes, Invisible Lives: The Multiple Worlds of Runaway
 and Missing Women and Girls in Upper Sindh, Pakistan   19
 Nafisa Shah

2. Education, Tradition and Modernization: Bedouin Girls in Israel   35
 Sarab Abu-Rabia-Queder

Part II. LISTENING AND LEARNING

3. More than One Rung on the Career Ladder: Examining Barriers
 to the Labour Market for Young Women Living in Poverty   53
 Lucy Russell and Louisa Darian

4. 'We're Not Poor – The Others Are': Talking with Children
 about Poverty and Social Exclusion in Milton Keynes, England   70
 Anna Lærke

5. Dancing with an Angel: What I Have Learnt from My
 'Special Needs' Daughter, Elisa   83
 Elsa L. Dawson

Contents

6. Being Parented? Children and Young People's Engagement
with Parenting Activities   92
Julie Seymour and Sally McNamee

Part III. CROSS-CULTURAL MOBILITY

7. Children's Moving Stories: How the Children of British
Lifestyle Migrants Cope with Super-Diversity   111
Karen O'Reilly

8. Children Negotiating Identity in Mallorca   126
Jacqueline Waldren

9. Identity without Birthright: Negotiating Children's Citizenship
and Identity in Cross-Cultural Bureaucracy   146
Ignacy-Marek Kaminski

10. Doing Fieldwork with Children in Japan   170
Roger Goodman

Notes on Contributors   179

Index   183

LIST OF ILLUSTRATIONS

5.1. Elisa with her Mum at WOMAD festival.   84

5.2. Elisa has fun at Towersey Folk Festival.   89

9.1. Akane-Liv Okamoto-Kaminski wearing her Polish National Dress in the family Tokyo home, 1982.   149

9.2. Akane-Liv and Ken-Stanislaw preparing for their first Swedish Midsummer celebrations, Stockholm 1986.   162

10.1. Children as young as six walk to and from school every day carrying all of their equipment for the day with them.   171

10.2. Parents regularly attend classes to watch what their children are doing and how they are taught.   172

10.3. All children, whatever their musical or theatrical talents or instincts, must participate in regular public performances in front of parents and other children.   176

ACKNOWLEDGEMENTS

❦

We would like to thank our contributors, members of the International Gender Studies Centre (IGS) at Queen Elizabeth House, Oxford University, and the many people who attended these seminars and offered valuable comments. Not all the speakers were able to contribute chapters due to other commitments and we acknowledge the input of Paula Heinonen, on Street Children, whose book *Youth Gangs and Street Children* was published in 2011 (Berghahn Books). We were delighted that Roger Goodman agreed to revise and update his article from *St Antony's College Record* 2004 and Sarab Abu Rabia her chapter from the *British Journal of Social Education*. We were able to access the fine research done by the children's study unit at QEH from which we have gained insights and we greatly appreciate comments by Barbara Harriss-White and Deborah Bryceson who very patiently read some of the chapters. Thanks also to IGS and Linacre College, Oxford University, for granting Kaminski a Visiting Senior Fellowship during the period of the seminars and while working on this book (2007–2012). We are also grateful to readers, reviewers and staff at Berghahn Books for their comments and support.

PREFACE

The discipline of childhood studies has revolutionized the study of children and demanded that they be looked at as important subjects in their own right (Montgomery 2001, James 2007). This book developed from a seminar series for International Gender Studies at Queen Elizabeth House Development Centre, Oxford University. The theme of the seminar, 'What Have We Done to the Children?', evolved from conversations between the editors of this volume, Kaminski and Waldren, concerning the experiences of bringing up children in transnational circumstances. Kaminski's Polish–Japanese children, one born in Sweden and the other in Japan, were subject to various forms of discrimination and identity readjustments as they lived and studied in Japan, the UK, Sweden and Poland. Waldren's children, born in Spain to American parents, also experienced adaptation and identity problems but insist they are 'at home in Spain', and say 'We grew up in this culture'.

We invited contributions from anthropologists, community workers, sociologists and development consultants to gain varied cross-cultural approaches to identity, childhood, youth, education, poverty and disability. An important aspect of the chosen chapters is the direct involvement of the researchers as parents, teachers, subjects and policy makers and the voices they offer of children and young people. The authors argue that cultural values regarding the meaning of children, parenting, gender, family and belonging vary greatly, and notions of the child, childhood, youth and identity alter across time and space. Our title for the seminar series was meant to be rhetorical and the issues broadened more widely, drawing in global concerns involving the exploitation of children in forced marriage, kidnapping, honour killings, the sex trade and poverty. Once the question was posed, there was no end to the possible discussions.

Perhaps in most situations children are perceived to be dependent on their parents. However, our experience, the studies we present here and much that we had read (Mead 1929, Boyden and Levison 2000, James 2007, Montgomery 2008) suggested that children in these complex social dynamics were not passive recipients nor infantilized mere receptors of environmental stimuli or of adult culture and ideas but rather social actors. As our materials illustrate, a child may choose to reshape her/his social role while actually performing it, and parents may only realize its consequences later. The growing contrast between the values and behaviour of young people and adult parents is certainly connected with the speed of social change. In a static view of the meaning of 'adult', it is often much harder for adults to change their views to meet new circumstances than it is for children. Continuous learning by adults begins to blur the boundaries between life stages but it would go a long way towards bridging what has been called the 'generation gap' (Mitterauer 1992: 240). The drawing together of thresholds that were previously strongly differentiated according to gender or age is certainly one of the most evident changes in the social history of childhood. Parents and children have very different roles and relationships in the contemporary world of rapidly changing mobilities and technology. As Signe Howell notes in her book on adoption, 'moving children from one sociocultural, geographical and national reality to another has wide social and political implications' (2006: xi). Children live in and negotiate worlds they create themselves (play, peer groups or games) as well as worlds others create for them and worlds in concert with others (their families, neighbourhoods and public spaces) (James 2007).

References

Boyden, J. and D. Levison 2000. Children and Social Actors in the Development Process. Working Paper 2000:1, Expert Group on Development Issues, Ministry for Foreign Affairs, Stockholm, Sweden.

Howell, S. 2006. *Kinning Strangers*. Oxford and New York: Berghahn Books.

James, A. 2007. 'Giving Voice to Children's Voices: Practices and Problems', *American Anthropologist*, 109 (2): 261–72.

Mead, M. 1929. *Coming of Age in Samoa*. New York: New American Library.

Mitterauer, M. 1992. *A History of Youth*. Oxford: Blackwell.

Montgomery, H. 2008. *An Introduction to Childhood: Anthropological Perspectives on Children's Lives*. Oxford: Wiley-Blackwell.

INTRODUCTION

Jacqueline Waldren and Ignacy-Marek Kaminski

'I ain't a child, and I shan't be a woman 'til I'm twenty, but I'm past eight, I am'[1]

Children, teens, and youth are some of the categories used to describe phases of growing into adulthood. Anthropologists resist universal definitions of children and childhood, recognizing the socio-cultural differences in children's lives around the world. Childhood can be said to be fabricated, invented or constructed in the sense that ideas and practices associated with positive child development are not the same around the world or even within a single society (Shweder 2009: xxviii).

Adults once assumed children everywhere represented something weak and helpless, in need of protection, supervision, training, models, skills, beliefs, education (Mead and Wolfenstein 1955: 7). This approach is no longer accepted. Families, like local communities, are undergoing socio-cultural and educational transitions faster than ever before. Transnationalism, multi-cultural education, technology and globalization affect neighbourhoods and offer children lifestyle choices their parents were never prepared for (Westin et al. 2009). Are parents and teachers ready to have their roles redefined by children and youths' rapidly changing desires and needs? If so, what are the common cultural and social mechanisms that both the state, children and parents can benefit from in an increasingly interdependent global community? The studies here tackle these issues and give us concrete examples of *Learning from the Children* in diverse contexts.

Before the advent of fieldwork, British anthropologists examined the nature of human society and the child, like the savage or primitive, stood in opposition to the rational, male world of European and North American civilization (Montgomery 2008). An inherent part of the colonization mission in Africa, Oceania and the Americas in the nineteenth century was the 'civilization' of the children of the 'savages'. Children were regarded as relatively easy to influence, and it was thought they could be instrumental in civilizing 'the rest', that is the adult population and society at large. 'The idea of civilizing through children has continued with the development of mass schooling systems and various other child-focused development projects' (Valentin and Meinert 2009: 23).[2]

Sociologists argued that 'the child as a social role and childhood as a social category separate from adults' began to develop in eighteenth-century Britain among the nobility. They were concerned that the social, emotional and physical growth of children as members of society were properly inculcated (Mitterauer 1992: 135). As a result, from 1880 to 1920 childhood was increasingly formulated in what might be called pediatric and pedagogical terms: new and radical ideas about the family, women and child rearing. Children were to be raised 'scientifically' instead of by custom. By the 1930s childhood was an established topic in ethnographic description, often in the context of kinship or ritual, education or socialization. 'The "child" as a person was rarely at the centre of transactions – the impact on a child's identity varied with the goals of adults. An heir is acquired, a bride promised, a worker provided – interests focused on giver and recipient and a child maintained social, economic and political relationships between adults' (LeVine 2007: 248).

The differentiation and specialization of age groups was associated with the emergence of the school as a place of moral training separate from the home. Before this period children were more integrated into the world of adults. New educational theories argued that concerns for an appropriate moral environment for children required new attitudes towards parental responsibilities. The importance of privacy and domesticity for the nurturing of the child was encouraged (Mitterauer 1992). Children were considered to be innocent and needed protection from adult society in order to be prepared for maturity at a later stage. This is a very western perspective on childhood and this book will add needed cross-cultural understandings to childhood in wider contexts.

Anthropologists have long been sensitive to the significance of liminal positions and persons and their potential to enhance, disrupt or threaten ordered relations. Despite much criticism, Margaret Mead's book, *Coming of Age in Samoa* (1928), placed children on the anthropological agenda. It soon became clear that the lives of children, their voices and concerns needed expression in a direct manner rather than always through adult representations of them. This required taking children seriously as both research subjects and as analysts of their own lives and circumstances (Scheper-Hughes 1992).

However, the methodological challenges of conducting in-depth qualitative research on children's and parents' perceptions of their lives, of social inclusion or exclusion, cultural adaptations, and the myriad of complex negotiations sometimes practised is daunting. The anthropologist is made self-conscious, critical and reflexive about her encounters and the possible power relations involved. The papers here led us to reassess our seminar title, 'What Have We Done to the Children?', to reflect the highly complex and dynamic processes involved in cognition and behaviour and re-balance the social power dynamics and value judgements embedded in the previous title. We felt 'Learning from the Children' was a more provocative description of the interdependence between parents, children and the ethnographer. As Toren (1990) notes, 'Children inevitably differentiate themselves from their parents and, in so doing, they establish historically specific forms of social relations that will manifest at once both cultural continuity and cultural change'. Shirin Gamarudi (2010) quotes an Iranian school teacher's response to contemporary childhood in Iran:

> When I was small, it was the time of patriarchy and the father's words; when I grew up and got married, it was the turn for wife dominance over me and the time of matriarchy; in hope of practicing dominance over my offspring, I had a child but Alas! It was time for him to rule. I doubt if there comes a time when I will be ruling.

The child was for the first time made the exclusive subject of an international human rights treaty with the adoption of The United Nations Convention on the Rights of the Child (UNCRC 1989).[3] This was a pivotal event for children worldwide that developed policies based on three main principles: protection from discrimination based on race, colour, sex, religion, national origin or other status; the principle that the best interests of the child must be a primary consideration in all actions concerning them; and the principle ensuring, to the maximum extent possible, the survival and development of the child (Shweder 2009: 516).

However, the UNCRC definition of a child is 'a person under 18'. This clumps children together as a category irrespective of class or culture and disempowers them (James 2007: 262). One wonders if the West is fully competent to set standards for 'the child's best interests' internationally or if 'all children should have rights' is agreed everywhere? The 'children' in the studies here range from pre-birth to 30 years of age. Definitions of the terms include age, agency, development, roles and responsibilities. If a girl can be married at 11 or a son or daughter still lives at home at 30, there are some conflicting notions of the stages composing these categories. Should childhood perhaps be a self-defined concept, as Heather Montgomery asked, citing a 13-year-old 'child' who is a mother, 'No I am not a child'.[4] Childhood is an ever-changing artifact – not simply a biological stage of life. Komulainen suggests:

> we need as researchers to become more aware of how children's voices are constantly constrained and shaped by multiple factors such as our own assumptions about children, our particular use of language, the institutional contexts in which we operate and the overall ideological and discursive climates which prevail. (2007: 23)

Today, children's position in societies around the world is seen to be more precarious with wider awareness of early marriage, exploitation, domestic violence, poverty and war, and they have become increasingly important in social policy issues. Childhood studies brought children's views and perspectives into focus. It became clear that children were not only victims but also perpetrators. We hope to add insights to the discussion of the concept 'child', which has been a socially and historically shaped interpretation of anatomic elements and physiological processes (Mitterauer 1992: 13). As Shweder (2009) notes, 'Any particular definition of the beginning and end of childhood is somewhat arbitrary and it is impossible to specify boundaries of life stages from all possible cultural and historical perspectives'. In the following studies we see 'childhood' change from one context to another, and this process now needs to be understood relatively, subjectively and multidimensionally in cross-cultural contexts. The contextualized approach to the study of children avoids both essentializing and universalizing traps that have long affected what we say about children, their identities, roles and behaviour.

A discourse on social inclusion and exclusion within developed as well as developing countries has drawn attention to various ways democratic societies are impoverished when voices of different gender, age or lack of economic resources are excluded. The children's voices that appear in our texts are context specific and do not speak about 'children' in general or 'the child' in abstract . As James notes, 'giving voice to children is not just about letting children speak; it is about exploring the unique contribution to our understanding of and theorizing about the social world that children's perspectives can provide' (2007: 264).

Based on a number of qualitative studies, this book offers insights into the lives, education and cultural identities of children and youth in Britain, Japan, Spain, Israel/Palestine, Sweden and Pakistan. Attention is focused on the social-power dynamics involved in child–adult relations from children's own perspectives and reveals agencies, power dynamics, interdependencies and the dilemmas of policy, planning and parenting in a changing world.

The transmission of social and cultural practices from parent to child is changing with advances in technology, mobility and globalization. Children have increasingly come to the forefront as culture makers and not just as extensions of adults. With knowledge and imagination they overcome confines of family, religion, poverty, traditions, state or national boundaries and devise strategies to cope with or improve their circumstances. Montgomery recognized that 'It is important to remember that some children continue to hope, dream and work their way out of poverty or desperation in which they find themselves' (2001: 12). These themes resonate in the voice of Emmanuel Mathias, one of 3,500 street children from Dar es Salaam, whose self-narrated and self-illustrated stories were made available by Kasia Parham (2008) through the Internet and the Dogodogo Project. 'I had been in a dark room, searching for a way out. But then I found a door; that door was Dogodogo. No one opened it for me. I opened it myself' (Mathias, cited in Cambridge Outlook 2009).[5]

The need for a broader cross-cultural understanding of childhood (as exemplified by the chapters in this book), and a need for reconceptualization of children as active participants in their own lives (as suggested by Montgomery et al. 2003) are as vital as securing the children's rights to communicate their changing needs to the other children and international policy makers at large. The Internet is increasingly allowing even the most socially vulnerable children living in the borderlands of global economies to communicate their individual needs directly and instantly (and frequently without the interference or even knowledge of adults). As these fast accelerating processes will continue to generate new dynamics in relations between children and adults, we may need to continue re-adjusting and to broaden our fieldwork methodologies accordingly.

In these studies, children and young adults are the active agents of change and adults are learning from them. The social and cultural practices that are being transmitted (and re-transmitted) across family networks are often as intricate as the changing life realities that both children and their parents have to cope with. These rapidly changing family dynamics may affect generational ties and family roles at first, and generate changes in our social fabric and state legislation later; or as the contributions to this volume suggest, these changes can take place at several levels simultaneously.

The importance of gender resonates through all of the chapters. Gendered studies reveal women as social actors and the need to place them in theories of behaviour, culture and society. The same applies to children. At first, it may seem that the majority of chapters are explicitly focusing on girls and women as social and cultural actors. However, the two opening chapters (by Shah and Abu-Rabia-Queder) are structured around the women's inter-relations with men as fathers, brothers, sons and husbands. While the young develop strategies to overcome restrictive traditions, older generations are concerned about the new responsibilities placed on youth and try to make meaning out of the changing norms of female and male relationships. The chapters in Part II provide examples of how these complex female/male inter-relations are manifested in different socio-cultural and economic systems. Those in Part III are narrated by globally active anthropologists, fathers and mothers. They not only reflect on their offspring's impact on reshaping their parental roles in various social and cultural contexts, but also focus on the changing socio-legal environments that change the parental role and increasingly turn the child and the parents into active agents of change.

Part I. Traditional Norms and Quiet Revolt

We begin Part I with Shah who shares her experience as Mayor of Sindh district in Pakistan and the systematic incidence of honour killings in that tribal region. Her research shows that the rigid notions of childhood and adulthood may become irrelevant as categories when gendered division constructs women as children with respect to men and girls as sexual adults. 'Husbands refer to their wife and children collectively as *bare*, a Sindhi word meaning "children"'. However, 'when it comes to their sexual role, women are adults at the age of eleven, an age considered to belong to childhood in the western legal system'. Shah concludes that though the systems of marriage and concepts of honour both turn women and girls into cultural children in relation to men, the act of running away constructs women and girls as social actors, capable of transforming their future, thereby reversing their roles as 'cultural and societal minors' in the custody of men. She also reveals the conflict between domestic law and constitutional law in prosecuting perpetrators or providing protection, medical and legal assistance for run-away victims of gender-based violence.

Abu-Rabia-Queder in Chapter 2, like Shah, examines the rigidity of tribal notions of honour and modernity that have prevented Bedouin girls from entering social space on equal terms with men. Abu-Rabia-Queder focuses on the plight of young Bedouin girls in the Negev region of Israel who are dropping out of school due to conflict between the Israeli Institute's perception of modernity (which promotes co-education) and Bedouin traditions that remain the cultural ethos of the girls' fathers. Her study reveals the modernizer's lack of consideration for local feminine codes and a lack of gender sensitivity with regard to hierarchal relationships in non-western societies. Abu-Rabia-Queder uses extensive quotations from her field interviews to reveal that 'the planner's ignorance of local cultural codes only created a greater control over the Bedouin women, who became more restricted by Bedouin men'. Thus the girls and women essentially become the victims of this modernizing process.

Both the less-educated families and the educated families believe strongly in the importance of keeping their daughters honoured in public, and acknowledge the forbidden romantic relationships between the two sexes in school. However, the educated girls, with the support and trust of both parents, are able to manage in the co-educational framework, embedding their traditional values in the modern space. This reflected a sort of quiet revolt against traditional norms and the young women who succeeded in attending the schools assumed pride in creating trust and confidence from their parents, whereas the dropout girls and their parents perceive the co-educational school as a dangerous place and are threatened by the possibility of the bad rumours that attending such a school could arouse. The fathers of these girls do not believe their daughters could both attend a mixed school and maintain their honour. In other words, both groups are unwilling to surrender feminine traditions of honour, but the educated families found ways to embed this tradition within the modern space of the mixed schools, while the families of the dropouts perceive that space as an unacceptable danger to their daughter's honour. Abu-Rabia-Queder suggests that 'the best solution is not to change the space already dominated by men, but to grant women their own separate, but equal spaces'. In her role as educated Bedouin woman, she was able to gain access to these family dynamics and the girls' confidence in ways that might not have been possible for non-Bedouin investigators.

In both of these studies some young women are shown to be neither passive recipients nor infantilized mere receptors of adult culture and power, inventing strategies that both maintain traditional values and allow for moderate change.[6] These studies agree with Cornwall's (1994) distinction between 'strategies' and 'tactics', and makes it clear that young women's struggles for survival or success are waged in domains where their positions as agents are relational, situational and, above all, provisional. As members of families, their abilities to make active, purposive, choices are constantly reconfigured in relation to others. Young women experience tensions between autonomy and connectedness throughout their lives and as they develop possess vulnerability and agency (LeVine 2007).

Part II. Social Policies and Current Realities

Global promises of international rights for children contrast with current realities. Chapters 3–6 deal with the interpretation of children's and young persons' rights in Britain and reveal how British young women and men are redefining the meanings of poverty, exclusion and inclusion (Russell and Darian, Lærke), disability (Dawson), exploitation and socialization (Seymour and McNamee).

Lucy Russell and Louisa Darian's chapter, based on their YWCA project work, 2004–8, among impoverished young women aged 11–30 in Britain, acknowledges that many ways to combat socio-cultural and economic exclusion among young women have been tried and failed. They found that as the UK became more multicultural, young ethnic minority women have subsequently become even more exposed to social and cultural exclusion in contemporary Britain. They suggest that a more community-oriented social policy is urgently needed and the YWCA 'More than One Rung' campaign has successfully challenged British governments' flawed social policies and offers practical solutions for routes out of poverty. Their plan promotes support and training for young women in ways that mobilize their personal and ethnic resources, challenge gender and cultural stereotypes, and most importantly lead to employment through paid apprenticeship recognizing that the co-ordination of political and business community's support for apprenticeship programmes is vital as work must be financially beneficial to be sustainable. However, they also note the inequalities in pay for women and men in many levels of employment which undermine young women's income-generating potential.

Gaynor Cohen, a retired anthropologist, made some interesting observations after attending Russell and Darian's seminar. Drawing on her extensive research and social policy publications in 1980s Britain (Cohen 1987) and her past involvement in equal opportunity education for 14–18-year-olds, Cohen discussed her advisory work with the unique mobilization project for British youth TVEI (Technical, Vocational Education Initiative) and reflected on how government-funded programmes focusing on young women in the UK have evolved during the past thirty years. She argued that there were less than expected 'social returns' from the governmental programmes she had participated in and those, thirty years on, examined by Russell and Darian. In fact, she found the goals for gender advancement to be less today than in the 1980s. These comments highlight the lapse in policy makers' understanding that various social meanings are given to males and females in a wide range of ethnographic settings and these gender constructs continue to effect a person's identity, access to knowledge, power and claim to resources.

In Chapter 4, Lærke discusses what it means to be 'impoverished' or 'poor' in Milton Keynes, and finds the emphasis put by government on young people's inclusion in the labour market particularly disadvantages single mothers with young children. She points out that any long-term, secure and decently paid employment is out of the reach of many parents who, forced by the notorious lack of state-funded childcare for the under fives, have spent years outside paid employment or further education. Lærke, who used a 'reflexive participant observation method' to conduct an independent qualitative evaluation of the Children's

Fund services in Milton Keynes (2005–2008) found that for both child and adult service users poverty and social exclusion are seen as 'problems faced by others' rather than themselves. She argues 'The fundamental approach to poverty – as manifest in social policy formulations as well as in Milton Keynes residents' views – is one that avoids explicating poverty as a collective problem to be understood in sociological terms. It is an approach that emphasizes the individual's unique "pathway out of exclusion"'.

Lærke's study of children as dynamic agents, who learn culture and society in interaction with other children and with adults, includes the children's understandings of gender and poverty in contrast to that of adults and policy makers. Lærke reflects on her anthropologically collected field data among the impoverished and/or excluded children and their families in terms of her own experience as a single mother (and a social researcher). Her reflexive method resonates with earlier works documented by other anthropological researchers.[7]

The birth of children whose bodies differ from the expected is, as Rayna Rapp and Faye Ginsburg (2001: 536) point out, an important occasion for meaning making. A growing ethnographic literature explores the social processes by which the personhood of disabled children is questioned, negotiated or asserted (Gammeltoft 2008). This literature focuses on the way in which parents come to reject or embrace children whose bodies differ from the norm by being weak or sickly (Scheper-Hughes 1992). Chapter 5 by Dawson adds a reflexive literary essay on the experience of a working mother and consultant who found herself learning parenting from her severely handicapped child. Their home in a British village community represents a model microcosm of society responding to what the protagonists of the social model of disability have identified as 'society's' failure to provide appropriate services and adequately ensure the needs of disabled people are fully taken into account in its social organization (Oliver 1990). Dawson describes the manner in which her daughter can live out her unique capacity for enjoying the moment to its full, without any fear of being considered out of place or inappropriate in this sensitive village setting. Disability here is presented through the experience of mother and daughter in different ways, at different times and different social settings and reveals the 'fluid interdependency of culture, structural and individual issues in a disabled person's life' (Corker and Davis 2001: 19–20). Dawson wonders if 'maybe I am guilty of trying to "normalize" her, but "normal" covers so many variations that it is almost meaningless in a multi-cultural, multi-ability society'. This is a unique insight into reciprocal caring experienced by society, a mother and her daughter. Dawson tells us: 'Of all the years of advice I have received on how to parent my daughter, one of the most memorable was to follow her lead, her unpredictable movements and laughter.'

These chapters also highlight how ethnicity, youth and gender clearly compound poverty or disability and remain largely unnoticed or unrecognized by the majority of policies. Despite the evidence that children should become increasingly important in social policy issues as their position in society is seen to become more precarious with conflict, divorce, domestic violence, single parenting, migration or poverty, social policies continue to propose programmes that repeat the mistakes of the past and often ignore the empirical studies of anthropologists and sociologists in the field.

In Chapter 6, Seymour and McNamee argue that, while parenting is a growing area of policy intervention in the UK, the research focus on children separate from the family's daily reality may lead to a partial view and inadequate social policies. They therefore suggest that the policy-oriented research should examine parents and children's views together as this will elucidate more clearly the realities of everyday life. Without this, parenting practices and children's roles within families cannot be properly understood. Seymour and McNamee's work recognizes the power differentials which operate in adult–child and indeed child–child relationships but seeks to explore what Katz (1994) has referred to as the 'spaces of betweenness' where children are able to employ personal strategies or resistances to influence parenting practices (as we see in Chapters 1 and 2 here).

This chapter contributes to a more nuanced approach to the social study of childhood employing Katz's concept to examine the way in which children acknowledge, work with and manipulate the power dynamics that exist between them and their parents. However, in order to fully explore these power dynamics, the authors consider it necessary to reiterate earlier calls for research on children to refocus on other players in the interaction and to re-situate children within their families (and other institutions). In order to develop and widen the research agenda on the social study of childhood, what may (apparently paradoxically) be required is that parents' and children's views are heard together. However, in practice, children being given the opportunity to make decisions means that adults must give over their power, or at least submit to children's priorities – which they may find difficult. James suggests the voice of the child holds rhetorical power and the researcher has to be aware of whose point is being made: that of the children, the anthropologist or the parents (Hockey and James 2003: 5).

Human Rights?

Humanity as a global fact is subject to critique. Human rights state that every man, woman and child has a right to such things as security, freedom and dignity, regardless of their race, gender, religion or beliefs. A UN General Assembly Resolution in October 2002 set out 'a joint commitment and issued an urgent, universal appeal to give every child a better future', stating among other things that 'The achievement of goals for children, particularly for girls, will be advanced if women fully enjoy all human rights and fundamental freedoms, including the right to development, are empowered to participate fully and equally in all spheres of society and are protected and free from all violence, abuse and discrimination'. However, Montgomery et al. make it clear that 'while a broad measure of agreement can be achieved about what constitutes children's needs and their well-being, any definition is necessarily rooted in time and culture' (2003: 2). The chapters here show that beliefs about childhood vary between different cultures, societies and historic periods, particularly in terms of the kinds of care, play and learning conditions that are considered 'good' for children as well as the goals of socialization, development and education.

However positive such human rights claims may sound, the reality of children's experiences discussed in these papers reveals unimagined inequalities, political pressures, economic and social involvements worldwide. As anthropologists we recognize the inherent dynamism of culture and its diversity and asymmetrical power relations. Regardless of the international conventions ratified by the UN, there is a substantial gap between the meanings of childhood and protection of children in various societies and cultures. There seems to be a universal tendency to identify and evaluate children and childhood not on their own terms but relative to the adult members of society. Ensuring children's rights means reconceptualizing children as active participants in their own lives (Montgomery et al. 2003: 217). The chapters here make it clear that there is no shared concept of childhood within or across societies. Through these anthropological and sociological discussions about the individual and society, structure and agency, we may gain some insights into diverse meanings and practices in the inter-relationships between parents, children, mobility, education, inclusion, exclusion, gender and identity that reveal some shifts in power from adults to children.

Part III. Identity, Mobility and Childhood

Structures established by the European Network of Ombudsmen for Children (ENOC) in 24 countries of the 47 member states of the Council of Europe are particularly active in protecting the rights of children with migrant backgrounds. In Sweden, for example, early implementation of bureaucratic action for children's rights was based on the ideal of a homogeneous society and the state undermined the security previously provided by families. Changing the ideal into social practice became more difficult when one out of four families had immigrant backgrounds. Though double citizenship (as discussed here in Chapter 9 by Kaminski) is becoming an option in increasing numbers of countries, the number of children born as stateless remains high even in economically advanced countries (e.g. the US, Japan and Spain). Two common ways of recognizing citizenship are *jus sanguinis* (right of blood: if your parents are citizens, you acquire citizenship) and *jus soli* (right of the soil means that you acquire citizenship if you are born within the country). However, neither applies if parents have different nationalities, only the father's nationality counts or nationality is only provisional until the 'child' comes of age and can choose. Anthropologists are in a position to explore these relationships and, as previously noted (Arhem 1994), they have long been sensitive to the significance of liminal positions and persons and their potential to enhance, disrupt or threaten ordered relations.

Chapters 7–10 reveal how children of expatriate parents in Spain (O'Reilly, Waldren) and Japan (Kaminski, Goodman) are seen to be altering their parents' lifestyle choices. In all of these chapters, children and young adults are negotiating new identities, interpreting new cultures and taking on roles once reserved for adults. As these cultural processes, adult/child dynamics and needs change, so must the approaches of academics and policy makers. O'Reilly, Waldren, Kaminski and Goodman suggest that children living with their parents in a second or third culture from that of the parents often find themselves in an ambiguous set of circumstances.

Movement involves change and bringing up children in 'foreign' countries and the diverse experience of transnational children and their parents has recently become an important area of research not only in anthropology but equally in educational studies.[8] As Goodman notes, 'Although I have been teaching and researching at all levels of Japan's educational and child welfare system for the past twenty years, seeing the system through the eyes of a parent has significantly altered my perception of it'. Multiple aplications of new technologies introduced into classrooms, changing teaching approaches, ages and stages of learning as well as the possible real and visual variations in mobility of students impact on concepts of schooling and education. What Goodman surprisingly had learned from his children was that against his initial expectations (based on his earliest studies of anthropological literature), his children's biggest challenge was not adjustment to the competitive pressure of Japanese schooling and mastering of a new language, but their re-adjustment to the English educational system that they and their parents were so familiar with.

In many ways parents in the developed world live their lives through their children: protecting them from unseen perils, structuring their work lives around school hours, helping with homework, organizing after-school activities, and planning for their futures. This child-centred focus from parents, teachers and researchers gives the children multiple modes of personal expression.

Waldren's study of children negotiating identity in Mallorca also sees children subjected to new forms of language, social and educational requirements adapting to their new environments more readily than their parents. In both Japan and Mallorca, the children's experience of being able to walk to school gives them a new independence. The children in these chapters are also highly technologically literate. They interact directly with others in a virtual world that has few boundaries, and parents find it increasingly difficut to mediate their interactions. These chapters make it clear that any engagement with children by parents, teachers or policy makers requires understanding them as dynamic, 'social actors', seeking their views, facilitating their roles and their decision making, to learn from them, engage with them and grow with them as circumstances change. Mothers or grandparents can help children read but the children often teach them to use a mouse, an iPod or a DVD player.

O'Reilly reflects on these issues in the Costa de Sol, Spain, where many British children are living with and internalizing the contradictions that mark their parents' lives. While their parents want to remain permanently in Spain, their children are not well integrated. Many children have been to Spanish schools but, uncomfortable with Spanish culture and social life, opted for international schools. O'Reilly's research finds contradictory trends among expat children: while 'their North-European postcolonial habitus demonstrates some antipathy towards the local Spanish', this is also 'mediated by a class habitus that perceives the Spanish in the school as "different" and better' (p. 123). These chapters illustrate that transnational migration, rather than being a homogeneous system, encompasses a wide range of different and situationally varied practices.

The research here is socially situated in a variety of places and changing circumstances, some personal and subjective yet derived from observation, participation and lived experience. While the contributors' personal involvement may provide new research insights into a wide span of complex issues and real-life situations involving both societies, parents and children, we recognize that it is also an emotionally and methodologically challenging experience for the researchers themselves. Signe Howell, writing about adoption and identity in her book *Kinning of Foreigners*, captured these concerns when she reflected on her own personal and professional experiences in these 'anthropological borderlands' and found them a source of strength: 'I have, at times, become more emotionally involved than I am accustomed to as an anthropologist, and this has made it necessary to exercise a high degree of reflexivity. The empathy that I experienced with the anxieties and happiness of the couples that I studied has, I am convinced, proved a strength rather than a weakness' (2006: xii). Many of our authors report similar experiences. Anthropologists (Callaway and Okely 1992, MacClancy and McDonough 1996, James and Prout 1999) consider how issues in their personal and academic life impinge on their research process and the authors here reflexively consider their positions as parents as well as ethnographers. Auto-ethnography of fieldwork is about lived interactions, experiences and embodied knowledge and aids in dismantling the positivist, neutral, impersonal accounts of the past. The anthropologist is made self-conscious, critical and reflexive about her/his encounters and the possible power relations involved in this kind of child-centred research.

Children as Social Actors

James and Prout (1999: ix) made it clear that

> The traditional consignment of childhood to the margins of social science or its primary location within the fields of developmental psychology and education has begun to change: it is much more common to find acknowledgement that childhood should be regarded as an important part of society and culture than a precursor to it; and that children should be seen as social actors not beings in the process of becoming such.

Research on childhood has advanced since then and we hope the studies here add to the insights and understanding of children's lived experience, their ideas about the world and themselves, and their relations to peers, adults and the wider realms they inhabit. Boyden and Levinson (2000: 1) stress that 'Achieving a widespread recognition and successful implementation of child centred policy ultimately depends on extended social discourse and action that incorporates all major interested parties'. Fundamental issues such as ending traditional forms of discrimination against girls and children with disabilities and children's participation in social decisions are some of the requirements needed in order to arrive at socially supportable solutions.

These chapters reveal the processes of identity formation and changing parent–child relations in Britain, Spain, Israel/Palestine, Sweden, Japan and Pakistan. This clearly involves a constant struggle within the individual, family, peer groups, traditional value systems, social and political perspectives that are not easily overcome. However, they illustrate how children acknowledge, work with and negotiate across the power dynamics which may exist between them and their parents, and often teach their parents and societies about the changing worlds they share and the new communication technologies they frequently use to link their family past and genealogies with rapidly accelerating globalization.

Notes

1. This quotation from Mayhew's *London Labour and the London Poor* (1861–62) poignantly illustrates a street child's concept of indeterminate age and the editors' difficulties in defining childhood and youth other than in each context.
2. This process is more fully examined in Valentin and Meinert (2009).
3. The UNCRC goes far beyond the rudimentary rights set out in the 1924 Declaration of Human Rights by providing children with a comprehensive and detailed range of entitlements.
4. Seminar given in the Fertility and Reproduction Series at Oxford University Institute of Social and Cultural Anthropology, 8 November 2010.
5. *Dogodogo* means the 'young ones' in Swahili. Kasia Parham, a Dogodogo volunteer field educator of multi-ethnic heritage (Giedroyc 2010: 188) had applied her broad cross-cultural experiences (including Japan, the UK and the US) to continuously provide the 'street survivors' with access to her own personal network of civic activists, scholars and international policy makers. She also globalized their voices by compiling their self-told street experiences into a book disseminated through the Internet (Parham 2008). Parham made the children aware that the funds generated *by them* through the Internet sales of *their book* will be directly used for their *and* the other street children's protection and educational development (see Cambridge Outlook 2009; www.cie.org.uk).
6. Research findings suggest that children are often far more competent in numerous ways than is commonly thought and also that growing up without responsibilities is not necessarily the most effective way to promote children's wellbeing and best interests (Knutsson 1977: 41).
7. As Pierre Bourdieu has pointed out, the 'objectivist' anthropologist, starting from the observation of practice, sets an ideal 'constructed object' as his (sic) theoretical goal. Once he has reached his goal, he can only see the continuing (and changing) practices of informants as an imperfect falling short of the ideal, as if his own theory were ontologically prior to the practices described. He therefore proposes a 'theory of practice' rather than an opposition between theory and practice (1977: 23–26).
8. Bryceson and Vuorela write that 'the thesis of transnationalism implies a radical change in the conceptualization of relations between movement and home: not only can one be at home in movement, but that movement can be one's very home' (2000: 158).

Bibliography

Arhem, K. (ed.) 1994. *Den antropologiska erfarenheten*. Stockholm: Carlssons Bokforlag.

Bourdieu, P. 1977. *Outline of a Theory of Practice*. Cambridge: Cambridge University Press.

Boyden, J. and D. Levison 2000. Children and Social Actors in the Development Process. Working Paper 2000:1, Expert Group on Development Issues, Ministry for Foreign Affairs, Stockholm, Sweden.

Bruner, E. 1986. 'Experience and its Expressions', in V. Turner and E. Bruner (eds), *The Anthropology of Experience*. Urbana, IL: University of Illinois Press, pp. 3–30.

——— 1993. 'Introduction: The Ethnographic Self and Personal Self', in P. Benson (ed.), *Anthropology and Literature*. Urbana, IL: University of Illinois Press, pp. 1–26.

Bryceson, D. and U. Vuorela 2002. *The Transnational Family: New European Frontiers and Global Networks*. Oxford: Berg.

Callaway, H. and J. Okely (eds) 1992. *Anthropology and Autobiography*. London: Routledge.

Cambridge Outlook 2009. 'From Street Child to Top Student', *Cambridge Outlook*, Issue 7, p. 10.

Cohen, G. (ed.) 1987. *Social Change and Life Course*. London: Tavistock.

Corker, M. and J. M. Davis 2001. 'Portrait of Callum: The Disabling of a Childhood', in R. Edwars (ed.), *Children, Home and School: Autonomy, Connection or Regulation*. London: Falmer Press.

Cornwall, A. E. and N. Lindisfarne (eds) 1984. *Dislocating Masculinity*. London: Routledge.

Cornwall, A.E., E. Harrison and A. Whitehead (eds) 2007. *Gender Myths and Feminist Fables: The Struggle for Interpretive Power in Gender and Development*. London: Zed Books.

Dresch, P., W. James and D. Parkin (eds) 2000. *Anthropologists in a Wider World*. Oxford: Berghahn Books.

European Commission 2007. Children in Communication about Migration – CHICAM. EUR 23113 – EU Research on Social Sciences and Humanities. Luxembourg: Office for Official Publications of the European Communities <www.chicam.org>.

Gamarudi, S. 2010. Paper given at Fertility and Reproduction Seminar Series, University of Oxford.

Gammeltoft, T. M. 2008. 'Childhood Disability and Parental Moral Responsibility in Northern Vietnam: Towards Ethnographies of Intercorporeality', *Journal of the Royal Anthropological Institute*, 14 (4): 825–42.

Giedroyc, M. T. 2010. *Crater's Edge* (with a preface by Norman Davies). London: Bene Factum Publishing.

Hockey, J. and A. James (eds) 1993. *Growing Up and Growing Old*. London: Sage.

Hockey, J. and A. James 2003. *Social Identity Across the Life Course*. London: Macmillan/Palgrave.

Howell, S. 2006. *The Kinning of Foreigners: Transnational Adoption in a Global Perspective*. Oxford and New York: Berghahn Books.

James, A. 2007. 'Giving Voice to Children's Voices: Practices and Problems', *American Anthropologist*, 109 (2): 261–72.

James, A., A. James and S. McNamee 2004. 'Turn Down the Volume – Not Hearing Children in Family Proceedings', *Child and Family Law Quarterly*, 16 (2): 189–202.

James, A. and A. Prout (eds) 1999. *Constructing and Reconstructing Childhood*. London: Falmer.

Katz, C. 1994. 'Playing the Field: Questions of Fieldwork in Geography', *Professional Geographer*, 46: 67–72.

Komulainen, S. 2007. 'The Ambiguity of the Child's "Voice" in Social Research', *Childhood*, 14 (1): 11–28.

Knutsson, J. 1977. *Labelling Theory*. Stockholm: Scientific Reference Group.

Lancy, D. 2007. 'Accounting for Variability in Mother-Child Play', *American Anthropologist*, 109 (2): 273–84.

LeVine, R. 2007. 'Ethnographic Studies of Childhood: A Historical Overview', *American Anthropologist*, 109 (2): 247–60.

MacClancy, J. and C. McDonough (eds) 1996. *Popularizing Anthropology*. London: Routledge.

Mead, M. 1928. *Coming of Age in Samoa*. New York: New American Library.

Mead, M. and M. Wolfenstein 1955. *Childhood in Contemporary Cultures*. Chicago, IL: University of Chicago Press.

Mitterauer, M. 1992. *A History of Youth*. Oxford: Blackwell.

Montgomery, H. 2001. *Modern Babylon: Prostituting Children in Thailand*. Oxford: Berghahn Books.

—— 2008. *An Introduction to Childhood: Anthropological Perspectives on Children's Lives*. Oxford: Wiley-Blackwell.

Montgomery, H., R. Burr and M. Woodhead 2003. *Changing Childhoods: Global and Local*. Chichester: John Wiley & Sons.

Oliver, M. 1990. *The Individual and Social Models of Disability*. Paper presented at Joint Workshop of the Living Options Group and the Research Unit of the Royal College of Physicians.

Parham, K. 2008. *Dogodogo: Tanzanian Street Children Tell their Stories*. Basingstoke: Macmillan.

Rapp, R. and F. Ginsburg 2001. 'Enabling Disability, Rewriting Kinship, Reimagining Citizenship', *Public Culture*, 13 (3): 533–56.

Rapport, N. and J. Overing 2000. *Social and Cultural Anthropology*. London and New York: Routledge.

Scheper-Hughes, N. 1992. *Death Without Weeping*. Berkeley, CA: University of California Press.

Schiller, N., L. Basch and C. Blanc-Szanton (eds) 1992. *Towards a Transnational Perspective on Migration*. New York: New York Academy of Sciences.

Shweder, R. A. (ed.) 2009. *The Child: An Encyclopedic Companion*. Chicago: University of Chicago Press.

Spyrou, S. 2011. 'The Limits of Children's Voices: From Authenticity to Critical, Reflexive Representation', *Childhood*, 18 (2): 151–66.

Toren, C. 1990. 'Childhood', in *Encyclopedia of Social Sciences*. London: Routledge.

Turner, V. and E. Bruner (eds) 1986. *The Anthropology of Experience*. Urbana, IL: University of Illinois Press.

Valentin, K. and L. Meinert 2009. 'The Adult North and the Young South: Reflections on the Civilizing Mission of Children's Rights', *Anthropology Today*, 25 (3): 23–28.

Westin, C., J. Bastos, J. Dahinden and P. Gois (eds) 2009. *Identity Processes and Dynamics in Multiethnic Europe*. Amsterdam: Amsterdam University Press.

Part I

CHANGING NORMS

Chapter 1
INVISIBLE ROUTES, INVISIBLE LIVES:
THE MULTIPLE WORLDS OF RUNAWAY AND MISSING WOMEN AND GIRLS IN UPPER SINDH, PAKISTAN

Nafisa Shah

Introduction

This case study of runaway women and girls in Upper Sindh[1] has a twofold objective: first, to examine what role gender, or being a female, plays in the social making of the girls and by that premise, what roles notions of childhood and adulthood play in women's identity.[2] This is also primarily the reason why both girls and women are the subject of this case study. I propose to examine how notions of adulthood and childhood are gendered by seeing how women and children are constructed jointly as minors.[3] Here I look at systems of marriage and concepts of honour which both make women and girls as cultural children in relation to men, or even boys.

A second objective is to understand these notions especially with respect to runaway girls and women.[4] This study helps me to look at women and girls as agents, who are able to effect social transformations by changing structural forms of marriage. The act of running away constructs women and girls as social actors, capable of transforming their future, thereby reversing their roles as 'cultural minors' in the custody of men.

My work shifts away from looking at these acts as aberrations that lead to delinquency, prostitution and crime. Runaway action is an assertion of women and girls challenging the dominant forms of marriage and possibly a strategy to social mobility and change. The closest anthropological discussions are in the field of bride capture as a form of marriage (Barnes 1999). However, bride capture is studied in a structural model and women's own agency; their choices of life paths are rarely considered in these studies. In the following, runaway action is shown as positive action towards social mobility, where women, otherwise considered children, become momentary 'adults'.

This study is informed by my experience as a native woman, but also as someone in an official position. As a Syed woman from Upper Sindh, I belong to a status group that is revered and respected, as Syeds are considered to be genealogically linked with the Prophet Mohammad. In addition, in 2001, I was elected as the Nazim, a mayor, in my home district Khairpur, which is part of Upper Sindh. My involvement both as a Syed woman and as a woman in power involved me in such a way that I can say that I am my own informant. Both these positions made me a nucleus of my own fieldwork, and its subject as well, and the problem solving, especially concerning women and girls, became routine. My home served as a meeting place, where women from the district would bring applications, requesting mundane provisions, food, clothing, shelter, but also sometimes for resolution of marital disputes, custody, or protection against violence. 'We have heard that you listen to women', they would come and tell me. Where women's direct access to political space is restricted, my access to women was considered empowering, so much so that during my period in office, men would come and tell me that the women of their family warned them that they now have a female representative to turn to, should they not behave with them, and some even threatened to have them locked up behind bars using my office.

Upper Sindh: The Field Area

Upper Sindh is geographically located in the south of Pakistan, bordering three provinces: Sindh, Balochistan and the Punjab, with a combined population of eight million people. This area is marked as one of the most violent regions in Pakistan, reporting not only a high crime rate as reported by the police but also cultural forms of violence such as killings in the name of honour, and group feuds.

Upper Sindh represents the confluence of three groups of peoples – the western Baloch, eastern Rajput-based groups, and the northern Jats.[5] Historically, it is influenced by the Balochi tribal system, and social rules are based on the normative honour values. Apart from territorial identities there is also a caste-like social stratification with many identity formations based on divisions of labour, especially in towns where there are many different groups of people. For instance, there are rank identities mimicking Hindu caste structures like the Syeds, considered to be descendants of the Prophet, as the highest and the Sheikh, low-caste Hindu converts at the lowest, and profession-based identities like the artisan communities. Numerous migrations of nomadic pastoral, camel and sheep herders from Afghanistan have meant a constant turnover of the population and frequent invasions have brought to this region Pashtoon, Afghan, Turkic and Mongol groups as well. The languages spoken are largely Sindhi, Seraiki, but Balochi and to a lesser extent Brahui are also spoken.

Economically, Upper Sindh is an agricultural area, growing cash crops like wheat, rice and cotton, and seasonal fruits. The perennial canals from the Indus have brought new settlements. Farming in Upper Sindh is a mixed set of social practices and social relations. On the lowest scale are the landless cultivators called *hari*, who are also sharecroppers farming for bigger landlords. These are followed by small farmers, whose farm sizes are so small that they have to supplement their own farm income by working on other farms as well, so they are both *hari* and owner cultivators. Medium-sized farms tend to be exclusively owner operated, and the larger farms may be cultivated by wage labour, *hari* operated farms or both. Then there are tenant farmers, who contract land from one season to the next on fixed rates and finally there are the absentee landlords, who lease out their lands in any of the ways described above.

Farming settlements are organized into villages, which are largely uniform groups of people organized around common landholdings with shared values and intermarriages. Village size can range from a single household to hundreds of households. There are several names for groups used in everyday relations – *qaum*, for large group identities, *raje* is another general word for the people, and *birathar* is used more as groups of interrelated lineages with a common identity.

The territorially organized group identities all seem to use honour ideologies to protect and shape their identity, resources and boundaries. Power, both political and social, is vested in heads of tribes, called *Sardar,* landed elite, called *wadera,* and various manners of religious heads, called *Pir,* who hold lineages that link them to the Prophet. Upper Sindh has historically had a strong local mediation system, and the *Sardar, Pir* and *wadera* reinforce their political power by participating in mediations over various conflicts. State power is largely based on the former colonial structure with a powerful bureaucracy and local elite given indirect powers.[6] The area is divided into districts and each district has its administrative machinery headed by a district officer and law and order managed by a police officer. Increasingly today, the state representatives assist the strong informal networks, and the chiefs and mediators strongly influence state institutions as they are part of the political power.

In the following discussion, I will use the local notions of honour as the context within which gender relations are shaped. The people of Upper Sindh follow Islam, and symbols of Islam such as the Quran are widely used in social relations. Here I may be questioned on how Islam constructs the local notions of honour. Some anthropologists like Rosen (2000) say that customary norms and values and religion are not really far apart but a continuum. However, the notion of honour rarely uses the rhetoric of Islam. Marriage practices also contradict official Islam, which emphasizes will and agency of two people, men and women who enter into contract. But going into details of whether customs are Islamic or not or how Islam has shaped custom and how custom is shaped by Islam is in itself a circular debate. If the society in Upper Sindh follows Islam, by that logic, all practices are subsumed under religion. But if the Quran is to be taken as a fixed form of Islamic injunctions then many practices find no basis in religious texts. And to reverse this argument, many practices mentioned in religious texts are not found in Upper Sindh. Here it is enough to say that in the local discourse, the laws of God, the laws of the state and the laws of the people, or *qaum*, are set out as distinct by people and all three are important, and the contradictions between all three result in conflicts all the time. Although there are resonances between the three and one can be set up as the other, in the community they are set up as distinct discourses. All three are used and applied in differing contexts, and why custom is a complicated category is because it undergoes changes over time, depending on how laws of the state, laws of God and laws of tribe interact.

Women and Girls as 'Children' in the Honour Value System

The social and political relations of Upper Sindh are based chiefly on the local honour values of *izzat* and *ghairat*. The anthropology of honour is a large body of material concerned with defining what honour is, but also recognizes that it is an elusive term.[7] My experience in the field is that honour is a relational term, used differently by men, women and by people across hierarchies in the same society. I am oversimplifying but, for basic context, *izzat* refers more to material honour, and *ghairat* is reactive honour, especially used as a self-help instrument, with respect to women. The honour value system involves much more than these two words. There is a whole repertoire of social behaviour, of modesty codes, of hierarchies within and across sexes and ages and manifests itself differently in different hierarchical settings.[8]

In Upper Sindh, one is simultaneously struck by the brutal forms of honour-related violence against men and women, and girls and boys, in the customary shape of *Karo kari* (a compound word meaning black man, black woman), when women and men are accused of sexual transgressions,[9] on the one hand, and the frequency with which women and girls run away from their homes and villages every day and contract marriages of love, challenging social control of women's movements, on the other. Both these worlds present a contradictory tension, one in which women or girls and boys are victims, and the other where they take control of their lives, one where the honour value system is articulated in self-help notions, and the other where it is challenged actively.

When women are suspected of sexual transgressions, it is the *ghairat* in men that provides the moral basis of violence against women. So much value is placed on women's status, especially with respect to marriage, if there is a violation, as in the case of women in relationships, women are accused as black, along with the men who are suspected with them. This practice, called *Karo Kari*, perhaps aims at marital rights and gender roles. Black men and women, and even girls and boys, are usually evicted from the community, and black men/boys fined to compensate for the women lost in the process. But many times, women and girls accused of being black are killed too, as are the men.

Men are considered women's natural guardians and protectors in the honour value system. Even though *ghairat* is considered to be a male reaction to violation of honour, women actively engage with the politics of *ghairat*. And older women in the hierarchy, such as mothers and mothers-in-law, may also be guardians of *ghairat.* For instance, I have met two mothers who defended the death of their daughters as black women, saying that there was no regret in such an action as it was about *izzat* and *ghairat.*

Like women, the fate of girls in Upper Sindh is linked to their productive and reproductive role. Very early on, the girl child is involved in domestic labour, as an assistant to the mother, especially to look after the younger siblings. Her role is to collect fuel wood, to run errands, to help their mothers in weeding, cleaning, washing and cooking. Further, teenage girls are likely to be punished in the same way as older women for violation of honour. Physically, girls also embody sacred honour with power to heal relations. This can be observed in the girl's capacity to resolve disputes. Girls are referred to as *niani,* which is a sacred term, denoting virginity and purity. As *niani,* a girl and sometimes an unmarried woman, who is a girl even at 40 if she is not married, can resolve disputes. In blood feuds women and girls can go to an aggrieved side, in a ceremony called *niani mairh,* and this method is sure to resolve disputes.

In the honour value system then, women of reproductive age are in the custody of men, and therefore cultural 'minors'. With respect to men, all such women are children. Husbands refer to their wife and children collectively as '*bare*', a Sindhi word meaning 'children'. They would never speak of wife in the singular as a person, but in the plural inclusive in the term '*bare*'. Women of reproductive age would, generally speaking, not go into public spaces alone. In most cases they are accompanied by a male, even if the male is a child. Young women are often chaperoned by brothers or nephews half their age. Married women would take their sons to the market with them; middle-aged women would be chaperoned by teenage students. In other words, a male child is a protector of an adult woman because he is a male, even when he is a child. Mentally too, women are considered minors, and women rarely speak in front of men in the presence of guests or other male members of the family. This permanent childhood conferred on women with respect to men erases boundaries between girlhood and womanhood. Women are girls and girls are women, and both are children with respect to males, who even as children have custodial and protection rights over them. This configuration reconstitutes notions of childhood and adulthood as gendered entities: children are primarily those who are dependent and need protection, and women of Upper Sindh are children, in relation to men. But when it comes to their sexual role, women are adults at the age of eleven and twelve, an age considered to belong to childhood in the western legal system. But many marriage transactions in Upper Sindh come into effect at this age. Girls become women when they marry at puberty but both girls and women are societal minors.

It follows therefore that childhood and adulthood are culturally constructed and their meanings related to social roles of men and women. The difference between girls and women is then only of comparative value and puberty is what marks the difference. Girls who are prepubescent are valued less than those who enter active childbearing age. But girls between eleven and fifteen, while defined as children from a legal perspective, are sexually adult and begin to symbolize the honour of the family. In order to further understand the difference in value between women and girls, I will now discuss the marriage systems in Upper Sindh.

Marriage Systems in Upper Sindh

Marriage systems in Upper Sindh are related to the agrarian economy, building on the domestic unit as the agricultural farm unit.[10] Marriage in Upper Sindh is essentially a system of exchange in social relations. It is called *sang*, which means a relationship.

In Upper Sindh, there are two recognized forms of marriage transactions, and both involve exchange. The first and the most common marriage is exchanges of sisters by brothers. This would also include exchanges of daughters, nieces and cousins among two men who could be brothers, cousins or just tribesmen.[11] This is called *de wath* – literally meaning 'give and take' or *avezo*, which means 'exchange', or 'in lieu of'. A woman who is given in marriage has always as a rule to be replaced, either immediately or after a period of time. When girls are not available, pledges for the future are made. The first girl child of the woman given in marriage may be pledged, hence establishing the right of the woman's family to the return of a woman. Pledging of unborn girls in marriage is called *peth liki diyan* – to write down a pregnancy – implying the contractual obligation of *sang*. Families never seem to forget an outstanding *sang*, and claims and counterclaims rumble on even generations later if *sang* remains against anyone.

Women who are exchanged refer to women they were exchanged for as their *avaz*, or *avezo*. In every discussion, women would refer to their *avez* women as a shadow of their own selves, a mirror image. 'I came in *avez* of my aunt', one woman would say; another would say, 'My *avez* has six sons' or 'The woman given in my *avez* has gone back to her paternal kin' and so on.

It follows then that men with many daughters are privileged. But from this follows that a man with many daughters would transact girls at a far earlier age than one with fewer daughters. The age and timing of women are calculated as factors in exchanges. For instance, if *sang* of a woman of reproductive age is exchanged with pre-pubescent younger girls, then two pre-pubescent girls would be due in lieu of one. The everyday difference between women and girls is then simply of value where puberty is the marker between two stages.

The second form of marriage is almost an inverse of the exchange marriages. This is by getting a woman or a girl in marriage after paying for her. This is more common among nomadic pastoral communities, but I have noted settled farming communities practising it as well. In Sindh, this is referred to as '*vekro*' – sale, or *takan mein diyan* – to give in exchange for money. *Vekro* is often of young women or girls, and parents – mothers and fathers – use girls for marriage for everyday expenses, like settling a loan, building a house, spending on health care, buying a buffalo. The older men are the best bidders for the girls, as they may have more property or buffaloes.

There seem to be some resonances between *vekro* transactions and trafficking of girls in the rural and tribal areas. However, this is a cultural transaction and to date I have not really come across middlemen or systemic networks that make money in the process. Hence I would be wary of calling this an organized form of trafficking. But in Upper Sindh, Balochi herders come from faraway lands, loaded with sheep and girls, and leave some girls behind and go back into the hills. Girls are given in *vekro* marriage across provinces and borders, sometimes taken as far out as Quetta, Loralai, Kandahar, or brought to Upper Sindh from there. At the time of this fieldwork, in Upper Sindh girls were given in *vekro* marriage for a price averaging Rs60,000 ($1,000).These transactions take place through active participation of immediate relations of women. One woman, a Lolai Baloch, repaired the roof of her house from the Rs60,000 she received when she gave away her daughter to a far older man from the Pal community in the neighbouring village.

There are also strong discourses of resistance against the *vekro* marriage of girls to older men. A woman, a widow with four girls, came to me asking for help when her second daughter, Rukhsana, only ten years old, had already been pledged in marriage by her brothers-in-law to a man called Qasim for Rs30,000. A deposit had been given for this pledge by the bridegroom to be. Qasim, who is about fifty years old, was already married and childless, and moreover killed his father's sister after accusing her of being black, and received payment of Rs200,000 from a neighbouring Rind Baloch he accused of being the black man. Her brother-in-law now calls him *ghairatmand* because of this act and thinks he will be an appropriate husband for the ten-year-old niece. Rukhsana's mother would like to have her brothers-in-law arrested to deter them from seeing through the contract. In fact, Rukhsana's mother had run away from home and was in hiding with her little girls. But there is no guarantee that tomorrow Rukhsana's mother does not negotiate marriage of the same daughter by getting the money for her from her own kin. As it is, Rukhsana's elder sister was sold by her father, when he was alive, to the Buriro community, also for Rs60,000. At that time, Rukhsana's mother did not resist. Most of the money from the first daughter's marriage was gambled away. About Rs10,000 was loaned to his brother Maula Bux, who, according to her, has still not returned this money to his brother. But often, those who mediate these runaways or support them in running away may resell them to another gentleman or marry them themselves. Sometimes these middlemen are fathers and mothers themselves. In fact, in one case, a mother who had already taken Rs60,000 and built her roof with that money, wanted me to get a divorce for her daughter, who had run away from her elderly husband. Some people from the village told me that she would probably do another *vekro* marriage for her daughter after the divorce.

So to summarize, in *de wath* marriages, men with many daughters transact minor girls in exchange for older ones, sometimes even three for one, leading to girls marrying older men. In *vekro*, older, more settled men end up with more wives and young men are at a disadvantage, because they do not have the means to afford the bride price. In exchange marriages, fathers may transact marriage by giving their daughters in exchange for brides for themselves, as well as for their sons, or use the cash money as the bride price not to get wives for their sons, but for themselves. Hence both marriage forms may lead to transactions of girls with older men, and both marriage forms make girls into social adults. In a large number of the *vekro* marriage cases I have come across, the transactions are often of girls.

25

In most cases, these girls use running away as a strategy to escape from these marriage transactions. When young brides run away, their older husbands rise up in arms because they have paid a bride price and must therefore be compensated if the woman they have paid for runs away. I would get a number of applications from older men, chasing after their runaway brides, who would wait for hours in the sun, trying to get me to help them get back their little wives. One man persistently came for five years. His bride had run away and contracted marriage with a *wadero*, and this poor man kept coming to me to phone the police to arrest the *wadero* for taking his wife away from him.

Often running away becomes a bridge to yet another form of marriage: the *pyar jo parano* or marriage of love. These are unlike the structured arrangements described above, and I have noted a great deal of social mobility, as normally forbidden marriages across groups, sects and ranks would take place through runaway action. The *pyar jo parano* – marriage of love – is a cultural form of marriage that takes place in the spaces between law and custom. Pakistani marriage laws based on Islamic personal law allow women a choice in marriage, and many of these marriages take place with support of state officials.[12] This marriage form merits a separate study, for it is a marriage that results from rejection of exchange marriage, and is considered an anomalous form, and yet it has created for itself a cultural place. To conclude this section, marriages then seem to be both the cause and the outcome of runaway actions of girls. Many girls leave their homes to find a better future in a tradition where they know their life may be under threat. Yet they do so, hence reversing their role as a minor who is dependent and totally subservient to the will of elder men and women as parents, husband, in-laws or kin.

The Runaway Experience: When Women and Girls Decide to Break Away

Women and girls, otherwise cultural minors, effect social change and transform their roles when they leave their homes. Hence women and girls become agents and reverse their social role of being in male custody. In this section I describe why they leave their homes and where they go when they do. Some women run because they are chased, others because they want to leave their husbands and yet others because they are forced into a marriage they do not want. But all of them say it was only when they felt they could not live in that situation any longer, that they decided to leave their homes. Many times they are supported in this action by men whom they may wish to marry. But even then, almost all women or girls I have met leave their homes on their own, and support comes only indirectly from these men in the background. No matter how much they may have planned or thought about it, the action itself remains full of uncertainty and danger.

While older women leave home with a clearer sense of where they want to go, girls are vague about their future, even though they are very clear about the cause of their running away. Some girls accompanied by their mothers would sit silently as their mothers speak on their behalf.

I will now show how a liminal place is constructed by society for runaway girls and women, and argue that despite being considered a deviant practice, society creates spaces for women and girls who run away. These spaces help women to negotiate their past, present and future with the help of mediators.

Invisible Routes: Cultural Spaces for Girls and Women as '*Saam*'

It is difficult to prepare estimates of runaway women and girls in Upper Sindh. Newspapers on average report two to three cases of runaways daily. There are two state shelters in Upper Sindh, and the one I frequently visit, in the city called Sukkur, reports a turnover of six to seven women every month. In the four years that I was the district head, I received more than two score runaway cases, one third of whom were girls.

When they leave their homes, the immediate objective is to find a neutral place where they can narrate their story and seek intermediaries. This right to seek protection is recognized in the social world in Upper Sindh, and the cultural sanctuaries give them a right to renegotiate their relationships with husband, parents or kin, and demand mediation, through which they can re-enter society. The protection given to women and girls is called *Saam* or custody, and women/ girls who enter these spaces become *Saam* women. The state of *Saam* embodies a transition where women are moving from one form of life to another. In some cases family men, fathers, brothers, uncles and husbands, who accuse girls or women of being 'black', may also voluntarily bring them to the local mediator to resolve the issue.

Although women or girls who become *Saam* come from different age, class and religious settings, there is an uncanny similarity in the choices they make and the routes that they follow. In their escape, there seem to be fixed pathways and centres, in and through which women move. I call these routes invisible for two reasons: first, they denote the secret knowledge that is critical for the runaway plots or actions to be successful, and second, because they are physically non-exis-tent as routes, but are simply social directions. The escape routes are strategic po-sitions of and for negotiations as well. For instance, very few of the girls who leave home and call for help ask to be taken to state shelters, called Darulaman. Private institutions, especially informal homes of tribal chiefs, Syeds and Pirs, those with indirect political and social power, receive many more girls and women. The first option is often the local mediator, and when there is no refuge there, the women may go to chiefs of tribes. Shrines provide space for indefinite stays and, when there are no mediators available, women would take refuge in shrines.

Although the standard routes are as above, there are a number of girls who may initially not have a plan of where they would run to. They are just 'leaving home' and find themselves on buses or in train stations. The link of the railway with runaway women and children has spawned a network of middlemen who hang out at the railway station looking for runaway children and girls to hand back to the parents for a paltry sum. In Sukkur state shelter, I met three girls who had come to the railway station. One said she was going to the mega city of Karachi, another was just standing there waiting for destiny to come to her, when the police came, and yet another girl, without parents, ran away from her uncles, and was found loitering aimlessly in the railway station by a policewoman.

After having traversed through various places of transit – the Pir, the Sardar, the Syed, the neighbour, the Shrine, the train, the bus, even the police station – for most women the state shelter home is the last destination. Attached to the Darulaman is also a legal world plied by lawyers, local magistrates and police officers. For instance, a typical narrative of women who reach Darulaman would be: 'My uncle was forcing me to get married to my cousin. I refused saying that he was too old, but they got batons to silence me, and brought a mullah. They forced me to contract the marriage. But I escaped, went to the *autaq* of Wadero, and gave him a Quran. They took me to the Police Station in Kot diji, and then took me to the court the next day and from there to the state shelter.'

State shelters are the last option because both entry and departure from Darulaman criminalize and judge women. Firstly, the runaways have to go through a session judge or the police before they can be admitted. Secondly, state shelters may help these girls seek their rights within the state system but may at the same time isolate them from their community forever. Not surprisingly, while it is permitted for women and girls to run away to the '*saam* places', it is the state shelter that is considered the most injurious to notions of honour.

The runaway movements of girls are neither single track nor one time movements. According to Darulaman officials, almost fifty per cent of the women and girls who register come more than once. When the issues are not resolved, then runaway becomes a cyclical condition. An example is Zohra, a girl in her mid teens, who has made four stops at my place during her three-year runaway cycle, several stops at her husband's village several hundred kilometres away, several at her father's equally distant village, more than five stops at a zemindar's house, and an equal number at her sister's in Khairpur. Zohra's running away from her parents' house, her husband's home and her sister's home is cyclical. In between, there have been stops at friends', at another sister's, and perhaps at places not known.

Zohra has moved long distances, all the way from the Punjab to Upper Sindh. She got married four years ago, and forcibly, to Mohammad Ali who paid Rs35,000 to her father. Her husband was old, and Zohra decided to escape shortly after her marriage. But she was caught and returned repeatedly to her husband, and sent to my area, where her sister lived. I saw Zohra five times over the years. She would come, stay overnight and then vanish. Every time, she would demand help with divorce and I engaged lawyers for her.

Invisible Lives: Social Responses to Runaway Women and Girls

How do these runaway women and girls re-enter society? There are three possible ways society responds to runaway women and girls.

Girls who Returned and Survived

In most cases, women and girls seem to apply pressure on parents or spouses to do things required of them: in the case of parents, to give up on certain marriage arrangements of a daughter; in the case of wife, a statement to the husband to stop beating her, or provide more money to her, or divorce her. These are short symbolic runaways – for a day or two, to relations, friends, local mediators, who would negotiate on their behalf and help them re-enter their social world.

As a rule, most girls who run away will be returned, and will revert to the parents' decision of marriage, or earlier life with their husband or will be married off to a distant relative. This is especially the case when girls are unmarried, and run away with inexperienced men, who do not stand up for them, leaving them half way. The younger the woman, the greater is the pressure to have her back. Interestingly, girls are 'returned' with the help of the mediators, police, even judges, and then remarried to anyone but the person she may have escaped with.

For instance, a girl student ran away with a young man in the village of Mithri in the year 2003. The girl was Hajano and the boy was Shahani. A kidnapping case was registered against the Shahanis, and some of the men in their family were brought to the police station. She was returned with the intervention of a mediator, who put pressure on the elders of Shahanis, and the girl was returned to the Hajano community and married off to a distant relative, in another city, Shikarpur. She now has two children by that man. Meanwhile, the Hajanos and Shahanis are still fighting, implicating each other in false claims, and spending hundreds of thousands of rupees contesting 'damaged honour'.

Sometimes, women do not accept such forced marriages, and manage to escape after they are remarried. In a recent case, Zeenat, who contracted a court marriage, was forcibly remarried to the local chief's nephew, but she managed to escape after contacting human rights organizations.

Girls who Returned and were Killed

The second possibility, not as likely as the first, is that girls are returned and then killed. Although girls take refuge for security, and there are spaces to do so, their life is in no way guaranteed. On the contrary, the intense violation of honour by escaping the boundaries of society is replete with dangers of categorizing the runaway girls as black women, and getting even with them in ritual. Here, girls are more vulnerable and susceptible to violence. There have been women who have been returned by mediators on guarantees through an extensive guarantee system in the community but have been subsequently killed. Two girls, Abida and Tehmina, 16 and 18, went to Sukkur telling their mother that they were going to a beauty parlour. When the kin learnt the girls could have possibly eloped with two boys, they were chased and returned and then killed. I encountered two other cases in the field. In one case a Manganhar girl had run away with a young man. They got married through the civil courts and went away to the north for several months. Yet she was returned with the intervention of a mediator after guarantees that she would be spared her life. Within a month of her return, her father and uncles killed her. In yet another case, a girl called Pervez Khatoon from Larkana ran away with another young woman, to a local Syed mediator, because she claimed that she was being sexually abused by her husband's nephews, since her own husband was impotent. Pervez Khatoon was returned on the mediator's guarantee and subsequently killed.

Becoming Invisible: The Girls and Women who Succeed in Changing their Lifepaths

The third possibility is a change of lifepath for women and girls. This is less common than the first possibility, but nonetheless a significant one. The girls end up marrying men they may have liked, either through a mediator or through the court through a *pyar jo parano*. If these girls have been branded as black and brought to the local mediator, they may be given in a *vekro* marriage through the mediator. Although I have no evidence other than hearsay, people do say that chiefs and mediators keep a part of the sum as the cost of keeping women in their homes. Women, especially married ones, are more likely to succeed in changing lifepaths. For runaway girls, only those with support will succeed, for example if the boy's family will fight for her rights.

But how does the social world respond to the women and girls once they are out of the *Saam* state, and begin to live regular lives, especially in marriages that their families do not accept? The missing women are, like the black women, 'socially dead'. Parents often say '*ho asan je lai marri wai ahai*' (for us, she is dead) about women who leave homes and survive. Hence no one speaks openly of them, nor weeps for them, nor misses them. Chasing them, and locating them, and even talking about them is socially taboo, once these women are beyond the reach of society. For the community, time stops as far as these missing women and girls are concerned – they become invisible – as they remain unacknowledged in the social world they left behind.

Concluding Remarks

The notions of childhood and adulthood become irrelevant as categories when gendered division constructs women and girls as children with respect to men, and boys and girls as sexual adults. In runaway actions, we can see the role of both women and girls as social actors exerting choice in their lives even under extreme threats. The lives and narratives of runaway women show that these women are making clear choices when they decide to leave their homes. Most women leave homes when they have the option of a marriage to a man other than the one they are forced into.

The conflicts resulting from this action reveal tensions in society. When women succeed in changing their lifepath through a *pyar jo parano*, they are also signifying a transition in society from a marriage of sister exchanges to seemingly a marriage of choice. Here then, both women and girls reverse roles as cultural minors in the permanent custody of the men, momentarily becoming adults who exercise their will in marriage.

Looking through the prism of gender shows the ambiguities of rigid notions of adulthood and childhood. Age as a grade of numbers is not a clear marker; there are other factors, such as gender, sexual experiences and sexual age. There is a relational aspect as well, as women are children with respect to men, but in relation to their children they are adults.

But despite this agency that constantly reshapes the social system, girls and women will return to their status as cultural minors. Once their status as wives is restored, even through a marriage of choice, they would return to their older gender role of the '*bare*', children when compared with men. No matter how women and girls assert their choices, these momentary inversions fall back into place as women re-enter social worlds through a marriage, whether it is *pyar jo parano*, the marriage of love, exchange marriage, or a *vekro* one. After this, they once again become the quiet wives and mothers, symbolizing the honour of the village and tribe they marry into. There is little space for women or girls to be on their own, and run away just to run away as a social action, leading to an autonomous life. Ultimately, the runaway women and girls, despite their multiple lives and agencies, are Upper Sindh's children of men.

Notes

1. This paper is a part of my doctoral research on violence and the honour value system in Upper Sindh. I did my fieldwork mainly from 2001 to 2004 but since I am a resident of the area, I have also updated my work from time to time. During the time of fieldwork, I also served in a position of power, as an executive head of one of the six districts of Upper Sindh, and many of the cases cited are personal encounters.

2. Although there are significant ethnographic works on children (for a historical overview of ethnographies on children, see, for example, LeVine 2007), study of childhood poses multiple theoretical problems (James and Prout 1997). Some of these are definitional issues on what a child is, the problem of binarism and positioning of the child as opposed to an adult, and the question of agency in children (James and Prout 1997). A significant contribution of anthropology of childhood was that early on, it was recognized that children and their roles are socially embedded and differ from one society to another (e.g. Mead 1928). But the anthropological literature assumes that childhood is a separate unified category and, even when children are shown to be social actors, they are nonetheless considered different from adults (Toren 1996) and actors in their own right. Lærke's (1998) methodology of working on children

tries to blur the child–adult boundaries as it involves processes 'whereby both adults and children continuously position and identify each other and their selves'.

3. Children in anthropology, until the 1970s, were rather like 'muted groups', just as women were, whose voices eluded anthropologists studying simple societies (Hardman 2001 [1973]). Theoretical comparison between women's studies and that of children is an important methodological issue that needs to be addressed when studying children (Oakley 1994). This approach allows us to understand how many adult social roles, such as women, or the disabled, ill and feeble, old parents, are perceived as dependent and needing care and protection and treated as if they would be children in everyday discourses. Hall and Montgomery (2000), for instance, have pointed out how discourses of youth and childhood are used politically: they may talk of young people as children to conceptually place them in a favoured category to which certain entitlements apply, whereas in other times young people may be positioned as beyond childhood, but short of adulthood, to assign them to a more ambiguous phase. In the material I will be presenting, gender challenges categories of adulthood and childhood, as women and children are positioned differently to men.

4. There seems to be little comparative work on runaway women and girls. Most current literature is based on data from Iran where it seems to have become a social phenomenon. There are some sociological studies of runaway action as 'deviance' related to crime, delinquency and prostitution (e.g. Flowers 2001). However, bride capture is studied in a structural model and women's own agency; their choices of life paths are rarely considered in these studies.

5. Samatr are related to the Rajput communities of Western Rajasthan.

6. The Indirect Policy was the main method through which the British administrators appeased the tribes and yet maintained their stranglehold on local forms of power (Bruce 1900). The Frontier Crimes Regulation, 1872, 1890 and then 1901, a law regulating tribal code, was the main instrument through which power was negotiated between tribal groups and the British imperialists.

7. For ethnographies of the anthropology of honour in the Mediterranean, see Pitt-Rivers (1954), Campbell (1964), Peristiany (1965), du Boulay (1974), Herzfeld (1985 and 1987), Gilmore (1987) and Sciama (2003). For Middle East/Maghreb ethnographies, see for example, Black-Michaud (1975), Abu-Zahra (1982), Wikan (1982), Dresch (1989) and Gilsenan (1996).

8. In Pakistan, some anthropologists have discussed Pukhtunwali – the Pukhtun honour code (Barth 1965, Lindholm 1982, Ahmed 1988), emotion and honour (Grima 1993), adultery in Baloch (Pehrson 1966) and more recently studied honour shaped by vengeance in a historical context (Keiser 1986), wealth from remittances (Lefebvre 1999) and honour crimes and criminal justice (Chaudhary 1999).

9. This implies adultery mostly; however, sex before marriage, or by widows or divorced women would also draw accusations of blackness. Hence I have used the word sexual transgression to encompass the different roles of women who are accused of violating honour.

10. Cf. Tapper (1991).

11. In other ethnographies and crime writings, women and marriage disputes are shown as the cause of honour-related crimes as well, for instance Kanwar (1989) and Chaudhary (1999).

12. Pakistan Muslim Family Laws Ordinance 1961 allows marriage according to personal laws of the contracting parties. Muslim personal laws as applied in Pakistan allow adult women the right of choice in marriage. Where women are coerced, they are entitled to go to the nearby magistrate to report this and further to contract marriage through the magistrate, called a 'court' or civil marriage, by giving a statement, which is called the 'free will affidavit'.

Bibliography

Abu-Zahra, N. 1982. *Sidi Ameur: A Tunisian Village*. St Antony's Middle East Monograph Series No. 15. London: Ithaca Press.

Ahmed, A.S. 1988. *A Pukhtun Economy and Society: Traditional Structure and Economic Development in a Tribal Society*. London: Routledge and Kegan Paul.

Barnes, R.H. 1999. 'Marriage by Capture', *Journal of the Royal Anthropological Institute*, 5 (1): 57–73.

Barth, F. 1965. *Political Leadership among the Swat Pathans*. London: University of London.

Black-Michaud, J. 1975. *Cohesive Force: Feud in the Mediterranean and the Middle East*. Oxford: Basil Blackwell.

Bruce, R.I. 1900. *The Forward Policy and its Results, or 35 Years Work among the Tribes on our North Western Frontier of India*. New York and Bombay: Longmans, Green and Co.

Campbell, J.K. 1964. *Honour, Family and Patronage: A Study of Institutions and Moral Values in a Greek Mountain Community*. Oxford: Clarendon Press.

Chaudhary, M.A. 1999. *Justice in Practice: Legal Ethnography of a Pakistani Punjabi Village*. Oxford: Oxford University Press.

Dresch, P. 1989. *Tribes, Government and History in Yemen*. Oxford: Clarendon Press.

du Boulay, J. 1974. *Portrait of a Greek Mountain Village*. Oxford: Clarendon Press.

Flowers, B. 2001. *Runaway Kids and Teenage Prostitution: America's Lost, Abandoned, and Sexually Exploited Children*. Westport, CT: Greenwood Press.

Gilmore, D. 1987. *Honor and Shame and the Unity of Mediterranean*. Washington, DC: American Anthropological Association.

Gilsenan, M. 1996. *Lords of the Lebanese Marches*. London: I.B. Tauris.

Grima, B. 1993. *The Performance of Emotion among Paxtun Women*. Karachi: Oxford University Press.

Hall, T. and H. Montgomery 2000. 'Home and Away: "Childhood", "Youth" and Young People', *Anthropology Today*, 16 (3): 13–15.

Hardman, C. 2001. 'Can there be an Anthropology of Children?' *Childhood*, 8 (4): 501–17. First published in 1973 in *Journal of the Anthropology Society of Oxford*, 4 (2): 85–99.

Herzfeld, M. 1985. *The Poetics of Manhood*. Princeton, NJ: Princeton University Press.

——— 1987. *Anthropology through the Looking Glass: Critical Ethnography in the Margins of Europe*. Cambridge: Cambridge University Press.

James, A. and A. Prout 1997. *Constructing and Reconstructing Childhood: Contemporary Issues in the Sociological Study of Childhood*. London: Routledge.

Kanwar, M. 1989. *Murder and Homicide in Pakistan*. Lahore: Vanguard.

Keiser, L. 1986. 'Death Enmity in Thul: Organised Vengeance and Social Change in a Kohistani Community', *American Ethnologist*, 13 (3): 489–505.

Lærke, A. 1998. 'By Means of Re-Membering: Notes on a Fieldwork with English Children', *Anthropology Today*, 14 (1): 3–7.

Lefebvre, A. 1999. *Kinship, Honour and Money in Rural Pakistan: Subsistence Economy and the Effects of International Migration*. Richmond, Surrey: Curzon.

LeVine, R.A. 2007. 'Ethnographic Studies of Childhood: A Historical Overview', *American Anthropologist*, 109 (2): 247–60.

Lindholm, C. 1982. *Generosity and Jealousy: The Swat Pukhtun of Northern Pakistan*. New York: Columbia University Press.

Mead, M. 1928. *Coming of Age in Samoa*. New York: William Morrow and Co.

Oakley, A. 1994. 'Women and Children First and Last: Parallels and Differences between Children's and Women's Studies'. In B. Mayall (ed.), *Children's Childhoods: Observed and Experienced*. London: The Falmer Press.

Pehrson, R. 1966. *The Social Organization of the Marri Baloch*. New York: Wenner-Gren Foundation.

Peristiany, J. 1965. *Honour and Shame: The Values of Mediterranean Society*. London: Weidenfeld and Nicolson.

Pitt Rivers, J. 1954. *The People of Sierra*. Chicago, IL: University of Chicago Press.

Rosen, L. 2000. 'From Courtroom to Courtyard: Law and Custom in Popular Legal Culture'. In *The Justice of Islam*. Oxford: Oxford University Press.

Sciama, L. 2003. *A Venetian Island*. Oxford: Berghahn Books.

Tapper, N. 1991. *Bartered Brides: Politics, Gender and Marriage in an Afghan Tribal Society*. Cambridge: Cambridge University Press.

Toren, C. 1996. 'Childhood'. In A. Barnard and J. Spencer (eds), *Encyclopedia of Social and Cultural Anthropology*. London: Routledge.

Wikan, U. 1982. *Behind the Veil in Arabia: Women in Oman*. Baltimore, MD: Johns Hopkins University Press.

Chapter 2
BETWEEN TRADITION AND MODERNIZATION: UNDERSTANDING THE PROBLEM OF FEMALE BEDOUIN DROPOUTS

Sarab Abu-Rabia-Queder

Introduction

This study discusses the problem of Bedouin girls dropping out from the public school system in the Negev region of Israel.[1] Data show that this phenomenon results from a conflict between the modern Israeli institutes' perception of modernity (which promote coeducation) and the Bedouin traditions that remain the cultural ethos of the girls' fathers. Israeli institutions' perception of modernity (enlightenment theory) aims to modernize the Bedouins according to Israel's modern principles, thus revoking traditional Bedouin values (sex separation). This paper promotes a postmodern theory that calls for embedding feminine traditional values of local communities as a necessary process in the development of modernity.

Modernization movements and efforts, especially those aimed at improving women's status, have occupied a central place in the political discourse of the Middle East and other non-western countries since the nineteenth century. A great symbol of modernization has been advocacy of women's greater participation in both the public sphere – through education, employment and un-veiling – and in the political arena. In her book on gender and social change in the Middle East, Valentine Moghadam explains why she focuses on women: 'It's my contention that middle-class women in the Middle East are consciously major agents of social change in the region, at the vanguard of the movement to modernity' (1993: xiii).

Until recently, modernity discourse was characterized by the dominant western understanding of these regions in terms of modernization theory. This approach

35

creates a dichotomy between the modern and the traditional, perceiving all that is non-western as primitive and archaic, in contrast to the progressive, enlightened West. Several scholars from non-western countries (Abu-Lughod 1998, Kandiyoti 1998, Ilkkaracan 2002) have criticized the 'western impact of modernization' on women. As Lila Abu-Lughod claims:

> even more crucial for understanding the projects of remaking women over the last century is to ask how modernity – as a condition – might not be what it purports to be or tells itself, in the language of enlightenment and progress, it is. (1998: 7)

Paidar (1996) argues that those who have benefited from modernization are mainly women from the urban middle and upper classes or the dominant race, whereas for lower-class and minority women, modernization often means a restriction or loss of traditional modes of power.

The main measure of women's emancipation as an indication of enlightenment has been their entrance into the public sphere in general, and the educational arena in particular, especially in Arab countries. Data from the United Nations Development Program (2002) *Human Development Report* indicate that, even though the Arab world shows the fastest improvement in female education in any region since the 1970s, more than 50 per cent of Arab women are still illiterate.

While there are numerous studies about the unsuccessful attempts of modernization projects to enhance the status and emancipation of Middle Eastern Bedouin women in the realms of employment, planning and veiling (Abu-Lughod 1986, Fenster 1999), the educational sphere has received virtually no academic attention. The aim of this paper is therefore to reveal another aspect of the challenge of helping women – in the context of Bedouin girls dropping out of the school system in the Negev. Specifically, the study aims to show that these girls leave school because of the clash between the Israeli (Western) institution's views of modernity and the traditional values of the Bedouin minority. Rejecting the modern enlightenment approach, which calls for modernizing local communities according to the new standards of the state, the current research adopts a postmodern approach (Giddens 1994), arguing for the embedding of local traditions in modern societies.

Gender and Education in the Bedouin Context

Schooling for the Bedouins of the Negev in the south of Israel did not begin until the late 1960s and early 1970s. This region was under military administration from the establishment of the Israeli state in 1948 until 1966 and, as such, the Bedouins were secluded from other Arab populations in the country. As most of the region's schools were closed during this period, Arab education was only available in the north of Israel. Thus, in order to gain educational and employment opportunities, Bedouins had to ask for special permission. As a result, an entire generation of Bedouin tribes had virtually no access to formal education, especially the women. It was not until the close of the military era in

1966, when the Bedouins could once again freely visit their relatives in the Gaza Strip and West Bank, that attitudes towards schooling changed.

At the same time, during the 1960s and 1970s, the Israeli government built seven permanent settlements for the Bedouins with the aim of 'modernizing' them. The government's approach to this project is reflected in the words of the Israeli statesman, Moshe Dayan:

> We should transform the Bedouins into an urban proletariat – in industry, services, construction, and agriculture. Eighty-eight percent of the Israeli population are not farmers; let the Bedouins be like them. Indeed, this will be a radical move, which means that the Bedouin would not live on his land with his herds, but would become an urban person who comes home in the afternoon and puts his slippers on. His children would be accustomed to a father who wears trousers, does not carry a *shabaria* [traditional Bedouin knife] and does not search for vermin in public. The children would go to school with their hair properly combed. This would be a revolution, but it may be fixed within two generations. Without coercion but with governmental direction ... this phenomenon of the Bedouins will disappear. (*Ha'Aretz* interview, 13 July 1963, cited in Abu-Saad 2001: 241)

Despite this 'modernity approach', the towns that were built lacked workplaces, banks, post offices, sewage systems, public libraries and recreational and cultural centres (Abu-Saad 1995). Even as education became more widely available, the Bedouin school system did not receive the same considerations or resources as its Jewish counterpart. The Human Rights Watch (2001) report found that the Israeli Ministry of Education treated the Arab and Jewish educational systems differently. While the latter is subdivided, allowing for educational pluralism (e.g. into secular and religious schools), the Arab system (including the Bedouin's) is monolithic. Thus, while the Israeli government concedes to Jewish religious traditions, it does not make similar accommodations for Bedouins.

Dropout rates among the Bedouins are the highest in Israel, especially for girls. A report by Katz (1998) indicates dropout rates of 10 per cent in the Jewish sector, 40 per cent in the entire Arab sector and more than 67 per cent among the Bedouins. In Rahat, the first Bedouin city in Israel, the overall dropout rate among 17-year-olds reached 40 per cent in 2002, and several of its neighbourhoods had a 100 per cent dropout rate for girls (Rahat Local Council 2003). The number of female Bedouin students increases every year, but the size of this increase decreases from one grade to the next (Katz 1988; see also Central Bureau of Statistics 1999: 78, table f/9).

Most studies investigating Bedouin girl dropouts (Kressel 1992, Hos and Kenan 1997, Ben-David 2000) blame the traditional nature of Bedouin society. That is, they attribute this phenomenon to traditional values of gender separation, restriction of women to the domestic sphere and the need to protect girls and their families from sexual shame. Hos and Kenan (1997) indicate that many parents do not send their daughters to school for fear of contact with boys from other tribes, which could damage the family honour. Many girls have to walk to a distant school or travel in mixed-sex buses, placing them in a dangerous zone over which parents have no control. In Meir's (1986) study, interviewed Bedouin men stated that girls who have reached puberty are ready for marriage; therefore, they cannot attend school and be exposed to boys. Abu-Saad (2001) points to the inherent conflict between the modern demands of Bedouin schools and the traditional obligations instilled upon girls at home.

These studies, which all perceive traditional Bedouin obligations as the main cause underlying girl dropouts, have offered no workable solution to lower the dropout rate. Most of them simply suggest that Bedouin society should adapt itself to modern demands, sending girls to school in the existing conditions. The current chapter proposes an alternative approach to the 'modern/traditional' dichotomy, perceiving the traditional nature of Bedouin society not as an inhibitor, but as a possible vehicle to promote women, by weaving the modern and traditional together. In order to better understand this approach, we need to first examine the woman's place in modernity approaches in other traditional societies.

Gender and Modernization Discourse in Traditional Societies

Many scholars attribute the difficulty of western modernization efforts to promote women in traditional societies to the pull of local traditions. Yet, these very attempts to modernize women in non-western countries – in terms of space, planning, sexuality and employment – have actually added to their suffering and marginalization. Munson's (2002) study of nineteenth-century and twentieth-century Spain describes how women were granted economic and civil rights and access to some public professions, but the debate revolved around how women would and should use space. Modernization gave them physical access to public space, yet they were still restricted culturally in this space. For a man, walking down the street involved watching others; but for the middle-class woman, it meant watching herself. A woman who did not guard her body was no longer protectively cloaked by social convention and was exposed to untold sexual danger. Eventually, in the mid-nineteenth century, women were restricted from public spaces.

In Turkey, which has been the main symbol of a modernizing nation, women's presence in the public sphere was the deliberate aim of reformers, especially in the 1950s. Yet, despite new laws on education, participation in economic and political life, and inheritance rights, women's participation in public activities was still limited in the 1950s. Few women were seen on the streets, in parks or in recreation centres (Ozbay 1999).

In their study of the impact of attempts by the West to modernize Third World countries, Belen and Bose (1990) show how, in the long term, these projects have served the western country's interests more than the intended beneficiaries. At times of economic crisis in these developing nations, women are controlled and placed in subordinate positions by those who own the means of production and dominant access to capital – namely, the men.

In a similar vein, Kurian's (2000) research on India's Narmada valley shows how the environmental justice movement, which aims to promote environmental sustainability, ignores local feminine cultural needs. Funded by the World Bank, the Sardar Sarovar Project built 3,000 dams on the Narmada River, with the aim of irrigating 1.8 million hectares of land, providing drinking water to the people, supplying electricity and offering employment opportunities. However, this project displaced tribal people living on the valley, and the adverse impact on women was great as they now had to walk further and work harder to obtain water, food, electricity and fuel. Denying women compensation for displacement contributes to their economic and social disempowerment. Not recognizing the role they can play in maintaining the environment thwarts the goal of environmental sustainability. Thus, these women perceive modernizing development projects as a means to institutionalize oppression.

The common thread running through these studies is the implications of modernity projects for women. Aiming to modernize a nation, reformers perceived it as monolithic and assumed women and men would give the same meaning to modernity. By neglecting to recognize the special needs of women, these projects have done little to improve women's status and emancipation. Similar effects are apparent among the Bedouin women in the Negev region of southern Israel.

Bedouin Women and Modernization Discourse

Resettlement of the Bedouin community in urban-style towns was the main thrust of modernization efforts in the Israeli Negev. Yet this process had a particularly adverse impact on Bedouin women, which was not taken into account in the planning process. When one-half of the Bedouin population of the Negev was displaced from the desert to recognized villages (in the late 1960s and early 1970s), they benefited from a variety of services – stores, banks, parks, schools. However, most of these benefits were, for all intents and purposes, denied to the women, owing to their lack of access to and familiarity with the public sphere (Jakubowska 1988).

Before the move to the villages, the Bedouin woman was a partner in the home, with relatively equal responsibilities. This partnership was evident in the elementary tasks she was responsible for performing, which were critical to the sustenance of the family, such as goat milking, preparing food and building the tent. Such activities increased her status as a provider and a producer during the hard way of life in the desert (Meir 1997). However, with the transition to the village, her roles were abrogated by modern services, and she became useless and unproductive in her own domestic space. At the same time, she lacked skills to work outside the house and the state did not provide her with an appropriate workplace that embraces traditional Bedouin customs. As a consequence, most of the men work outside the village, while the women stay at home without any vital employment, left solely with the roles of wife and mother (Abu-Lughod 1986, Fenster 1999).

Fenster (1999) has shown how the modernization planning process did not consider cultural constructions of space when creating Bedouin towns in the

Negev, effectively creating a situation that increased control over the women. Since the resettlement, Bedouins live in neighbourhoods within towns, according to tribal affiliation, and men avoid moving in other neighbourhoods because of accepted traditional rules of territoriality and respect for women's modesty. This does not, however, prevent the men from moving in public spaces, while it does restrict the women. It is not culturally acceptable for Bedouin women to be seen in public, as this can taint their honour. Thus, modernization efforts have created what Fenster calls 'forbidden' and 'permitted' spaces for women: the home and the neighbourhood become their permitted private place, where they are free to move, and outside this area is the forbidden public place – the park, the bank and the town centre.

A comparable reduction of women's freedom of movement occurred among Bedouins in the new settlements built in Jordan, Egypt, Saudi Arabia and Iran, as demonstrated in Abu-Lughod's study of the Awlad Ali Bedouin tribe in Egypt. As a result of the move to towns, the Bedouins began to receive more visitors. Owing to modesty norms that forbid women to have any contact with men, even eye contact, women were limited in mobility to domestic arenas. Restrictions on movement meant that they could not even take advantage of social and welfare services located outside their neighbourhoods. As a consequence, these women felt worthless and did not perceive any improvement in their status or self-image (Abu-Lughod 1986). These studies reveal the modernizer's lack of consideration for local feminine codes and the lack of gender sensitivity with regard to hierarchical relationships in non-western societies. Thus, the women essentially become the victims of this modernizing process.

The aim of this chapter is to challenge this modernizing approach in the field of education among the Negev Bedouins, an area that has not received scholarly attention. Specifically, I question the existing coeducational structure of Bedouin schools, which clashes with traditional values, and suggest that this is a primary factor in the high dropout rate among girls. This is in contrast to the approach that perceives coeducation as 'the most optimal strategy to assure equality of opportunities' (Berkovitch and Bradley 1999: 487). In their promotion of women's education and status, the United Nations, non-governmental organizations and other international organizations have tended to perceive local opposition to schooling as a hindrance to modernization, and have focused on changing traditional beliefs rather than embedding them in their modernization efforts. In doing so, they disregard cultural sensitivity to the educational experience (Berkovitch and Bradley 1999).

Research Methodology

In examining Bedouin attitudes to girls' education, I conducted ethnographic interviews with girls and their parents from two groups: those who were enrolled in school (educated) and those who had left school (dropouts). There were ten girls, ten mothers and five fathers interviewed in each group, with a total of 50 interviewees. To ensure that Bedouin girls and women had an opportunity to express themselves, I used a qualitative research method that bases itself on the actions and meanings of the individual person, who can be understood best through his or her language and attitudes (Berg 1995). This method helped me get to know the interviewees' proximate world, which had not thus far been explored in research. This allowed me to ask the women personal questions in privacy (without the presence of a male figure), especially about their marriage and family life. Participants were asked to express their perceptions of why girls continued in school or dropped out, as well as their perceptions of Bedouin norms and the Bedouin woman's role.

The process of locating the women, especially those in the less-educated group, met obstacles from the fathers, who were sensitive to the issue being studied and were afraid of their daughters' exposure. To locate the dropout girls, I first obtained the names of 17-year-olds who had stopped attending the local high school. Finding that inaccuracies in school registration undermined my efforts, I carried on by locating the relatives of these girls on the basis of surnames in a 'networking' process (Feldman 1981). To encourage people to respond, I used my role as a teacher in the community and, through my colleagues, was able to visit girls who were not attending school in their homes. Sometimes it became necessary to ask a man's permission to interview his daughters and wives. To reach the girls' fathers, other males in the community needed to help me make the initial contact. Most fathers refused to open up or even to meet me because I am a Bedouin woman. It took me a year to locate ten girls who had left school whose parents agreed to participate. The girls were interviewed in their homes, sometimes in the presence of their mothers and sometimes alone. For cultural reasons, all interviews with fathers took place in their homes with at least one additional family member present.

I accessed the schoolgirls – all of whom were 17 years old – through the local high school. These interviews took place at the school in a classroom that the principal made available to me. To reach their parents, I asked the girls to obtain permission. At this stage, too, I had to replace one girl with another whose parents would agree to have her interviewed. My status as a Bedouin woman facilitated my access to the community – but as an independent, modern Bedouin woman by appearance, I represented the antithesis of my interviewees. That is, I did not express the expected behavioural norms of a traditional Bedouin woman; for example, I do not usually cover my head with a scarf. However, it was necessary for me to accommodate myself to the traditional attire (by wearing a long skirt and a long-sleeved shirt) and traditional norms (by not looking directly at men during the interview and by accepting the presence of a woman while interviewing her husband). These methodological concerns exemplify the conflict of a modern researcher researching her traditional community. In order to minimize this distance, she fits in by approaching traditional values as something that can benefit her research, and not by considering them a barrier. The researcher's approach should be to integrate tradition, not reject it.

My sample consisted of two groups of interviewees. The educated group had mothers with nine years of schooling, although a few of the mothers had no education at all. Their average age was 40–45 and they had seven to nine children. All their husbands were employed and most of the fathers had finished high school. The less educated group had mothers with no education at all. Their age was 40–45, they had more than ten children, 40 per cent of their husbands were unemployed and the fathers had an average of seven to nine years of schooling.

Findings

A Bedouin Girl's Honour: Attitudes of the Less-educated Families

All the girls who had dropped out of school emphasized the importance of keeping their honour in terms of their behaviour and dress, and the difficulty that girls in this modern age face in doing so. For instance, when asked about Bedouin norms, Tofaha answered:

> The norms that I am going to tell you about all exist, but not among all the Bedouins. Most of them don't want their daughters to go out on the street, because then they will be bothered by boys and they will start calling her *sayaa* [not honoured]. They say that going out of the house ruins the girls. Even going to school ruins the girls in their eyes, because they will start to gossip about every girl walking in the street.

Farida says:

> A girl must not go too far. She has to have someone escort her. Because if someone sees her in the street, he will start a rumour about her, gossip, and then they will ruin her name and honour. Even if she is honourable, if she goes to school by herself, they will always gossip about her. That's why I always do what my parents ask me. I don't go out by myself.

Mothers' attitudes were very similar. In the words of Samia, the mother of a dropout girl:

> [T]he most important thing is her *sootra* [protection], that God protects her by marrying her and keeping her honour. We should protect her from the *aar* [shame]. It's better to get her married instead of someone seeing her and causing problems for her family.

Similarly, Lila explains the connection between honour and school:

> [I]f a girl goes out, even to school, she will be worthless. Because if people see her by herself, they will start to think she is not honourable. Then she will have too much freedom, go out with boys and do bad things to her honour. And people today are not compassionate.

Keeping the girl's honour is also the father's primary concern, as Majid, father of one of the dropouts, says:

My daughter, Manal, had too many men asking for her hand. So we preferred to get her married instead of being seen in school by different men. You know what happens with boys and girls in school. I don't want there to be any bad rumours about her.

Clearly, all interviewees in the less-educated group perceive keeping the girl's honour as the most important value in the girl's life and for her family. It seems that the parents' perception of honour is transferred to the second generation, who cannot and will not disobey the norms by which they were raised.

A Bedouin Girl's Honour: Attitudes of the Schoolgirls' Families

The schoolgirls emphasize how their parents warn them to keep their honour in school by watching themselves and distancing themselves from the boys. As Nasreen stated:

My parents always tell me that I am not allowed to speak to boys at all. It's shameful to speak to them or even to sit near them in class. Because people would be suspicious and ask what is going on between [us].

Suad explains why a father who catches his daughter having a secret relationship with a boy from school has the right to stop her from attending school:

I think the parents are more experienced than us and we need to pay attention to what they say. I think it's a good thing to have a relationship with boys, but a pure relationship, not a romantic one. A girl who has romantic relationships, I think I would tell her father to explain to her that these things are not allowed among us, but if she continues, he has every right to stop her from attending school.

The mothers of the schoolgirls also indicate the importance of their daughters' honour, but, unlike the mothers of dropouts, they perceive the need to keep one's honour not as something that prevents their daughters from attending school, but rather as a condition for them to attend school. As Miriam says:

I know my daughter protects her honour, acts in an honourable way – that's why we don't mind her going to school, it's up to her. Even if there was some boy who flirts with her, she would put him in his place and react as required, then he would not even talk to her again.

She also indicates her role in educating her daughter to maintain good manners:

I always tell her not to cross the lines, not to be outside by herself. To come home before sunset. I don't allow her even to go to the store after dark, you know all the boys are out at that hour watching her. I don't want them saying any bad things about her. Why should people gossip about her?

The fathers of schoolgirls, unlike the fathers of dropouts, seem to acknowledge the modern mixed space in which they live. Like their spouses, they do not see the need to maintain their daughter's honour as an inhibitory factor for schooling, but rather as a primary condition for allowing her to attend school. Najeh, another father, claims: 'The first thing is her honour. As long as she keeps her honour and her *oroobia* [being an Arab girl], she will honour herself and be honoured by others.'

In order to deal with modern demands, these families embed local traditions within the modern space. For instance, if girls have to walk to school, fathers arrange transportation to keep their honour protected. As Rami says:

> I don't want people looking at her in the street and saying she is dishonoured because she is by herself. That's why we have a car taking her to and from school. This I don't disapprove of. I prefer to have a permanent car taking her to and from school instead of standing in the street and hitchhiking.

One father claims that he gives his daughters controlled freedom, effectively embedding traditional values within the space of modernization:

> Traditional Bedouin norms are our weapon. The good thing in them is the honour. I prefer my daughter to wear traditional dress but I don't force her. I just try to direct her, because in this dress boys in school will not look at her. Their age is very difficult. I give my daughters freedom but in a critical way, for instance, we don't let our daughter go out dancing in clubs, I will not let her! [But] I will let her go to a close girlfriend to do homework together.

Whereas the less-educated families seem to perceive honour and traditional norms as something that cannot be maintained in the modern space, the educated families see such norms as a condition for their daughters to move in this space. Consequently, they allow their daughters to attend school, while acknowledging the difficulties in keeping these norms.

The Importance of Paternal Support

Girls who drop out do not benefit from their fathers' support to attend school because of the difficulties in keeping their honour. In contrast, schoolgirls not only receive their fathers' support, but also have their trust and confidence despite the difficulties and expected bad rumours.

Among the less-educated group, the mothers spoke of how their spouses would not support their daughters' schooling. As Mariam says, 'We stopped her from attending school. You think she can resist her father? She has nothing to do but accept it'. One daughter who tried to resist the decree of her father suffered for it, as her mother explains:

She is angry and sad, but what can she do? When she wanted to go to school, her father start yelling at her and even hit her. When she went to school, her relatives went there and took her out by force.

In contrast, the schoolgirls had more support from both parents. As Alia indicates:

When I started studying in high school, my uncle started asking me questions and was very angry at me. But thanks to my father, he did not pay attention to him, because he trusts me and has a lot of confidence in me.

The fathers of the schoolgirls indicate their trust in their daughters even though they know these norms are very hard to follow in school. As Rajeh says:

I know that boys and girls in school party, but as long as I trust my daughter and I know who I raised, I don't have to be afraid for her. Even if she was alone with another boy inside a closed room, I trust her not to do anything wrong. As long as I trust her, there is no need to worry.

It seems that these fathers place greater importance on their daughters' education; as Ali says, 'If I wanted [to impose] these norms, I would have stopped them [his daughters] from attending school a long time ago'.

In summary, all fathers and mothers of both groups acknowledge the importance of keeping the girl's honour, but the educated fathers trust their daughters to attend school while the less-educated fathers do not raise this issue at all and place the norms above the education of the girls.

Reasons for Dropping Out: Boys, Girls and Bad Rumours

In the less-educated families, the importance of maintaining their daughter's honour seems to have had a major impact on decisions about her attending school. When asked why they left, most dropout girls ascribed this to the fear of romantic contact with boys in the classroom. Suha explains her reasons for dropping out:

I studied in a weak class, where most of [my classmates] were boys. So I was not used to them. That's why I felt like a stranger and stopped attending school. Also, my best friend stopped, so I did not want to be left alone with the boys.

Suhaila also describes the school as a dangerous place for a Bedouin girl:

School is also important, but we cannot mix with boys. Here we don't encourage girls to study, since we don't have a school for girls only. Because dangerous things happen to girls in school, and girls are not aware of these dangers. Because every girl who goes out to a mixed school, even if it is not her fault, she will suffer from bad rumours [about her].

The mothers of dropout girls give similar reasons for why the latter left school. Speaking about her daughter, Amira says:

> Her uncle and father prevented her from going to school. If people see a girl who goes out alone by herself, they will start gossiping about her and ask, 'How come she goes out alone?', 'There is no honour', 'We should protect our daughters these days; you can't trust a daughter to go to school by herself'. They are afraid for their daughters, because we had a lot of rumours about girls who ran away with their lovers, or you hear about a girl who was killed for family honour, or about a girl who was raped. There are a lot of accidents. That's why they prefer their daughters to stay home instead of attending school, in these hard times where boys and girls always see each other.

The fathers' explanations are of a similar tone. Wahib's statement is typical:

> I disapprove of my daughter studying in a mixed school with boys. My daughter studied until grade 9 and then we stopped her from attending school. In school there are some young boys who could shift her from the right way, you see, girls and boys are like fuel and fire, they just wait to meet each other.

Girls' Schools: The Preferred Scholastic Framework

Both generations of the less-educated group prefer separate schools for the girls. Iman expresses her wish to continue her schooling, but on one condition: 'I would like to attend school, but only in a separate school. If there was a school just for girls, then girls would focus only on their studies and their future.'

The fathers describe the existing coeducational framework as something imposed by the Israeli government. Tamer says: 'The truth is that the government imposed this kind of school on us. And I don't accept it. Because when a woman and a man are together, Satan is between them.'

The dropout girls and their parents seem to see the option of separate girls' schools as a viable solution. Indeed, some of these girls, after marrying and bearing children, and with their husbands' approval, now attend a local school for completing studies that is open only to women. As Fatma says:

> I stopped attending school in grade 8. After I married I returned to this [women's only] school. What is special about this school is that the boys are separated from the girls ... Because there is no contact here between us [girls] and them [boys]. Here there are no problems at all and all the girls are together.

Sara's father explains why her continued education is now acceptable to him: 'She is not my responsibility anymore. When she is married, she can go to school if her husband approves. When I stopped her from attending school, I wanted to protect her. The most appropriate framework for protecting her is marriage.'

Both the less-educated families and the educated families believe strongly in the importance of keeping their daughters honoured in public, and acknowledge the forbidden romantic relationships between the two sexes in school. However, the educated girls, with the support and trust of both parents, are able to manage in the coeducational framework, embedding their traditional values in the modern space, whereas the dropout girls and their parents perceive the coeducational school as a dangerous place and are threatened by the possibility of the bad rumours that attending such a school could arouse. The fathers of these girls do not believe their daughters could both attend a mixed school and maintain their honour. In other words, both groups are unwilling to surrender feminine traditions of honour, but the educated families found ways to embed this tradition within the modern space of the mixed schools, while the families of the dropouts perceive that space as an unacceptable danger to their daughter's honour.

Discussion and Recommendations

The phenomenon of Bedouin girl dropouts exemplifies the marginalization of women as passive victims in the process of modernizing a traditional society. The case at hand shows that, when a modern state offered Bedouins an education as part of the modernization process, it did little to consider the needs of the women or the community's traditional values. Israel's coeducation policy essentially discriminates against Bedouin women, creating obstacles to their education while Bedouin men have undeterred access to schooling. The modern concept of coeducation does not benefit a society that forbids women to appear in public. In fact, by giving the Bedouins a monolithic form of education, the Israeli state has extended a limitation of the private sphere to the public sphere. Delivering modern education to a traditional Bedouin community breaks the sacred traditional social norms of honour. Staudt (1988) argues that modernists endorse coeducation as the optimal strategy to assure equality of educational opportunities. However, while some cultural traditions do not oppose the educational access of girls and women per se, they do oppose full coeducation. In such cases, separate but equal facilities for men and women are considered a reasonable compromise (UNESCO 1995). If parents are unwilling to send their daughters to mixed schools, then more schools should be built for girls. This encourages access while not challenging those cultural beliefs underlying the differential treatment of sons and daughters. In the Bedouin context, married girls who had left school can return to a modern institute that endorses traditional values – a school just for women. This creates an option for those fathers who stop their daughters from attending schools with mixed classes. In this way, the Bedouin community can avoid producing an entire generation of uneducated women.

The discourse of the global campaign to educate women and girls repeatedly cites the aim of elevating the status of women. However, the international organizations that promote such modernity projects seem to find it necessary to counteract 'traditional opposition' to the education of girls in order to enhance women's status. The findings of the current study suggest that this is not necessarily the case. Traditional values did not fade when the Bedouin community moved to modern settlements, even when girls started attending schools. The Bedouins' perceptions of the girl's honour and other traditional feminine norms, such as veiling and exposure to men, continued to hold. In the more educated families, upholding such norms was a condition for daughters to appear in a mixed public space (the coeducational school); they were able to embed tradition in the modern space. In the less-educated families, the risk of breaking these norms kept fathers from letting their daughters finish their studies.

The modernity project in the Negev threatened the Bedouin culture by producing high residential density, increasing the likelihood of undesirable encounters for Bedouin women and thereby threatening deeply engrained cultural codes concerning women's modesty. As Fenster (1999) argues, the modernist outlook on society emphasizes a formal top-down approach of planning, which ignores the 'others' and therefore pays less attention to social relations and their expression in space. This type of western modernist theory views the direction of change as predetermined, rather than as a product of integrating cultural codes, norms, values and social attitudes. The planners' ignorance of local cultural codes only created greater control over the Bedouin women, who became more restricted by Bedouin men. The males' own ambivalence towards the transition resulted in their forming 'guards of honour' to shield their women from the new realities of the modernized towns.

This chapter embraces a postmodern view of society, challenging the grand theory of modernism and emphasizing the particular and the local. Feminist contribution to postmodernist theory is in adding not only cultural sensitivity, but also gender sensitivity. In feminist terms, the approach this study wishes to promote is called 'entryism' (a term coined by Helie-Lucas 1993), a strategy for women's action that develops from within the community and its traditional values. Entryism is suitable for women who wish to introduce changes in their communities but cannot use revolutionary approaches that contravene local traditional values. The solution of separate spaces in the educational system among the Bedouins respects distinctions based on gender and incorporates these distinctions into plans to urbanize and modernize. As Munson (2002) argues, for women whose modernist spaces limit their access to the public, the best solution is not to change the spaces already dominated by men, but to grant women their own separate but equal spaces.

Applying this postmodernist approach, we can understand how and why notions of modernity have not 'liberated' Bedouin women. When 'modern education' is imposed on the Bedouin community, women pay the price by dropping out of school. In the present case, the solution should come from the Israeli state. Bedouins in Israel are an ethnic minority that faces discrimination and lacks the means to create alternatives. If the state fails to provide the right solution, Bedouin women will remain torn between two types of otherness: as women in traditional society and as an ethnic minority in modern thought. Release from this otherness requires new discourse, a postmodernist perception of traditional communities.

Acknowledgements

The author would like to thank Sara Helman, Valentine Moghadam and Niza Berkovitch for reading the first draft of this paper.

Notes

1. This chapter is a revised and updated version of an article that was previously published as 'Between Tradition and Modernization: Understanding the Problem of Female Bedouin Dropouts', *British Journal of Sociology of Education*, 27 (1): 3–17. The article can be found at http://www.informaworld.com.

Bibliography

Abu-Lughod, L. 1986. *Honor and Poetry in the Bedouin Society*. Berkeley, CA: University of California Press.

Abu-Lughod, L. (ed.) 1998. *Remaking Women: Feminism and Modernity in the Middle East*. Princeton, NJ: Princeton University Press.

Abu-Saad, I. 1995. 'Bedouin Arabs' Education in the Context of Radical Social Change: What is the Future?', *Compare*, 25: 149–61.

—— 2001. 'Education as a Tool for Control vs. Development among Indigenous Peoples: The Case of Bedouin Arabs in Israel', *HAGAR-International Social Science Review*, 2: 241–61.

Belen, E. and C. Bose 1990. 'From Structural Subordination to Empowerment: Women and Development in Third World Existence', *Gender & Society*, 4: 299–320.

Ben-David, J. 2000. *Report of the Cultural and Environmental Factors Determining Bedouin Dropouts of the School System*. Jerusalem: Ministry of Education (in Hebrew).

Berg, B.L. 1995. *Qualitative Research Methods for Social Sciences*. Boston, MA: Allyn & Bacon.

Berkovitch, N. and K. Bradley 1999. 'The Globalization of Women's Status: Consensus/Dissensus in the World Polity', *Sociological Perspectives*, 3: 481–98.

Central Bureau of Statistics 1999. *Statistical Abstract of Israel*. Jerusalem: Center for Statistical Office (in Hebrew).

Feldman, E.J. 1981. *A Practical Guide to the Conduct of Field Research in the Social Sciences*. Boulder, CO: Westview Press.

Fenster, T. 1999. 'Space for Gender: Cultural Roles of the Forbidden and the Permitted', *Environment and Planning D: Society and Space*, 17: 227–46.

Giddens, A. 1994. 'Living in a Post-Traditional Society', in B. Ulrich, A. Giddens and S. Lash (eds), *Reflexive Modernization: Politics, Tradition and Aesthetics in the Modern Social Order*. Cambridge: Polity Press.

Helie-Lucas, M. 1993. 'Women's Struggle and Strategies in the Rise of Fundamentalism in the Muslim World: From Entryism to Internationalism', in H. Afshar (ed.), *Women in the Middle East*. London: Macmillan Press.

Hos, R. and A. Kenan 1997. *Report of Personal and Community Aspects Related to School Enrollment of Bedouin Girls*. Jerusalem: Ministry of Education (in Hebrew).

Human Rights Watch 2001. *Second Class: Discrimination against Palestinian Arab Children in Israel's Schools*. New York: Human Rights Watch.

Ilkkaracan, P. 2002. 'Women, Sexuality and Social Change in the Middle East and the Maghreb', *Social Research*, 3: 753–79.

Jakubowska, L. 1998. 'The Bedouin Family in Rahat: Perspectives on Social Change', in Y. Aini and E. Orion (eds), *Reshimot benoseh Habedouim*. Midreshet Sdeh Boker: Ben-Gurion University Press (in Hebrew), 34–48.

Kandiyoti, D. 1988. 'Bargaining with Patriarchy', *Gender & Society*, 2: 274–90.

Katz, Y. 1998. *Report of the Investigating Committee on the Bedouin Education System in the Negev*. Jerusalem: Ministry of Education (in Hebrew).

Kressel, G.M. 1992. 'Shame and Gender', *Anthropological Quarterly*, 65: 34–46.

Kurian, P. 2000. 'Generating Power: Gender, Ethnicity and Empowerment in India's Narmada Valley', *Ethnic and Racial Studies*, 23: 842–56.

Meir, A. 1986. 'Pastoral Nomads and the Dialectics of Development and Modernization: Delivering Public Educational Services to the Israeli Negev Bedouin', *Environment and Planning: Society and Space*, 4: 85–95.

—— 1997. *As Nomadism Ends: The Israeli Bedouin of the Negev*. Boulder, CO: Westview Press.

Moghadam, V. 1993. *Modernizing Women: Gender and Social Change in the Middle East*. Boulder, CO: Lynne Rienner.

Munson, E. 2002. 'Walking on the Periphery: Gender and the Discourse of Modernization', *Journal of Social Theory*, 36: 63–75.

Ozbay, F. 1999. 'Gendered Space: A New Look at Turkish Modernization', *Gender & History*, 11: 555–68.

Paidar, P. 1996. 'Feminism and Islam in Iran', in D. Kandiyoti (ed.), *Gendering the Middle East: Emerging Perspectives*. London: Syracuse University Press, 51–67.

Rahat Local Council 2003. *Education and Demography in Rahat*. Rahat Municipality: Unit for Strategy Planning (in Arabic).

Staudt, K. 1998. *Policy, Politics and Gender: Women Gaining Ground*. West Hartford, CT: Kumarian Press.

United Nations Development Program 2002. *Human Development Report 2002*. New York: Oxford University Press.

UNESCO 1995. *Education of Girls and Women: Towards a Global Framework for Action*. Paris: UNESCO Press.

Part II

LISTENING AND LEARNING

Chapter 3
More than One Rung on the Career Ladder:
Examining Barriers to the Labour Market for Young Women Living in Poverty

Lucy Russell and Louisa Darian

Young Women and Poverty – What is Poverty?

YWCA England & Wales understands poverty as primarily a lack of money and not having what others in society have for a decent quality of life. However, it is not just the condition of being without adequate food, money, etc., but goes beyond material things; living in poverty can affect the way a person is treated and how they feel. It can mean feeling powerless and excluded, leading to a loss of dignity and self-esteem. Some young women do reject it as a term, some feel it is a negative label and that to be poor is also to be worth less in, or to, society. Some do not see themselves as poor because they are just the same as other people around them. The 'poverty trap' is another element: being unable to raise one's standard of living because one is dependent on state benefits which are reduced if one gains any extra income. Through our youth work with young women, we encourage them to critically examine their own situation in life and to look at society around them. We encourage them to ask why they have a different income from other people. Following such work, young women often become enthused about tackling poverty and discrimination.

YWCA England and Wales works with the most disadvantaged young women in England and Wales to challenge poverty and overcome discrimination. In 2010 the organization changed its name to Platform 51. It runs youth and community projects in some of the most disadvantaged parts of the UK. Through these projects women are supported to overcome the barriers they face. The organization also has a national co-ordinating office which works with women to influence policy and campaign for change with disadvantaged women. This paper reflects research carried out by the authors and focus groups and interviews with young women and staff about living with poverty and what it means to them. The information gained was used to create the policy basis for YWCA's campaign 'More Than One Rung'. This campaign targeted the extremely low pay received by apprentices in the lowest paid professions. The majority of such professions are predominantly female. YWCA established that this low pay trapped working young women in poverty and therefore the government's approach to work as a means of escaping poverty was failing the most vulnerable young women. Following a year long campaign, YWCA successfully influenced policy change and the minimum income for apprentices was increased.

Figures from the Family Resources Survey (FRS) show that about one million young women between the ages of 16 and 30[1] live in poverty in Great Britain.[2] This means they are living in households with an income below 60 per cent of the average. In the British Cohort Study, Blanden (2006) found that 17 per cent of young men who were poor at ages 10 and 16 were still poor at age 30, compared to 29 per cent of young women. This shows that not only are women more likely to experience poverty, they are also more likely to find it difficult to escape it. The Poverty and Social Exclusion (PSE) survey (Pantazis et al. 2006) found that the risk of poverty was higher among young people than among the adult population as a whole, and that young women were more likely to experience poverty than young men.[3]

Findings from the PSE survey (16–24-year-olds):
- Nearly twice as many young women (42 per cent) as young men (24 per cent) were living in poverty.[4]
- When a subjective measure[5] of poverty was used, more young women (18 per cent) than young men (12 per cent) were living in absolute poverty.
- More young women (43 per cent) than young men (28 per cent) were deprived of necessities[6] than young men (28 per cent).
- Forty-eight per cent of young women with dependent children were living in poverty, compared to 23 per cent of young men in the same situation.

Young mothers are particularly at risk of experiencing poverty. Analysis of the Millennium Cohort survey found that teenage mothers were over three times more likely to be poor than mothers in their 30s and that 80 per cent of lone mothers under 18 were in receipt of Income Support (Mayhew and Bradshaw 2005).

What Are the Consequences of Poverty for Young Women?

Poverty has devastating effects for both the individual and society. It is linked to low educational achievement (Cassen and Kingdon 2007), ill health, being a victim of crime,[7] increasing vulnerability to abuse (see next section) and many other negative consequences. Some of the effects of poverty are unique to young women, or felt more intensely by them than by young men. Others are shared by women across the age range. Where possible we try to distinguish these.[8]

Economic Dependence

Women are more likely than men to be economically dependent on a partner or family member because of their greater responsibility for unpaid care work within the home, which can limit their access to a wage (Lister 2004). In some cases, this can lead to a lack of control over finances, which in extreme situations may result in abuse. For some young women, particularly young women from certain black and ethnic minority backgrounds, economic dependence means being prevented from carrying on with their education because their family or partner will not support them to do this.

A small-scale survey by YWCA revealed that one-third of the women aged 16 or over had experienced financial abuse (Moloney and Russell 2008).[9] This could include having money taken from them or being manipulated to control or harm them. A worrying number of the young women we spoke to were experiencing it and, worse still, many of them did not know what it was, so struggled in silence. Many experienced multiple types of financial abuse (Brannigan 2005). The survey found that the most common types of financial abuse were:

- being made to give a partner cash,
- having money taken from them without being asked, and
- having benefits or wages taken from them.

When we asked whether the young women's partners ever wasted money needed for essentials, over three-quarters said yes, they did. Examples of what partners wasted money on included holidays, computer equipment, going out, gambling and drugs.

Women as Managers of Household Poverty and Debt

While men are more likely to control household finances, women are more likely to be responsible for managing the household budget (Pahl 1989) and debt (Women's Budget Group 2005). Ali, YWCA Participation Development Manager, said: 'Young women are the ones responsible for managing the poverty – getting the shopping, managing the house, and ensuring the partner has enough money for their needs – the needs of the young women are often the last.' Their responsibility for managing debt can mean they are more likely to face criminal proceedings for unpaid debt. A 1998 report, based on evidence provided by over 200 Citizens Advice Bureaux around the country, found that of the 200,000 people prosecuted for non-payment of TV fines, 68 per cent were women. The researchers attribute this to the fact that women are more likely to be at home when inspectors call during the day (Citizen's Advice 2003). Von, YWCA Project Manager, notes: 'Young women tend to be the ones to put their name on loan agreements and to have their names on household utility bills. When financial difficulties occur they are often the ones facing the courts.'

The Shock Absorbers of Poverty

Wanting to protect loved ones from the effects of poverty can mean that women are more likely to go without things for themselves. It is because of this that they have been described as the 'shock absorbers' of poverty (Women's Budget Group 2005). Research found cases of mothers going without basic necessities such as food or heating to be able to provide for their children (Middleton et al. 1994). Although men also go without things during periods of poverty, they are more likely to go without luxury items such as visits to the pub, a hobby or holiday (Gordon et al. 2000).

YWCA's 2008 research with women in Wales found several cases of women living in very dire circumstances and going without healthy food or heating: 'I've got old towels around my window to stop a draught coming in and blankets, like, I'm just scared to put the heating on' (YWCA 2008). In her study on girls in school with low incomes, Ridge (2005) found that younger girls were very aware of and understanding about their parents' financial circumstances and therefore limited what they asked for out of the household budget. 'By striving to protect their parents from the painful awareness of how poverty is impacting on their childhood they engaged in a range of strategies, including the self-denial of needs and desires, moderation of demands and self-exclusion from social activities.'

Time Poverty

Women also go without non-material things, for example, time for oneself. Caring for dependent children or sick or elderly family members has to be juggled with domestic duties, employment or training. This makes them more vulnerable to being time poor (Floro 1995) than men. Being time poor means having little or no leisure time, leading to social isolation. Lack of time can also make taking part in community groups and politics more difficult (YWCA 2003). This can limit young women's ability to develop skills that could be beneficial for their personal development and in the labour market.

Stress and Ill Health

Time poverty and responsibility for managing the household budget can result in stress and anxiety. This can lead to depression and mental health problems, both of which affect women more than men, especially when they are mothers of young children and are lone parents (Women's Budget Group 2005). Ill health can, in turn, affect a woman's ability to find paid work and is a major barrier to the employment of lone parents, the overwhelming majority of whom are women (Marsh 2001).

Shame

'Fitting in' is vital for the development of friendships, especially for young women in school (Ridge 2002). Not having the right clothes, or not being able to go into certain shops, creates feelings of shame (Yeandle et al. 2003), contributes to low self-esteem and can be a source of bullying for young girls. Feelings of shame can be made worse in school: factors such as the free school meals queue and expensive uniform and trips, make poverty more visible. Ridge's study found girls adopted protective strategies to hide their poverty, for example by buying dinner separately from friends or not claiming their free meal: 'We used to have a paper token, which is little bits of paper and I'd go to the office and as soon as they'd give it to me I grab it in my hand and screw it in my pocket. I do this every day' (Ridge 2005).

Pride and Determination

Although poverty can be incredibly stressful for young women, many express a sense of pride and a determination to improve things for themselves and their children. Von, YWCA Project Manager, notes, 'Women can respond to their experience of poverty with great resilience and develop survival skills. Children can be a driving force'. Young women's determination to improve things for themselves is evident in their attendance at YWCA centres and events. Youth workers have reported cases of young women walking for miles to get to YWCA centres when they don't have the bus fare.

Recognizing Difference

Not all young women experience poverty to the same degree or in the same way. Youth and gender interact with other characteristics such as ethnicity, disability and sexuality to affect the way that poverty is experienced.

Why Do Young Women Experience Poverty?

The government makes flawed assumptions about the lives of young women, which have at times contributed to their poverty. These include:

- Young women rely on family members or a partner for financial support.
- Young women in the labour market have less responsibility than older workers.

- Young women are receiving training in work.
- Young women have lower living costs.

This affects their treatment and experience in the home and labour market.

In the Home

Young women's responsibility for unpaid care work in the home and the cost of formal childcare limits their access to a wage. This means that many have to rely on family members or a partner for financial support. While public attitudes are changing now, a strongly gendered division of labour is still evident in many communities (Department of Communities and Local Government 2006). Using no qualifications as an indicator for low income, 35 per cent of young women aged 20 to 24 without qualifications describe themselves as looking after the home, compared to 1 per cent of young men (Escott and Buckner 2006). This shows that a large number of disadvantaged young women are not in work and are not available for work because of their role in the home.

For government policy to assume that young women can rely on others for financial support is dangerous. Firstly, some young women do not receive support from their families, either because they are not in contact with them or because their families cannot, or do not want to, support them financially. Secondly, living in the same house as a partner or family member does not mean that a young woman is receiving her fair share of the household's resources. Women's lower contribution to the household's income can mean that they receive less money for themselves and consume fewer household resources, which can lead to poverty (Pahl 1989). Thirdly, financial dependence means a young woman is always at risk of experiencing poverty if support is withdrawn or a relationship ends. Young women need an adequate income of their own from work or the social security system. Many of the most vulnerable young women are not in work or able to access work easily and so do not receive this.

Poverty and the Labour Market

Many women living in poverty are also working. Certain labour market policies like the lower rate of the national minimum wage and young women's role in the home can result in disadvantaged young women faring badly in the labour market. Figures from the Annual Survey of Hours and Earnings (ASHE) (Office for National Statistics 2006) show that a quarter of the lowest-paid young women are receiving just £80 or less a week. This is less than the amount received by low-paid young men. The size of the gender pay gap is not the same for all young women. For example, the pay gap is smaller at the lower end of the pay scale, and at the lower end of the age range. Young women are also particularly vulnerable when it comes to training and gaining skills; the gender pay gap begins at 16 for female apprentices and 18 for female employees. We will explore apprenticeships below.

What Causes Young Women's Disadvantage in the Labour Market?

Occupational Segregation

Despite significant changes in the workplace over the previous decades, men dominate in the traditionally highly-paid sectors and women in the lower-paid sectors (Department for Education and Skills 2005) such as cleaning, catering, cashiering, clerical and caring. Young women, particularly those facing poverty and disadvantage, tend to choose careers in traditionally 'feminine' jobs. We shall explore reasons for this in the pathways to work section of this chapter. These jobs are usually low paid and lack opportunities for progression. Young women become stuck in a cycle of low income, impacting on their lifetime income so that it remains low and leads to, or perpetuates, poverty.

Traditional Gender Stereotypes

These influence young women's decision making. They and their families want to see them fit in with traditional ideas of what a young woman does. Lack of opportunity to explore non-traditional careers, combined with gender stereotypes, limit young women's career choices and mean they do not consider better-paid traditionally 'male' careers and occupations. Young women's constrained choices can move them onto routes towards low-level jobs in sectors traditionally dominated by women, characterized by poor pay and few career prospects. For example, the average hourly wage for sales assistants and retail cashiers, three-quarters of whom are female, is £5.44. This compares to £7.03 an hour for elementary goods storage occupations, where over 80 per cent of workers are male (Women and Work Commission 2006). Paula, YWCA Participation Development Manager, points out, 'Men who do not achieve educationally can become higher wage earners by training as plumbers, electricians, brick-layers, etc.'. Women are likely to move into jobs with less room for progression. For example, young women are less likely than young men to be in professional and technical occupations or skilled trades and are more likely to be in sales and customer and personal services (Escott and Buckner 2006).

Opportunity Costs of Caring

Women tend to experience a 'sticky floor' in employment, trapping them into low-paid jobs. This is because they have less work experience, training, occupational benefits and so on, which often follows from taking time out of the labour market to care – known as the 'opportunity costs' of caring (Joshi 1992).

Part-time and Vulnerable Employment

Ten per cent of women aged 20 to 24 work part-time, compared to 4 per cent of young men (Escott and Buckner 2006). This results in a large pay penalty because part-time work tends to pay less. A woman aged 20 to 29 working part-time earns on average £3.03 less an hour than her male counterpart who works full-time (Escott and Buckner 2006). Work in traditionally female jobs can also be very vulnerable, meaning unstable work that places employees at risk of poverty now and in the future. Young women may experience injustice – e.g. bad treatment or high risks – at work because of imbalances of power in the employer–worker relationship (TUC Commission on Vulnerable Employment 2007).

Discrimination

Research has found that ethnicity also has an impact: Pakistani and Bangladeshi women experience a very large pay gap, larger than that experienced by white women (Platt 2006). Although there are laws against discrimination on the grounds of gender, the government's reluctance to enforce compulsory pay audits means that some women may be getting paid less for doing the same jobs as men (Bellamy and Cameron 2006).

Youth Policy

Government policy has made a number of flawed assumptions about young people, which have been used to justify young women's low pay. The law still allows employers to pay young people less: there are lower national minimum wage rates for younger people aged 16 to 21. One justification is that it is assumed that young people have less responsibility in work, but many 16–17-year-olds are doing the same jobs as 18–21-year-olds. Cass, aged 21, told us: 'I had a friend, she was a year older than me she got £1.50 an hour more than me. We did exactly the same [job].' Secondly, it is assumed that young women receive training in work, but this is questionable. Research shows that the industries that predominantly recruit young workers are generally unlikely to invest in formal training (Sekharen and Lucas 2003). Thirdly, to assume that young women can rely on others for financial support is not always correct and is a dangerous assumption to make. Lastly, it is argued that young people have lower living costs. However, it does not cost a 16- or 17-year-old young woman any less to buy essentials than an 18- or 25-year-old.

Young Women and Apprenticeships

As we mentioned before, the gender pay gap begins at 16 for young women if they enter apprenticeships. This became a grave concern for us because of government proposals to double the number of apprenticeships available. YWCA believed that unless action was taken, this expansion would widen the gender pay gap for a new generation of young women. With this in mind, we chose to focus on apprenticeships in our 'More than One Rung' campaign.

Making Work Work for Girls

We agreed with the government's proposition that apprenticeships can be an important route out of poverty for young people. Such training is one explanation given for lower rates of youth poverty in Austria and Germany (Arnstein et al. 2006). The 2006 Leitch Review of UK skills concluded that apprenticeships are crucial to the UK becoming a world leader in skills and competing in the global market. The number of young men and women on apprenticeships is now largely equal (Beck et al. 2006). But the distribution of young men and women is not equal in all sectors and there are some that are traditionally dominated by just one sex. Women are overwhelmingly found in hairdressing, early years care and education and health and social care, and men in construction, engineering and the motor industry. Women are more likely to do apprenticeships, and men are more likely to do advanced apprenticeships which lead to higher qualifications and therefore higher earnings. The latest figures show that of the 100,000 young people on advanced apprenticeships in England, just 30 per cent are female (Learning and Skills Council 2007a).

The government's success in increasing the number of females taking part in apprenticeships has not been extended to black and minority ethnic young people. In 2006–7, only 5 per cent of people who started an apprenticeship in England were from a Black or minority background (Learning and Skills Council 2007b). As people who are younger tend to be more ethnically diverse than the rest of the population, this is particularly concerning: nearly 18 per cent of young women aged 16 to 24 are from an ethnic minority group compared to 11 per cent of women aged over 25 (Escott and Buckner 2006).

Apprenticeship Pay is Different for Girls

Data on apprenticeships are often inadequate, but a 2007 Department for Innovation, Universities and Skills (DIUS) survey revealed alarming findings on female apprentices' pay (DIUS 2008: 24). There was a 21 per cent weekly gender pay gap. The lowest paid trainees worked in hairdressing, where 91 per cent of the apprentices were female. Their average take-home pay was £109 a week. The highest paid apprentices worked in the electro-technical sector, where 99 per cent were male. Their take-home pay was £210 a week. In 2005 the situation was even worse: of the one in five apprentices receiving less than £80 per week, over 70 per cent were female. Half of the trainees in early years care and education and hairdressing earned £80 or less a week. Female apprentices' low pay is largely a result of the sectors young women train in. More males than females enter advanced apprenticeships, which are better paid. Apprenticeships in the female dominated sectors are less likely to be available at NVQ level 3, which is the higher end of the qualifications (Ullman and Deakin 2005).

Initial pay rates are lower in female dominated sectors. A 2005 survey found that looking at level two trainees only, the two lowest paid sectors were early years care and education (£78 a week) and hairdressing (£86 a week) and the two highest paid sectors were electro-technical (£160 a week) and customer services (£155 a week) (Ullman and Deakin 2005). The sectors girls work in make them more likely to have non-employed rather than employed status, known in England as programme-led apprenticeships (Fuller et al. 2005). This means that apprentices have not yet secured a contract of employment with an employer and receive support from the state rather than a wage. This can result in them receiving less money. In England, the average wage of an apprentice in 2005 was £137 a week (Ullman and Deakin 2005), whereas the maximum a young person's household can receive in state support is just over £90. Non-employed status is particularly common in the childcare sector, where employers can be reluctant to employ a young person until they are 17 because they cannot work unsupervised or be counted in staff ratios (Spielhofer et al. 2006). The types of apprenticeships young women do affects not only their current pay, but it also has long-term financial implications. For example, girls are more likely to do apprenticeships than advanced apprenticeships, so are less likely to get NVQ level 3 qualifications which are required for progression into higher education and professional programmes (Beck et al. 2006).

The Impact of Low Apprenticeship Pay

As we have already discussed, the first impact is that young women miss out through the gender pay gap and lower wages. Sadly, the second impact is that some young women end up missing out entirely on doing an apprenticeship. Financial pressures mean that some disadvantaged young people do not have the luxury of being able to invest in their futures by doing an apprenticeship. They may be forced into jobs without training if it means receiving better pay right now, especially as a 16–17-year-old can receive a minimum of £130.61 through the national minimum wage for a 37-hour week.

Laura's Story

Laura trained as an apprentice for six months and received £78 for a 40-hour week. She really enjoyed the programme and was looking forward to eventually becoming a fully qualified travel consultant. But after being thrown out of her mum's house she was unable to complete her programme. Once she had paid for her hostel and travel, she barely had any money left. 'I didn't even have that long left to complete it really but I just couldn't do it.'

The third impact is that some young women are forced to drop out of their apprenticeship courses. Evidence indicates that only 59 per cent of apprentices currently complete their programmes (Learning and Skills Council 2007c). We believe that low pay may be contributing to this. The National Foundation for Educational Research found that (Spielhofer et al. 2006):

- Half of the apprentices surveyed were not satisfied with their pay; 28 per cent were dissatisfied and 24 per cent were very dissatisfied. Trainees receiving more money were significantly more likely to be satisfied.
- Over two-fifths of respondents were so dissatisfied with their pay that they had considered leaving their apprenticeship. More than a quarter of trainees who had dropped out of their training stated 'not getting enough money' as the main reason.

Sian's Story

Sian gave up her hairdressing apprenticeship because of low pay which she felt was unfair given the amount of work she was doing. She calculated that she could earn more by working in a chip shop and going to night college. 'I'd work from 9am to 6pm sometimes and I'd have to clean the shop every day, do stock checks, make sure everything was always clean, wash people's hair, make the tea, wash the dishes, I used to do quite a lot for £60 a week. Some people pay £60 for one haircut!'

Pathways to Work

Bearing in mind our concerns about occupational segregation, we began to investigate what influenced young women's choices about work and training. The government has spoken a lot recently about raising young people's aspirations.[10] However, YWCA's own research has found evidence that the most disadvantaged young women do not know how the world of work functions and have limited options to choose from. Their aspirations are limited by many things: firstly, their social capital, for example the networks they can utilize to gain access to work and secondly, their access to information and knowledge about the options available to them. They do not know what impact their choices will have on their future income or where to go for support.

Careers Advice and Guidance

Our experience, and research in Scotland,[11] shows that good quality careers advice and guidance, combined with the right support, helps young people find pathways to work, make career choices and stay engaged, and it reduces the number of young people not in education, employment or training (NEET). Gender stereotyping affects the decisions young women make about careers. Connexions, Cheshire & Warrington (2003) studied the opinions of disadvantaged young women on career choice and work experience. The data on where disadvantaged girls go after leaving school showed high levels of gender segregation in the choices young people make after completing compulsory education. This is despite a range of initiatives to encourage broader career aspirations. Research by Construction Skills (2006), the Sector Skills Council for the industry, has found that young women feel let down by the careers advice they receive and are being put off traditionally male dominated industries. 'Almost one third (31%) said they had been discouraged from studying certain subjects at school on the basis of their gender ... Further, two in five (42%) girls felt they were limited in terms of the options they were given at school simply because they are girls'.

Young Women's Opinions

In 2007 YWCA conducted participatory research with young people in Wolverhampton to find out what their barriers to work were (Johnson and Percy-Smith 2007). Young women told us that their self-esteem and confidence were crucial as to whether they succeeded in careers and work or not. Many young women were dealing with emotional and psychological barriers as well as deciding about their future. These must be dealt with alongside basic careers advice and guidance as they inhibit a young woman's ability to enter the labour market. Career decision making was also influenced by the fact that many girls living in poverty felt the pressure to earn money immediately for survival and were aware that this did not balance with long-term education plans.

When it came to advice and guidance, a lot of young people felt they were not listened to and that they got pushed in directions they didn't want to go. They were rarely asked about their dreams but instead often felt pushed towards the courses that were readily available.

Katy, 14

Katy is going to go to college to study childcare because, '[T]hat's all there is ... I wanted to be a chef but the school has closed down food tech and no one can do it (This has wrecked my future) ... I don't want to do childcare but had to because there was nothing else. I won't put much effort in to it'. (Johnson and Percy-Smith 2007)

Young people said that careers advice is not useful unless you already know what you want to do; they wanted more help with talking through options. Young women felt careers advisors often didn't understand them. Many young women mentioned a particular worker (a teacher, youth worker or support worker, for example) that had made a difference, but equally many mentioned someone who had had a negative effect. Those with a clear vision of the future had often been inspired by a role model. Young women told us they wanted to be treated with respect; they wanted someone friendly and caring who listens to what they say.

In our experience young mothers in particular miss out because their education may be disrupted and they may not be in school when careers advice is available. Few services are tailored to meet their specific needs and help them combine work, education and training with childcare and flexible work. They also find that programmes do not take enough account of the range of individual young women's situations and goals (Harden et al. 2006).

Work Experience

Young women in YWCA centres tell us they often get offered gender stereotypical work experience, most of which is poor quality. Unsurprisingly, Equal Opportunities Commission (EOC) research (Francis et al. 2005) found that work experience placements were influenced by gender stereotypes and that girls received a stronger steer into low paid, gender stereotypical work. According to Learning and Skills Councils data, out of 10,258 national work experience placements covering mechanical, construction and engineering, only 520 (or 5 per cent) were undertaken by girls (Francis et al. 2005).

Research also found that Education and Business Partnership staff, who aim to link learning providers with the world of work, did not prioritize challenging gender stereotypes. They claimed they wanted to see freedom of choice for pupils. However, the freedom of choice model is likely to perpetuate inequalities, as different pupils have different levels of knowledge of, and access to, work placements through their social networks. The 'freedom of choice' model for work experience presumes all young people start from an equal base and have equal social networks. We know that disadvantaged young women often do not have the social networks to independently access non-stereotypical or high earning work experience.

The EOC also found that placement takeup was linked to race and socio-economic group. Young women who felt they would definitely not go to university, an indicator of being in the most disadvantaged economic groups, were more likely to take up jobs like hairdressing and caring. However, young South Asian women were often more willing to try new types of work, although advisors often stereotyped them as unwilling to do so (Francis et al. 2005).

Campaign Successes

YWCA has seen significant progression in its campaign calls and will continue to lobby for change. Our most prominent call was for English apprentices to receive the equivalent of the national minimum wage (NMW). In September 2008, the Skills Secretary, John Denham announced that the minimum income for apprentices will go up from £80.00 per week to £95.00. He said that, 'It will be young women – apprentices like those in hairdressing and care – who will benefit most'. Such words clearly demonstrate the impact of the campaign. The rate remains below the equivalent to NMW but it is a very positive step in the right direction. We also remain concerned that there is no minimum income for apprentices in Wales.

YWCA has also continued to address the matter of low pay for young women. In late 2008 young women living in poverty met with Commissioners from the Low Pay Commission to discuss low pay for young people. The More than One Rung campaign called for young women to receive support to learn about work and training in ways that broaden their horizons and challenge gender stereotypes. We are developing a number of pre-apprenticeship courses that will help young women develop the skills that prepare them for training and work so they can get on to high-quality apprenticeship programmes. YWCA has also created a number of youth work models to work with young women in YWCA centres to help them learn about work and challenge gender stereotypes. We intend to disseminate these widely in the future. We have also identified the fact that getting an apprenticeship or work experience placement in an atypical career is only the first step. Young women may then face sexism and prejudice once in work. To help them overcome such challenges, we are promoting mentors who will help guide young women in the world of work.

We have worked closely with government to make sure stereotypes and equalities are addressed in the guidelines for Careers Information, Advice and Guidance. We also continue to run our own personal development programme called 'Wise Up' which builds young women's confidence and self-esteem to increase their ability to seek out and take up good quality work and training opportunities. We will continue to be a voice for disadvantaged young women and to make sure their needs stay high on the agenda during the forthcoming changes to legislation around education and skills.

Can We End Young Women's Poverty?

There are many ways of tackling young women's poverty in England and Wales and this approach is only one option. It was, however, a wise option as it echoed the intentions of government and got the issues high on the political agenda. It has also been practical in that it looks for routes out of poverty through work, but recognizes that work must be financially beneficial to be sustainable. Youth and gender clearly do compound poverty, yet this remains largely unnoticed or unrecognized by the majority of policy. Young women still suffer from lack of voice and representation and there is a danger that in the economic downturn their needs will once again be de-prioritized. However, YWCA continues to evidence our argument and build a strong message that achieving equality in work and skills is vital to the success of education and skills programmes in the UK. Young women's equality is pivotal to the success or failure of such proposals and so, until this is achieved, YWCA's call for change will remain.

Notes

1. This figure does not include those aged 16 to 18 in part-time or full-time education up to and including 'A' level standard.
2. This is a measure of disposable income after housing costs and equivalized to take into account the size and makeup of different households.
3. Note that the sample they used was very small so the findings may not be applicable to the wider population.
4. In this survey, poverty is measured as lacking two or more necessities due to lack of money and having a low income – the income threshold varied by the size and composition of the household.
5. A subjective measure asked respondents, 'how many pounds after tax do you think are necessary to keep a household such as yours out of absolute poverty?' Absolute poverty is defined as an income insufficient to cover basic necessities such as adequate diet, housing, heating, clothing, water and prescription costs.
6. These are socially perceived necessities and include things like a television and money to spend on oneself weekly. To see a full list, visit: www.bris.ac.uk/poverty/pse/sum_find.htm#Socially%20perceived%20necessities.
7. See, for example, the Poverty Site: http://www.poverty.org.uk/summary/key%20facts.shtml.
8. In some cases we have been unable to distinguish which effects of poverty are unique to young women because of the lack of simultaneous gender and youth analysis in the available research.
9. Survey designed and conducted by Julie Moloney for YWCA England & Wales. For more information, see Moloney and Russell (2008).
10. For example in Gordon Brown's succession speech in Manchester.
11. Careers Scotland delivered Enhanced Resource Pilots with NEET (not in education, employment or training) young people to schools in Scotland. In the first pilot, NEET figures reduced from 31 per cent to 6 per cent over two years. Pilots are now being rolled out in seven local authority areas as part of the Scottish government's 'More Choices, More Chances' strategy. See http://www.careers-scotland.org.uk/AboutCS/Initiatives/EnhancedResourcePP.asp.

Bibliography

Arnstein, A., M. Iacovou and L. Mencarini 2006. 'Youth Poverty and Transition to Adulthood in Europe', *Demographic Research*, 15 (2): 21–50.

Beck, V., A. Fuller and L. Unwin 2006. 'Safety in Stereotypes? The Impact of Gender and "Race" on Young People's Perceptions of their Post-compulsory Education and Labour Market Opportunities', *British Educational Research Journal*, 32 (5): 667–86.

Bellamy, K. and S. Cameron 2006. *Gender Equality in the 21st Century: Modernising the Legislation*. London: Fawcett Society.

Blanden, J. 2006. 'Bucking the Trend – What Enables Those Who Are Disadvantaged in Childhood to Succeed Later in Life?', Working Paper 31, Department for Work and Pensions, London: HMSO.

Brannigan, E. 2005. '"His Money or Our Money?" Financial Abuse of Women in Intimate Partner Relationships'. A report by the Coburg Brunswick Community Legal and Financial Counselling Centre Inc. Victoria, Australia.

Cassen, R. and G. Kingdon 2007. *Tackling Low Educational Achievement.* York: Joseph Rowntree Foundation.

Citizens Advice 2003. 'Criminal Justice Bill', London.

Connexions Cheshire & Warrington 2003. *Career Choice and Work Experience: Perspectives from Young Women.* Northwich: Connexions Cheshire & Warrington. Cited in Hutchinson, J. and H. Lamb 2007. *Evidence for YWCA Campaign II: Review of Literature on Support for Work Choices.* Derby: Centre for Guidance Studies, University of Derby.

Constructionskills 2006. *Three Quarters of Young Women being Put Off Traditionally Male-dominated Industries by Poor Careers Advice.* London: Construction Skills. Cited in Hutchinson, J. and H. Lamb 2007. *Evidence for YWCA Campaign II: Review of Literature on Support for Work Choices.* Derby: Centre for Guidance Studies, University of Derby.

Department for Education and Skills 2005. *Apprenticeship Pay: A Survey of Earnings by Sector.* London: DfE.

Department of Communities and Local Government 2006. 'The Economies of Deprived Neighbourhoods: Summary of Research'. London: DCLG.

DIUS (2008) *Apprenticeship Pay: 2007 Survey of Earnings by Sector.* London: Department for Innovation, Universities and Skills.

Escott, K. and L. Buckner 2006. *Young Women's Employment: Growing Up Poor in England and Wales.* Oxford: YWCA England & Wales.

Floro, M.S. 1995. 'Women's Well-being, Poverty and Work Intensity', *Feminist Economics*, 1 (3): 1–25.

Francis, B., J. Osgood, J. Dalgety and L. Archer 2005. *Gender Equality in Work Experience Placements for Young People.* Report commissioned by the Equal Opportunities Commission. Manchester: EOC.

Fuller, A., V. Beck and L. Unwin 2005. 'The Gendered Nature of Apprenticeships: Employers' and Young People's Perspectives', *Education and Training*, 47 (4/5): 298–311.

Gordon, D., L. Adelman, K. Ashworth, J. Bradshaw, R. Levitas, S. Middleton, C. Pantazis, D. Patsios, S. Payne, P. Townsend and J. Williams 2000. *Poverty and Social Exclusion in Britain.* York: Joseph Rowntree Foundation.

Harden, A., G. Brunton, A. Fletcher, A. Oakley, H. Burchett and M. Backhans 2006. *Young People, Pregnancy and Social Exclusion: A Systematic Synthesis of Research Evidence to Identify Effective, Appropriate and Promising Approaches for Prevention and Support.* London: EPPI-Centre, Social Science Research Unit, Institute of Education, University of London.

Johnson, V. and B. Percy-Smith 2007. *Give Us a Chance! Young People's Reflections on Work Choices and Support.* Oxford: YWCA.

Joshi, H. 1992. 'The Cost of Caring'. In C. Glendinning and J. Millar (eds), *Women and Poverty in Britain.* Hemel Hempstead: Harvester Wheatsheaf.

Learning and Skills Council 2007a. 'Monthly Average in Learning Aug-Jan 07'. Available at: http://www.apprenticeships.org.uk (accessed 12 September 2011).

—— 2007b. 'Work Based Learning 2006/07: Starts by Ethnicity'. Available at: http://www.apprenticeships.org.uk (accessed 12 September 2011).

—— 2007c. 'Quarterly Cumulative Leavers and Successes'. Available at: http://www.apprenticeships.org.uk (accessed 12 September 2011).

Leitch, S. 2006. *Leitch Review of Skills: Prosperity for All in the Global Economy – World Class Skills*. Final Report. London: HM Treasury.

Lister, R. 2004. *Poverty*. Cambridge: Polity Press.

Marsh, A. 2001. 'Helping British Lone Parents Get and Keep Paid Work'. In J. Millar and K. Rowlingson (eds), *Lone Parents, Employment and Social Policy*. Bristol: Policy Press

Mayhew, E. and J. Bradshaw 2005. 'Mothers, Babies and the Risks of Poverty', *Poverty*, 121: 13–16.

Middleton, S., K. Ashworth and R. Walker (eds) 1994. *Family Fortunes*. London: CPAG.

Moloney, J. and L. Russell 2008. *Young Women and Financial Abuse*. Oxford: YWCA England and Wales.

Office for National Statistics 2006. 'Annual Survey of Hours and Earnings'.

Pahl, J. 1989. *Money and Marriage*. London: Macmillan.

Pantazis, C., D. Gordon and R. Levitas (eds) 2006. *Poverty and Social Exclusion in Britain: The Millennium Survey*. Bristol: The Policy Press.

Platt, L. 2006. 'Pay Gaps: The Position of Ethnic Minority Women and Men'. Manchester: Equal Opportunities Commission.

Ridge, T. 2002. *Child Poverty and Social Exclusion from a Child's Perspective*. Bristol: Polity Press.

—— 2005. 'Feeling Under Pressure: Low-Income Girls Negotiating School Life'. In G. Lloyd (ed.), *Problem Girls*. London: Routledge Falmer.

Sekharen, S. and Lucas, R. 2003. In EOC (2005) 'Consultation Response: Low Pay Commission, Extending the National Minimum Wage to 16 and 17 Year Olds'.

Spielhofer, T., J. Nelson, L. O'Donnell and D. Sims 2006. *The Role of Training Allowances in Incentivising the Behaviour of Young People and Employers*. London: DfES.

TUC Commission on Vulnerable Employment 2007. *Hard Work, Hidden Lives: The Full Report of the TUC Commission on Vulnerable Employment*. London: TUC.

Ullman, A. and U. Deakin 2005. 'Apprenticeship Pay: A Survey of Earnings by Sector'. London: DfES.

Women's Budget Group 2005. 'Women's and Children's Poverty: Making the Links'. Available at: www.wbg.org.uk/RRB_Reports.htm (accessed 12 September 2011).

Women and Work Commission 2006. 'Shaping a Fairer Future'. London: Department of Trade and Industry.

Yeandle, S., K. Escott, L. Grant and E. Batty 2003. 'Women and Men Talking about Poverty'. Manchester: Equal Opportunities Commission.

YWCA 2003. *Turning Opinion into Action – Young Women and Participation*. Oxford: YWCA England & Wales.

—— 2008. *Shock to the System: Real Life for Young Women in Wales*. Oxford: YWCA England & Wales.

Chapter 4
'WE'RE NOT POOR – THE OTHERS ARE':
TALKING WITH CHILDREN ABOUT POVERTY AND SOCIAL
EXCLUSION IN MILTON KEYNES, ENGLAND

Anna Lærke

❦

In 2005–2008, I conducted an independent qualitative evaluation of the Children's Fund services in Milton Keynes. My brief was simple, although the job was not: to provide an ongoing evaluation of how the Milton Keynes Children's Fund (MKCF) services were experienced and used, on the ground, by children and their families; to do so on the basis of ethnographic data collection; and to feed back my findings in interim reports regularly presented to the MKCF Management Board.[1]

Data were collected slowly and over a long period of time, mainly through participant-observation, focus group facilitation, and group interviews with children and parents living in so-called 'deprived' areas of Milton Keynes. For this chapter, I draw mainly on data collected from a sample of approximately 30 children, aged 4 to 16. I also refer to data collected among parents and service providers in the MKCF areas. Interviews were recorded and transcribed; focus group discussions and participant-observation data were not. Some of this material has been presented to the MKCF Management Board, albeit in a different format and for other purposes.[2]

My purpose here is to show that children (and their families) using the MKCF services were mostly unaware of the larger socio-economic and cultural bases upon which these services rest. 'Unaware', not because they were any less observant than we all are of the premises upon which cultural meaning rests, but as a key function of the production of that cultural meaning (cf. Bourdieu 1977). In Milton Keynes, this unawareness, or 'misrecognition' (*ibid.*), was expressed in two distinct ways. One concerns the children's noticeable silence as regards the issue of their own poverty; and the other has to do with the children misrecognizing the 'us' and 'them' divisions inadvertently produced by those children's own use of the MKCF services.

The Children's Fund and the *Every Child Matters* Agenda

The Milton Keynes Children's Fund Partnership was set up in 2003/2004 as part of the Third Wave of Children's Fund local initiatives in England. The Children's Fund (CF) is a National Government programme initiated in November 2000, targeting 5–13 year olds and their families. Its equivalent for 0–5 year olds and their families is known as Sure Start. The national CF programme is due to run until 2011.

There are 149 local Children's Fund partnerships in England, working with disadvantaged children and their families. Their overall aims were described thus on the national Children's Fund website in 2009:

> The Children's Fund aims to provide a responsive approach to meeting needs and developing good practice for services for children and young people at risk of social exclusion. It aims to develop services so that children and young people at risk of social exclusion are identified early. Its purpose is to fund services for children, young people, their families and communities which tackle the barriers and disadvantages they face and which help them to realise their potential. (Children's Fund)

The CF is part of a social, health, education and employment agenda instigated by the New Labour Government in 1997. Since then, a terminology replacing notions of poverty, inequality and class with the notion of 'social exclusion' has pervaded government family and child welfare policy as well as public discourse (Levitas 2005 [1998]: ix). The Social Exclusion Taskforce (formerly the Social Exclusion Unit) defines social exclusion in terms of individuals' ability to participate in mainstream society. Resources are seen as crucial to this ability and are broadly defined:

> Social exclusion is about more than income poverty. It is a short-hand term for what can happen when people or areas have a combination of linked problems such as unemployment, discrimination, poor skills, low incomes, poor housing, high crime and family breakdown. These problems are linked and mutually reinforcing. Social exclusion is an extreme consequence of what happens when people don't get a fair deal throughout their lives, often because of disadvantage at birth, and this disadvantaged [sic] can be transmitted from one generation to the next. (Social Exclusion Task Force)

Thus, social exclusion is the result of happenstance conspiring to disadvantage individuals and groups. But it is also the result of such disadvantage being 'transmitted from one generation to the next'. The contradiction is telling: being socially excluded both is and is not the responsibility of the individual. The Task Force's definition of 'social exclusion' is remarkably unclear. It depicts a cluster of causes but avoids explicating the nature of the relationship between them. This is typical of government social policy rhetoric. In close-up, the precise meaning and implications of phrases such as 'good practice', 'barriers', 'realizing potential' and 'social exclusion' unravel somewhat, providing scope for different, and even contradictory, interpretations. Arguably, it is precisely because such phrases evade clear and narrow definition – i.e. because they will mean different things to different people and in different contexts – that they can be so extensively employed – take up so much space – in public discourse.

The vacuities of family and social welfare policy discourse seem to me crystallized into optimum de-contextualization in the much quoted, and widely used, five 'core objectives' of the *Every Child Matters* (ECM) agenda:

> The Government's aim is for every child, whatever their [sic] background or their circumstances, to have the support they need to:
> • Stay healthy
> • Stay safe
> • Enjoy and achieve
> • Make a positive contribution
> • Achieve economic well-being (see Dept for Children, Schools and Families Archives website)

On the basis of such broad formulations, local CF partnerships, or management boards,[3] identify areas, communities or groups 'at risk' of social exclusion, and allocate funds supporting a range of services for children and families.

One such service is the Milton Keynes Community Mobiliser (MKCM) programme (now Community Action:MK, see website).

'Targeted Universalism' and the Community Mobilisers in Milton Keynes

The Milton Keynes Community Mobiliser (MKCM) service is worth attention for its unusually radical commitment to service user participation, training and empowerment (see Lærke 2006a, 2006b). At the time of my evaluation, the MKCM attracted about two-thirds of the Children's Fund budget in Milton Keynes. Unlike most local CF partnerships, the MKCF management board risked experimentation at its 2003 launch and formulated a new and unique service approach rather than supporting existing governmental and non-governmental services in the CF areas. According to the director of the MKCF board, this approach aims to de-stigmatize service use through a focus on what he calls 'targeted universalism':

> There's an analogy to the paint brush and the roller. If you imagine you have a wall that needs painting but not all of it needs painting, maybe 50 or 60% needs painting. It would be silly to use a paint brush on it. Because even though some of the wall is going to be painted that doesn't need painting it is much quicker to use a roller than it

is to use a paint brush. Targeted universalism is like that … what we do is … identify the high need areas, and then we set up open services in those areas. We target services, universal services, in those areas and therefore there is a very high hit rate. The added advantage of that is that you are helping people, but you are helping them in a non-stigmatizing way. You also tend to draw in people with no problems in that area who act as a spur and as a model to people who might be functionally at a lower social level … I think most social support systems in this country tend to target people as problem people, as problem families … with targeted universalism, we target a particular estate or cluster of estates, but we do it in a way which doesn't actually pick out people as problem people. (MKCF Manager)

Thus, the MKCF devotes resources and attention to so-called 'upstream' early prevention rather than more heavy-handed 'downstream' intervention. Doing so, it is argued, enables service users to identify, express and to some extent address their own needs, thus allowing space for grass roots participation and empowerment. However, the notion that people are empowered by 'participation' and by 'being heard' rests on an unexamined presumption – i.e. a belief – that all potential action is recognizable as such and that all manner of voices can indeed be heard. It rests on the belief that dominant discourse will and can allow, not only for dissent, but for resistance.

At the core of this belief lies a buzz-wordy invocation of 'empowerment' which fails to question the nature and extent of such empowerment. It is no coincidence, for instance, that I have been met with baffled silence when making comments such as this one in my evaluation reports:

Prevention, of course, must necessarily imply some specific – albeit not necessarily explicated – ideas about what it is that should be prevented. It also necessarily carries within it presumptions about who would be 'at risk' of whatever it is that is to be prevented. In other words, a preventative approach identifies groups or individuals 'at risk of social exclusion', thereby marking people as 'in need' *before* this need really manifests itself. (Lærke 2006b: 37)

Studying Poverty

At the best of times, it is difficult to ask people about their personal experiences of family life, money and social position. As a researcher, you may find yourself asking questions that people have not anticipated or which they find it difficult or upsetting to contemplate. In her study of child poverty and social exclusion in England, Ridge notes:

Poverty is in many ways a socially unacceptable word, heavily imbued with stigma and prejudices. Therefore, research which seeks to explore the nature and impact of poverty needs to be conducted with great sensitivity. (Ridge 2002: 9)

In other words, doing research with individuals and families considered 'at risk of social exclusion' is potentially very difficult, methodologically, analytically, and also inter-personally. Moreover, as poverty nearly always escapes direct scrutiny, so does its cultural manifestation: 'class', as a mode of identification, runs deep in the foundation of Englishness (Thompson 1963, Willis 1978), whilst at the same time escaping behind 'polite manners' that render it near-impossible, but also unnecessary, to speak explicitly about class (Williams 2006). As Steedman puts it: '[i]n Britain there is no ... everyday, laconic understanding that here it is class attitudes ... that shape the quiet, genteel and sentimental oppression of working-class children' (Steedman 1982: 3).

Thus protecting itself from being addressed directly, class becomes a mode of being which cannot easily be challenged. In Milton Keynes, among adult service users, class was a way of speaking and dressing, a way of moving through the room, a particularly defiant way of going outside for a cigarette, a way of carrying one's handbag or sweetening one's tea. Class *was* challenged, as a tag or stigma attached to unwilling residents: 'I *hate* that "deprived area" tag. What's "deprived" about us? This is a good place to live' (Mother, resident of Milton Keynes).

But it was also not challenged, as a mode of identification confining groups of people to a category. A group of mothers engaged with the Community Mobiliser Service spoke about community, participation and different kinds of neighbours:

Parent 1: 'You see kids walking around the estate ... doing nothing, really. They could be doing arts and crafts or football or food fun or what have you. It's a shame'.

Parent 2: 'Yes, there are children who are not taking it [the Mobiliser Service] up'.

Anna: 'Why do you think that is?'

Parent 1: 'Oh, because they can't be bothered'.

Parent 3: 'It's not the kids, though ... it's the parents. If they didn't have to stay with their kids, they'd send them'.

Parent 4: 'But it isn't a child minding service'.

Parent 1: 'They'd rather stay at home on the sofa'.

Anna: 'Does anyone here know families who don't use the service? And why they don't?'

Parent 4: 'Of course ... they just can't be bothered'.

Parent 3: 'You know X [named neighbour]? When we had Food Fun in the Community Centre at half-term, her youngest went and I kind of looked after him ... I shouldn't, really ...'.

Parent 4: 'You shouldn't *have* to ....'.

Parent 3: 'I know, but I did ...'.

Parent 2: '... and all the time, X sat around with her mates and a can of lager'.

Parent 1: 'She [parent not using the service] is bone idle, she is'.

Parent 2: 'Yes, that's all there is to it'.

(Focus group, Milton Keynes)

Thus, these mothers rejected a 'label' by assigning that 'label' to others. In their own way, children did that too.

Children Talking about the *Every Child Matters* Objectives

As I began asking children questions about the five *Every Child Matters* objectives, the first four objectives were swiftly and articulately addressed. The children were almost too ready with phrases of received wisdom such as 'you feel safe when there's no graffiti', 'we tidied up our neighbourhood, and it makes you feel good when things look nice – it's more clean now', 'being healthy is about healthy eating' and 'when you achieve something it makes you proud'. Less contrived replies, such as 'being safe means you look out for perverts' and 'achievement is going to school, but I hate school', were rare.

However, the fifth objective, 'economic well-being', seemed to make little sense to the children in terms of own everyday experiences. Poverty, in fact, appeared to be a distant, literally foreign, issue. Asked what they took 'achieving economic well-being' to mean, the children typically replied:

Child 1: 'give to charity'.
Child 2: 'like Red Nose Day … give to charity'.
Child 3: 'it's about the environment. You have to look after the environment'.
Child 4: 'like Live Aid and that … some people in Africa don't have clean water'.
(Children aged 7–11 years)[4]

It was clear to me that I was not asking the 'poverty' question right, so I turned to my own immediate and personal experiences for help – as one does. I told the children about my own situation, as a single mother with young children and a very low wage. I told them about the grief of not being able to afford to take my children to see the new Harry Potter film, about holidays I could not afford, about my children's embarrassment at bringing 'Tesco Value' crisp bags in their lunch boxes, and about the difficult choice between paying our TV licence or having a birthday party. The children recognized all that. Of course they did. They just did not recognize it as poverty.

My approach may have been unusually direct, asking specifically about money and poverty, and I may have pushed more than I should have. Undoubtedly, I pushed harder for clear answers than would be deemed ethically right by some (see Alderson 2004). However, it would have made little sense for me to express myself more vaguely when my objective was to uncover how the children made sense of the phrase 'achieving economic well-being' – itself, arguably, a euphemism. This observation alone – that poverty cannot be outspoken even by the government setting the agenda for these 'inclusive' and 'preventative' services – may go a long way to explain the children's mute responses. But although the embarrassment of poverty should not be underestimated, the children's alienation was more than a defence against potential stigmatization. It was also, I suggest, a more deeply rooted *misrecognition* (Bourdieu 1977) of their own 'othering' of a poverty; an 'othering' of which they were themselves, in the larger societal context, the victims.

The 'Othering' of Poverty

Two episodes have stuck in my mind.

I was meeting with five children, aged 9–10, to facilitate a focus group discussion among them, in the room used for Breakfast and After School Clubs in their school. All five children regularly used the CF services. As we were talking about classmates or neighbours not using the service, a small group of boys gathered at the open door, making faces at us. I invited the boys to join us but was immediately informed by one of the group participants that these boys should not take part, as they did 'not know anything about the Children's Fund' and consequently would have nothing to contribute. The boys themselves simply giggled and ran off, in apparent agreement.

This exchange struck me as odd, since we were in fact talking about the usefulness (for me) in knowing about people who did not use or know about the Children's Fund. Even with evidence literally on the doorstep, the focus group children failed to see their peers as potential service users. This, I would suggest, is not because these children were deliberately exclusive, but it might be because an un-challenged distinction between 'us' and 'them' – between those who take part and those who do not – was so deeply embedded in users' as well as non-users' perceptions of self and others that it simply did not occur to either to question it – not even when that particular question was the focus of our discussion at the time.

That an 'us' and 'them' distinction was at work was later confirmed in my brief conversation with three of the boys who had been at the door earlier. As I left the focus group, I met these three in the car park. 'Is that your car?', asked one. I said it was and asked why they had not joined us earlier in the Club Room. 'Oh, we don't go there,' said one. 'The After School Club is stupid.' said another. Pointing at the third boy, his friend explained, 'he was excluded'. Asked for what, the third boy replied that he had been caught smoking outside the Club Room during After School Club.

On another occasion, I went with families on a day trip, organized and partly funded by the MKCF, to a local amusement park. As we were leaving on the coach, I spotted three bored-looking boys kicking a drinks can around the pavement by the local shops. I asked the children next to me if they knew those boys, and why it might be that they were not joining the trip. I was told that, yes, the children knew the boys, and, of course, they were not on the trip because they never took part in anything organized by the Children's Fund. A mother behind me commented that these boys were 'always looking for trouble' and that their parents were 'no good' and would never take them on a trip. The boy sitting next to me explained that the boys did not even go on the Cadbury World trip last year because their parents could not afford it.[5] The mother behind me commented that these boys' families 'probably needed' the CF services more than anyone. Not only did these views echo the views of the service providers, that those not using the services needed the services the most (see Lærke 2006b), this was also the closest to a direct link between service use and poverty that I ever heard suggested by anyone using the CF services.

Among those who were engaged with the MKCF services, I often heard comments about parents 'depriving' their children of the benefits from using these services by refusing to accompany the children to outings, activities and parties. Many of the services were aimed at the whole family and for that reason required adult family members to take part. This was an issue of concern for a number of MKCF practitioners who were divided over whether or not to turn away an unaccompanied child. Regularly, young children would turn up for activities with teenage siblings, or no one, accompanying them. Most practitioners – such as the Community Mobilisers – were adamant that they would not turn any child away, but, strictly speaking, that is what they should have done. Thus, whilst the 'inclusive' family approach – and the 'targeted universalism' – succeeded in engaging some families, they were clearly flawed in their insistence on parental participation.

Children who used the services were aware of this flaw and often commented on the unfairness of this state of affairs. They consistently blamed parents for other children's non-participation. Asked why some children did not know and engage with the services, children typically replied that 'they aren't allowed', 'parents haven't got the time' or 'their mam won't let them'.

As illustrated by the children's responses to the fifth ECM outcome (which, puzzlingly, the National Evaluation of Children's Fund left out when collecting evidence from children and young people; see Edwards et al. 2006: 184–5), those who engaged with the Children's Fund services seemed to be generally unaware that those services were predicated on the assessment of 'deprivation', 'poverty', 'need' and 'lack' in the areas where they lived. Service users constructed non-users as a group distinct from themselves, that is, they divided the community into an 'us' and a 'them'. This is not, in itself, all that surprising. Arguably, all group identities are premised on the mutual construction of an 'inside' and an 'outside'. What is interesting is that this 'othering' did not extend to the wider societal context within and by which *all* residents of the community had been collectively identified as at risk of social exclusion.

As already mentioned, prevention – by its very nature – creates problems, because prevention must define, rather than simply identify, what is to be prevented in the first place. Thus, there is a tension between empowerment and social control. Whilst the young service users clearly felt empowered by the participatory agenda underlying the services, they – equally clearly – did not recognize the social control inherent in that agenda. Ironically, it was the consistency and success with which the MKCF sought to de-stigmatize service use that made those living in the target areas unaware of that targeting and its origin and purpose. Among the service users, many adults and all the children believed that the services were universally available. Arguably, that is testament to successful de-stigmatization, something which is notoriously difficult to achieve for services aimed at preventing social exclusion, family breakdown, school exclusion, teenage pregnancy, youth crime, anti-social behaviour and similar problems heavily laden with negative connotations (Lærke 2006a). However, because the de-stigmatizing agenda did not explicitly address and challenge the very notion of social exclusion/inclusion, nor the issue of social control embedded in all charitable and 'social' work, the discursive foundation from which the CF service drew its authority remained hidden from view and thus protected from scrutiny. This, I suggest, resulted in a transposition of us/them conceptualizations from the larger societal perspective into, on the one hand, the narrower and more immediate perspective of the local community and, on the other, a far-fetched global perspective rendering identification and recognition virtually impossible. In other words, the 'them' were sought out either among immediate neighbours, also living in council houses and on low incomes, or among the poor children in Red Nose Day Africa, rather than among fellow British citizens of the home-owning, comfortably off, car-driving classes. Thus the anti-stigma agenda of children's and family services did not so much challenge stigmatization as redirect its aim away from those who might have the strength to resist such stigmatization and towards those, in the margins, who did not. And when this happens, an 'us' and 'them' distinction prevents communities from acknowledging that, in terms of general stigma, everyone is 'in the same boat'. It 'protects' service users from seeing *themselves* as 'deprived' or 'at risk'. The 'targeted universalism', in other words, succeeded in de-stigmatizing the use of Children's Fund services by encouraging a distinction between the deserving and the undeserving (see Lærke 2006b: 29–31, 33; Lærke 2006c).

Individualizing Service Participation and Usage

It is common for publications and websites concerned with social exclusion and deprivation to stress the importance of support for individuals and individual families in building resilience, overcoming barriers to social inclusion, fulfilling their potential, and building pathways away from social exclusion, abuse, victimization, crime, unemployment, and so on (Social Exclusion Task Force). Emphasis is on the individual, as is also evident in the way the ECM objectives are formulated, and, indeed, in the very policy title 'Every Child Matters'. The following story illustrates how every child does matter, but it also shows that the way in which each child matters can only be understood in relation to the social context of that child. The story was told to me by two young people who, supported by the MKCF, worked with children in the local community. Among these children were three siblings who lived with their mother, stepfather and older brother:

> There are four children in this family. Three of them come to activities. The oldest one doesn't. The youngest is a girl of five, and then there are the two boys of eight and ten. They came from the beginning … They were naughty, a real pain sometimes, and the boys were constantly fighting and the girl didn't want to do any of the things we suggested. They were dressed inappropriately. Their teeth are really bad. Sometimes they come hungry and we've started giving the kids fruit and sandwiches […] We started off with sports, but the girl didn't like to do anything physical. So we got this idea to give her the option of being a coach assistant. We gave her a whistle, and she knew the rules through her brothers. She liked that. She is often refereeing in football

matches now … You could see that she began to see that rules are there for a reason … The middle child, he learned to behave … and the boys get on much better. Now they stick up for their sister … before they were just rude to her. The children have bonded. (Interview with young people working with children)

This was presented to me as a 'success story' about three children being helped to engage with their community and each other in constructive ways. But the underlying socio-economic conditions that allow children to go hungry and to miss proper dental health care remained unchallenged.

Needless to say, communities are made up of individuals, and social interaction – constructive as well as destructive – is rooted in the practices and beliefs of individuals. Nevertheless, services such as the Children's Fund must *also* be understood sociologically, that is, they must be understood as a form of social engineering. Failure to recognize the 'identification power' of charitable and preventative intervention would be to leave out of sight a crucial aspect of their impact. Or, to put it differently, as one group in society is identified as 'at risk', another is identified as 'protected', and, further, within the 'at risk' group, the process by which participants become involved is also the process by which non-participants become excluded.

Thus, a sociological perspective can reveal, not only that, but also how, among those 'at risk of exclusion', some are more 'excluded' than others (for a more detailed discussion, see Lærke 2006c). Evading this perspective not only allows for a popular notion that responsibility for poverty lies with the individual rather than with the structural dictates of a market-driven economy, it also enables (or compels) those who are (deemed) socially excluded to deny, individually, rather than challenge, collectively, that label. When responsibility for family welfare is thus individualized, not only do the systemic causes of poverty disappear out of sight, there will also be some categories of individuals who are held more responsible than the rest. In contemporary England, it is parents, and in particular single mothers, who bear that responsibility.

In her analysis of New Labour social policies, Ruth Levitas discusses a related – and similarly narrow – perspective on poverty. Over the past decade, she argues, employment, education- and social and health care policies have increasingly focused on participation in the paid workforce as the route *par excellence* out of poverty and exclusion (Levitas 2005 [1998]). As long-term, secure and decently paid employment is out of the reach of many parents who, forced by the notorious lack of full-time state-funded childcare for the under-fives, have spent years outside paid employment or further education, the emphasis on inclusion in the labour market particularly disadvantages single mothers with young children (Levitas 2005 [1998]). In line with Levitas' analysis, the majority of CF service users in Milton Keynes are children under the age of 13 and single mothers with no or poorly paid part-time employment.

Policing the Borders

Whilst it is central government discourse that produces dominant constructs of social inclusion/exclusion, and thereby also dominant constructs of 'the social' itself, it is front-line staff on the ground, such as the Milton Keynes Mobilisers, who must administer and negotiate that construct in practice.

The MKCF community workers are middle-class professionals and they do not themselves live in areas identified as 'deprived'. To put it perhaps too crassly: every morning when they go to work, they literally and figuratively cross the border between socially included and socially excluded. Moreover, they do not hide away in offices. They walk the streets of the neighbourhoods they work in. You could say that they embody and enact a discursive process that distinguishes the 'deprived' from the rest. Or you could say that they patrol the borders between the mainstream and socially included, on the one hand, and, on the other, the poor, the people 'at risk' of social exclusion and 'in need' of social services. Their work, as we have seen, also helps police and define boundaries *within* the 'deprived' communities, between those who can be included and those who cannot, between that which can be helped and that which cannot, and between the 'social' and 'the anti-social'.

Clear from the statements by both child and adult service users is that poverty and social exclusion are seen as problems faced by others. The fundamental approach to poverty – as manifest in social policy formulations as well as in Milton Keynes residents' views – is one that avoids explicating poverty as a collective problem to be understood in sociological terms. It is an approach that emphasizes the individual's unique 'pathway out of exclusion'.

If we look at poverty as activity or process, we can see that 'social exclusion' is a very social process, and one that involves society as a whole. Those who are deemed 'socially excluded' form an integral, and a key, part of the social fabric. Moreover, for this to 'work', for social distinctions to retain their power, we must, in the sociological sense, be unaware of producing them. Arguably, children, being less burdened by the repetition of *habitus* (that is, by time), may be more powerful agents of social change. But, being thus burdened, they are also forced to conform the more rigorously to the *status quo*. To assume that children can more readily 'break the mould' is to ignore the unique pressure upon children everywhere to become society's next generation of adults.

Notes

1. The first three interim reports are available on the Milton Keynes Children's Fund website (see Lærke 2006a, 2006b, 2007).
2. For an interesting discussion of different styles of writing for different audiences and purposes, see Neale (2008).
3. The MKCF Management Board consists of directors or deputy directors of various governmental and non-governmental organizations concerned with children's, family, health and crime prevention services. There is also a representative of the local communities on the Board. I believe this composition is fairly typical across the local CF Boards.

4. Like the majority of parents I spoke with, the children were, or claimed to be, unaware of the key premise upon which the service they used was based. In light of the children's focus on overseas poverty and aid, this was perhaps particularly ironic in relation to the Mobiliser service which is directly inspired by ideas underpinning overseas community-based aid projects (see Bigdon and Sachithanandam 2003, Care International 2002, Kampala Ministry of Local Government 2003, Korf 2002).

5. Although organized and partly funded by the MKCF, activities requiring coach hire and entrance fees usually cost £2–5 per person which must be paid in advance.

Bibliography

Alderson, P. 2004. 'Ethics'. In S. Fraser, V. Lewis, S. Ding, M. Kellett and C. Robinson (eds), *Doing Research with Children and Young People*. London: Sage in association with The Open University.

Bigdon, C. and S.A. Sachithanandam 2003. *Strengthening Local Governance through Community Mobilisation*, Working Paper 50, Integrated Food Security Programme, Trincomalee, Sri Lanka.

Bourdieu, P. 1977. *Outline of a Theory of Practice*. Cambridge Studies in Social Anthropology. Cambridge: Cambridge University Press.

Care International 2002. *Community Resources Training Manual*. Care International in Zimbabwe, Harare.

Children's Fund, see Dept. of Education Archive: http://www.education.gov.uk/vocabularies/educationtermsandtags/1492 (accessed 31 October 2011).

Community Action: MK, see http://www.mkweb.co.uk/mkchildrensfund/ (accessed 31 November 2011).

Department for Children, Schools and Families Archive: http://webarchive.nationalarchives.gov.uk/20110104141502/dcsf.gov.uk/everychildmatters/ (accessed 31 October 2011).

Edwards, A., M. Barnes, I. Plewis and K. Morris et al. 2006. *Working to Prevent the Social Exclusion of Children and Young People. Final Lessons from the National Evaluation of the Children's Fund*. University of Birmingham and Institute of Education, DfES Research Report No 734.

Kampala Ministry of Local Government 2003. *Community Participation and Mobilisation*, Participant's Handbook for Lower Local Governments, Kampala, Uganda.

Korf, B. 2002. *Promoting Communication and Dialogue*. Working Paper 32, Integrated Food Security Programme, Trincomalee, Sri Lanka.

Lærke, A. 2006a. *Second Interim Report. Independent Qualitative Evaluation of Milton Keynes Children's Fund's Services*. Milton Keynes: The Open University, Faculty for Education and Languages. Available at: http://www.mkweb.co.uk/mkchildrensfund/

——— 2006b. *The Milton Keynes Community Mobiliser Service. First Interim Report from an On-going, Independent, Small-scale, and Qualitative Evaluation of Milton Keynes Children's Fund*. Milton Keynes: The Open University, Faculty for Education and Languages. Available at: http://www.mkweb.co.uk/mkchildrensfund/

——— 2006c. 'Mobilising Communities – Policing the Borders? Participation and Social Inclusion as Key Principles in the Milton Keynes Children's Fund Initiative'. Unpublished paper presented at The Periphery and Policy Conference, 21–22 April 2006, Truro, Cornwall.

——— 2007. *Milton Keynes Community Mobilisers: The Views of Children and Young People. Third Interim Report from the Independent Qualitative Evaluation of Milton Keynes Children's Fund*. Milton Keynes: The Open University, Faculty for Education and Languages. Available at: http://www.mkweb.co.uk/mkchildrensfund/

Levitas, R. 2005 [1998]. *The Inclusive Society? Social Exclusion and New Labour*, 2nd edn. Basingstoke: Palgrave Macmillan.

Neale, J. 2008. 'Ranting and Silence: The Contradictions of Writing for Activists and Academics'. In H. Armbruster and A. Lærke (eds), *Taking Sides: Ethics, Politics and Fieldwork in Anthropology*. Oxford/New York: Berghahn.

Ridge, T. 2002. *Childhood Poverty and Social Exclusion: From a Child's Perspective*. Bristol: The Polity Press.

Social Exclusion Task Force, see http://webarchive.nationalarchives.gov.uk/+/http://www.cabinetoffice.gov.uk/social_exclusion_task_force.aspx (accessed 31 October 2011).

Steedman, C. 1982. *Landscape for a Good Woman: A Story of Two Lives*. London: Virago.

Thompson, E.P. 1963. *The Making of the English Working Class*. London: Penguin.

Williams, H. 2006. *Britain's Power Elites. The Rebirth of a Ruling Class*. London: Constable & Robinson.

Willis, P.E. 1978. *Learning to Labour. How Working Class Kids Get Working Class Jobs*. Aldershot: Ashgate.

Chapter 5

DANCING WITH AN ANGEL:
WHAT I HAVE LEARNT FROM MY 'SPECIAL NEEDS' DAUGHTER, ELISA

Elsa L. Dawson

⁊ঌৈ৾ৡৎ৹

The look of sheer wonderment in Elisa's eyes captivated me. She hugged me yet again as if to thank me for bringing her to this magical world. We were in the beer tent at Towersey Folk Music Festival, where we can be found every August Bank Holiday. A group of drinkers spontaneously strummed accordions, banjos and violins in a trance-like devotion to the Celtic spirit. Elisa moved in her version of dance around the tables – swaying her head and upper body from side to side to the music and running around, grabbing anyone who attracted her attention to join in. Onlookers gazed with sympathetic, or even perhaps empathetic, smiles, none seemingly finding her reaction out of place.

Towersey, with its tolerant atmosphere towards any kind of difference, outlandishly and colourfully dressed festival goers celebrating difference in the music on show, is one of the most 'enabling' environments I have found for Elisa, my fun loving 13-year-old daughter. At Towersey, Elisa can live out her unique capacity for enjoying the moment to its full, without any fear of being considered out of place or inappropriate. For me and Elisa, it represents a model microcosm of society responding to what the protagonists of the social model of disability have identified as 'society's failure to provide appropriate services and adequately ensure the needs of disabled people are fully taken into account in its social organisation' (Oliver 1990). At Towersey, all Elisa's needs are perfectly met: non-stop lively music, space and permission to dance, and in any way found appropriate by the person concerned, tasty food and drink (well, until Mum's cash runs out!), friendly people who don't mind being hugged at any time, and last but not least, clean and spacious disabled toilets, where she can be changed, usually necessary at least once a day.

Figure 5.1. Elisa with her Mum at WOMAD festival. Photo by Elsa L. Dawson.

Elisa was born with Angelman Syndrome, which is described by the medical profession as 'a neurogenetic disorder characterised by developmental delay, absence of speech, motor impairment, epilepsy and a peculiar behavioural phenotype, … caused by the lack of expression of the UBE3A gene associated with various abnormalities of chromosome 15q11–13' (Dan 2007). Other symptoms noted are 'severely impaired expressive language, ataxic gait, tremulousness of limbs, and a typical behavioral profile, including a happy demeanor, hypermotoric behavior, and low attention span. Seizures, abnormal electroencephalography, microcephaly, and scoliosis' (Guerrini et al. 2003). All of these manifest in Elisa.

The birth of children whose bodies differ from the expected is, as Rayna Rapp and Faye Ginsburg (2001: 536) point out, an important occasion for meaning making. A growing ethnographic literature explores the social processes by which the personhood of disabled children is questioned, negotiated or asserted (Gammeltoft 2008). This literature focuses on the way in which parents come to reject or embrace children whose bodies differ from the norm by being weak or sickly (Scheper-Hughes 1992). What I have learnt most from my daughter is the importance of being in the moment and enjoying it to the full, whirring around a dance floor to the music of a Celtic band, only stopping for the seemingly endless hugs she gives me. As a parent, knowing also how much she cries when she experiences discomfort or frustration, and with what feeling, I can only seek to maximize the situations in which she finds hilarity, and follow her lead. Of all the years of advice I have received on how to parent her, one of the most memorable was to follow her lead (by the Son-rise Autism Treatment Center of America). She has dragged me into innumerable music festivals (though Towersey will always be our favourite), funfairs, theatres, discotheques, pubs, restaurants, amusement arcades, cinemas, shopping centres, motorbike rallies – anywhere where there is life, music, dance and magic. Boats, buses and trains are great favourites too. I doubt if I would have gone to half of these without her.

There is no medical cure yet, but some significant progress has recently been made towards developing one. The medical profession is therefore unable to offer more than monitoring Elisa's development, although neurologists have contributed greatly to her very survival and comfort by managing her epilepsy, and providing emergency treatment for her when seizures occur. I would therefore not agree with a rejection of medical intervention for conditions intrinsically related to the disability of Angelman Syndrome as implied by the proponents of the social model.

However, I have regular struggles with the profession. For example, an endearing characteristic of all Angelman children is their frequent laughter. This is, however, frequently termed 'inappropriate' in the literature about the Syndrome, as in Lalande and Calciano (2007). 'Inappropriate' in whose opinion, I would ask. How do we know what makes Elisa laugh, since she cannot communicate through language? How can we therefore judge whether the laughter is appropriate or not? If we knew what it was, maybe it would make us laugh too. If we were as unfettered as she is by words and the rational thinking they facilitate, social mores, concerns about the future or the past, maybe we would laugh like she does. On the other hand, maybe it would not make us laugh, but what makes human beings laugh differs from culture to culture anyway, let alone where differing variations of physical and mental states are involved. So surely such laughter should not be the subject of judgements about what is appropriate and what is not. It is an example of the 'normalizing' efforts of society, so criticized by Oliver (1990).

Like Landsman, I would define my relationship with my daughter as valuable and enriching rather than tragic (1998), although, life with Elisa is by no means a bed of roses. She is extremely hyperactive, in addition to requiring total personal care and constant supervision. The lesson which is a corollary to 'live life to the full' is 'never take anything for granted'. Being able to sip a cappuccino quietly while reading a serious paper in a cosy coffee shop has become immeasurably more enjoyable than it ever was before and one of my most appreciated treats. This is impossible with my beloved daughter at my side. She adores tearing up paper and any food or drink on a table is considered fair game for another favourite occupation – throwing things on the floor and creating a loud clatter leading to dramatic adult attention. When I am trying to get her to sleep, which often takes an hour, even scratching my nose becomes a luxury that could cost me another 15 minutes of patiently (or not so patiently) waiting for the jerky movements and fidgeting to stop.

I received her diagnosis one dark painful evening in February 1997, when she was a year and three months old. The paediatrician had asked me to attend the appointment accompanied by a family member or close friend, so I knew the news was serious. At a year old, we had noticed that Elisa was not meeting the usual milestones – walking and talking, and asked our GP for an investigation. She had assured us all was fine with Elisa, and we were just over-anxious parents, but agreed to start up the process. Four months later we discovered that our precious daughter would never express herself in words, would have eating difficulties, a tendency to epilepsy, but live a normal lifespan. My life as a mother and a woman changed forever. My husband, and Elisa's father, was a Peruvian architect, who had been unable to develop his profession in the UK, and had returned to Peru to work on urban design projects with a group of colleagues. So apart from his occasional visits to the UK, and the two years which Elisa and I spent in Lima, Peru, I was to care for her as a single parent.

I cried more or less solidly for a week after receiving the diagnosis, despite family and friends rallying around with deeply felt sympathy. The idea which most helped dry the tears, suggested by a hypnotherapist, was that the big challenges in life help you become the person you are destined to be, bringing out characteristics and potential which would otherwise remain undeveloped. This gave me the motivation to set to work on finding ways to help Elisa make the most of her life, and to make the most of my life with her. At my age another child was out of the question, so this was my only chance to experience motherhood.

A story which helped me in a similar way was: you are on a plane, heading for a dream holiday in Italy, and suddenly it is announced that the plane is actually going to Amsterdam. At first you are shocked and disappointed, and then gradually you begin to realize that Amsterdam also has its charms – the tulip gardens, the canals, the windmills. Being Elisa's mother has led me along a series of journeys to new territories, most significantly, a spiritual path, as I try to find meaning in the situation in which I find myself.

Since the conventional medical profession had no remedies to offer for Angelman Syndrome, apart from the life-saving control and emergency treatment for her epilepsy, and physiotherapy, which has never made an obvious difference to Elisa, one such voyage of discovery was into complementary therapies. Out of the innumerable treatments I have tried, the two which proved most helpful have been homeopathy and cranial osteopathy. These both have the capacity to help Elisa to sleep better and be calmer. This has been crucial to my ability to bring her up on my own, which I could not have done without regular sleep. However, conventional doctors have been reluctant to recognize the practitioners who make such a difference to our lives, talking instead patronizingly about 'Mum being convinced that these therapies have helped' and warning me against being taken for a ride by expensive treatments in my desperate search for a cure.

Another journey of discovery was into the world of the education of disabled children. By chance I discovered conductive education, largely rejected by the

UK state special needs education establishment, but so effective with Elisa. Conductive education was developed mainly for children with cerebral palsy, in Hungary, at the Peto Institute in Budapest, and employs a series of routines to 'help children and adults with motor disorders learn to overcome problems of movement as a way of enabling them to live more active and independent lives'. The Birmingham Institute of Conductive Education, from whose website this description is taken, provided Elisa with several three-week courses, which resulted in her learning to walk, climb stairs and use the toilet – all essential skills without which our life and festival going would have been so much more restricted. A similar approach was used by the Ann Sullivan School in Lima, Peru, which Elisa attended on a daily basis for the two years we lived in Lima. At these schools, Elisa learnt more than in all her six years at a UK state special school, which has tended to prioritize the government's watered down version of the national curriculum over independence skills. None of this has made any noticeable impression on her development or understanding, although I really appreciate all the patience and imaginative efforts of the teaching staff to implement the government's approach.

Working at Oxfam, the ideals of inclusion in the mainstream were fixed firmly in my head by my work as a Gender Adviser, and when Elisa was due to leave their excellent crèche, I had searched around for a primary school which would accept her. After visiting every school in Oxford, I discovered Eynsham, a small village just outside the city, where the community primary school's head seemed enthusiastic about having Elisa in his school. We bought a house and moved in, only to be rejected by the school's teaching staff, who thought it would be impossible to manage with Elisa's wandering habits and hyperactive ways in their open plan classroom arrangement. This was despite solid backing for my wishes throughout the application process from the local education authority. I was extremely disappointed, and I still find it hard to accept that she has to attend a special needs school outside Eynsham, in Witney, which I did not choose for her. It is on a site together with a mainstream school, but the 'integration' they claim to organize appears tokenistic to me. The special school sits literally on the edge of the mainstream building, and most activities are organized separately. There is no joint vision or sense of identify for the school as a whole, mainstream together with special, and even the names of the schools are different.

Life with Elisa has taught me that other countries who lack our technical resources may actually have more effective methods for educating, in that the technical fixes we have are less available. Teachers at the Ann Sullivan School, or 'specialists' as they were called, determined that disabled people in a poor country such as Peru needed to be as independent as possible, reprimanded me for taking Elisa out in a pushchair. That way she would never learn to walk independently, they said, as she would always expect to be allowed to sit in a wheelchair. Spurred on by them, I struggled with taking Elisa out on foot. When she would try and sit down on the filthy pavements of Lima, I would sing her marching songs (difficult for me as I am not of a military nature!) to distract her and encourage her to walk. It was back-breaking, but I am so glad I persevered. Back in the UK,

I climbed with her to the top of Tintagel, something we could never have done before our two years at Ann Sullivan. When Elisa returned to the Witney School, I was asked if they could take a folding pushchair with them when they went for their weekly walk into town. I replied firmly 'on no account'.

In all my endeavours, it never occurred to me to doubt that Elisa was a person in her own right, with consequent rights to the educational opportunities of all her peers. Reading the article by Tine Gammeltoft (2008) about North Vietnam shocked me deeply, in its revelation of how many societies around the world would have considered her as merely a burden at best, and at worst not even worth saving from abandonment. I knew that Amazonian groups in Peru often abandoned such children at birth but I had thought this was because they realized they would be unable to care for them. The Lima society where I lived exhibited a similar affectionate response to Elisa as we experience in the UK.

However, I share Gammeltoft's view that the social model, and the view that it is society which disables impaired people, as originated by Oliver (1983), is insufficient. I cannot expect society to adapt to all the idiosyncrasies of Elisa, for example, hitting out at people's faces, pulling hair, grabbing their food, no matter how well I may understand and sympathize with her reasons for acting like this. I have to work on modifying this behaviour in the best way I can, by alternating between ignoring it and stating firmly to her that this is unacceptable. Whether this works is debatable, but I consider that I have to make every attempt possible to do this, as I see it as my responsibility as her mother to help her develop the kind of behaviour most likely to gain her acceptance in society. In this sense, maybe I am guilty of trying to 'normalize' her, but 'normal' covers so many variations that it is almost meaningless in a multi-cultural and multi-ability society.

Nor is Gammeltoft's idea of the corporeal model really relevant to Elisa, because her body is almost average, except for her slightly smaller head. The literature on Angelman Syndrome states that a typical characteristic is a wider than average mouth, but if Elisa's mouth is technically speaking larger than average, I do not as her mother notice this. It is mainly what she does with her body that is different to so-called normal human movement, i.e. the jerky nature of her movements, her unstable manner of walking, her arm flapping on hearing music and her frequent laughter. These characteristics actually endear her to most human beings with whom she comes into contact and seem to make her more valued.

This is not to say I do not push the boundaries of society's tolerance of her difference every time I go out with her, which is every day she is not at school, as we love life too much to stay at home. Restaurant goers have to cope with her messy eating habits and shoppers can be hugged at any moment without warning. I do all I can to mitigate these effects, planning our outings like a strategic foray. Which restaurant has tables big enough for me to have my plate on it out of her reach? Which are the seats at the theatre where no one will be sitting in front of us, and close to the disabled toilets? I have to say that I am amazed at the tolerance and infinite kindness we have received during our outings. On a recent occasion in a smallish restaurant in Brixham, Devon, I feared an old lady near us was annoyed with the commotion we were causing, but as she got up to leave, she came over and said 'You are an amazing mother!', bringing tears to my eyes as I felt the stress, which is such a constant part of my life, drain from me.

Elisa, moreover, exhibits absolute confidence that she is a person in her own right, and has built up her place in the community of Eynsham, where she is greeted constantly by name as she walks around the village. She is the most exuberant fan of the Eynsham Morris, whose leader, the owner of our endlessly helpful village DIY, welcomes her warmly at every dance. He is the heart of Eynsham and was recently rewarded with an MBE for his services to the community. Every May Day, you will find us in the village square, swaying to the sound of his accordion, Elisa brandishing a drum stick lent by one of the Morris Men to participate in the music making.

Her best Eynsham friends, four lively intelligent and caring girls of her age who have to my great delight attached themselves to us, hotly defend her right to personhood. They advise me on what clothes she should be wearing, and what music she should be enjoying, that is up-to-date music of their generation, not mine. Interestingly, Elisa loves their music more than mine, even though she spends more time with me. They get angry on her behalf at stares and signs of rejection which I have not even noticed. They are determined that Elisa should take her full part in the life of Eynsham, including competing every year to be a Carnival maid of honour. Much to our disgust, she has yet to be chosen. They

Figure 5.2. Elisa has fun at Towersey Folk Festival. Photo by Elsa L. Dawson.

help me organize her birthday discos in the village hall, inviting all their school friends and encouraging them to come along to celebrate Elisa.

Perhaps my most important discovery from being 'Elisa's Mum' is to begin to perceive what spirit might look like. When Elisa laughs in her enchanting manner, hugging herself with her arms, I ask myself where that laugh comes from. She cannot have learnt it, as on the one hand she does not seem to copy easily, either because she does not want to or because she is unable to, and on the other, I know of no one in her immediate circle who laughs in any way like that. Therefore it can only come from within her. It can only be her essential being expressing itself, her light and joy, which I have been told it is her mission to bring to the world. So perhaps my preferred model for relating to Elisa would be the 'spirit centred model' – although we are in danger, as Oliver points out that 'in discussing issues related to disability … we will end up with more models than Lucy Clayton' (Oliver 1990).

Such a spiritual model of understanding disability lies behind the approach of the Steiner movement, whose excellent Camphill villages are where I would most like Elisa to live when I or her father are no longer there to care for her. Their view is that people are disabled because their corporeal reality inhibits the full unleashing of their spirits, and their schools for special needs children have developed a series of interventions known as curative education which include such responses as Rhythmical Massage Play, Curative Eurythmy and Colour Light, which are designed to help them overcome these barriers. That is a view which makes much sense to me, and I believe Elisa would benefit from such therapies. Unfortunately, their schools are very expensive. I would have to prove that the state schools are inappropriate to Elisa's needs in order to get a funded place, and I have not been able to do this. I also feel that she would lose the advantage of the Eynsham community if she were to attend one of the Steiner schools, as there are none close enough for her to live at home and attend as a day pupil. They also generally seem to operate on the edge of society rather than within it, and Elisa loves society and society loves her. So Eynsham is where we will stay, at least until either I or someone else founds a Towersey where you can live throughout the year.

Bibliography

Dan, B. 2007. *Angelman Syndrome* (Clinics in Developmental Medicine). London: MacKeith Press.

Gammeltoft, T.M. 2008. 'Childhood Disability and Parental Moral Responsibility in Northern Vietnam: Towards Ethnographies of Intercorporeality', *Journal of the Royal Anthropological Institute*, 14 (4): 825–42.

Guerrini, R., Carrozzo, R., Rinaldi, R. and Bonanni, P. 2003. 'Angelman Syndrome: Etiology, Clinical Features, Diagnosis, and Management of Symptoms', *Paediatric Drugs*, 5 (10): 647–61.

Lalande, M. and Calciano, M.A. 2007. 'Molecular Epigenetics of Angelman Syndrome', *Cellular and Molecular Life Sciences*, 64 (7–8): 947–60.

Landsman, G. 1998. 'Reconstructing Motherhood in the Age of "Perfect" Babies: Mothers of Infants and Toddlers with Disabilities', *Signs*, 24: 69–99.

Oliver, M. 1983. *Social Work with Disabled People.* Basingstoke: Macmillan.

———— 1990. *The Individual and Social Models of Disability.* Paper presented at Joint Workshop of the Living Options Group and the Research Unit of the Royal College of Physicians.

Rapp, R. and F. Ginsburg 2001. 'Enabling Disability: Rewriting Kinship, Reimagining Citizenship', *Public Culture*, 13 (3): 533–56.

Scheper-Hughes, N. 1992. *Death Without Weeping.* Berkeley, CA: University of California Press.

Chapter 6
BEING PARENTED?
CHILDREN AND YOUNG PEOPLE'S ENGAGEMENT WITH PARENTING ACTIVITIES

Julie Seymour and Sally McNamee

~~~~~~~~~~

Introduction

There is currently a huge focus on the activity and outcomes of parenting. This occurs in the academic world – for example in terms of research on parenting post-divorce and separation, (Smart et al. 2001), step-parenting (Ribbens McCarthy et al. 2003) and fatherhood (Dermott 2008) – and in lay discourse and the media. In the UK, parenting is now also a growing area of policy intervention (Gillies 2005) including Sure Start schemes, Parenting Contracts and Orders related to youth offending, and recent reports such as *Supporting Parents* (CSCI 2006) and *Every Parent Matters* (DfES 2007). Much of this intervention focuses on parenting when it is perceived to have gone wrong. In all this, the majority of the emphasis has been placed on the adults/parents involved, but some attention has been paid to the children and young people who are the recipients of, or indeed participants in, such activities.

Such research in the social study of childhood has focused on the agency of children in several arenas of action but, as can occur with emerging theoretical and substantive areas, may have overstated the case. More recent studies are acknowledging the constraints (as well as the liberties) which children may be living within and are producing more nuanced accounts of childhood in relation to structure/agency debates. Rather than presenting the child as a free agent, this work recognizes the power differentials which operate in adult–child and indeed child–child relationships but seeks to explore what Katz (1994) has referred to as the 'spaces of betweenness' where children are able to employ personal strategies or resistances to influence parenting practices. This chapter will contribute to this more nuanced approach to the social study of childhood employing Katz's concept to examine the way in which children acknowledge, work with and manipulate the power dynamics that exist between them and their parents. However, in order to fully explore these power dynamics, we consider it necessary to reiterate earlier calls for research on children to refocus on other players in the interaction and to re-situate children within their families (and other institutions). In order to develop and widen the research agenda on the social study of childhood, what may (apparently paradoxically) be required is that parents' and children's views are heard together.

In order to illustrate our argument, we will draw on existing research in the field, including empirical evidence from three studies of children and family life conducted by the authors. These consist of McNamee's doctoral work on children's negotiations of the use of computer games in the home[1] (McNamee 1998a, 1998b, 2000), research on the construction of family life in single location home/workplaces[2] (Seymour 2005, 2007a, 2007b) and a data set from James, Christensen and Jenks' ESRC-funded research on children's understandings and perception of the social organization of time (Award No. L129251025).[3] In this latter project, Sally McNamee collected quantitative data, the results of which will now be revisited.

It is contextually important in this discussion of parenting practices to highlight at this stage Mayall's (2001) acknowledgement that, in the UK, the control of children is still constructed in policy as almost wholly the parents' responsibility (although they may be helped by the State). In the Ministerial Foreword to a recently published evidence paper on Families in Britain (Department of Children, Schools and Families (DCSF) 2008), Beverley Hughes, the Minister of State for Children, Young People and Families, comments that recent government policies are:

> patently not about government dictating but about empowering families and enabling them to make the right decisions for them. These successful policies are good examples of how Government can help strengthen families enabling them to help themselves and reduce the pressures they face.

The document goes on to confirm that the government should:

> work in a partnership with families based on fair rules: respecting privacy but expecting, and in some cases enforcing, families to fulfil their responsibilities too. (DCSF 2008: 105)

As Alanen (2001), in the same volume as Mayall, points out, using the comparison with Finland/Norway, this is only one model of parent–child–state relations.

Defining Parenting

In the UK, there appears to be broad agreement as to what parenting consists of between government agencies, researchers and in lay discourse. Significant research effort has been expended on defining the areas in which parenting takes place and examining parents' actions within these areas (e.g. Ritchie et al. 2005). Recent reports show a strong degree of consensus in the areas identified. The National Children's Bureau's report prepared by Madge (2005) for the Joseph Rowntree Foundation (JRF) identifies parenting behaviour in eight areas as follows: providing basic physical care, giving affection, assuring security, encouraging development of a sense of identity, providing stimulation, exercising guidance and controls, promoting growing responsibility and supporting and developing independence. These map closely to those of the Family & Parenting Institute's definition of parenting capacity (Henricson and Bainham 2005) which includes: basic care, emotional warmth, safety, stimulation, guidance, boundaries and stability. Similarly when children, young people and families were asked by UK government departments such as the Department for Education and Skills (DfES) to define important outcomes for children they listed: be healthy, economic well-being, stay safe, enjoy and achieve and make a positive contribution (DfES 2004).

This consensus as to the appropriate areas of parenting could be labelled parenting activities or parenting behaviour, but a more useful conceptual way of considering them would be to view them as 'parenting practices', drawing on and adapting Morgan's (1996) notion of 'family practices'. The term 'practices' is a theoretical tool which allows a more fluid and active dimension to the substantive area being studied by focusing on the activities and discourses which make up the doing of the topic under investigation. In this case, it is the doing of the family; that is the activities and discourses which construct relations based on marriage/partnership, parenting and kinship. This family practice approach widens the research focus from a concentration on a static location in a specific social institution (the family) or physical site (the home) to an examination of the active nature of the process of doing family. Clearly, one key component of doing family is doing parenting; that is, being involved in parenting practices. Yet, as acknowledged in the introduction, it is not only parents who are involved in such practices. The processual focus advocated by Morgan's theoretical concept acknowledges the roles and interactions of all contributory members, including the children and young people, who respond to adult parenting practices.

Morgan suggests a focus on feeding children as one example of an everyday and regular parenting practice (Morgan 1996: 162–3). On one level, its performance is to achieve the very real requirement of nourishing growing children. Yet the specifics of how it is done (when, where and with whom) is influenced by family traditions and beliefs, cultural mores, moral discourses such as those relating to waste, health or childhood obesity, and perhaps more pragmatically income and children's food preferences. Hence the doing of feeding the family's children can take place away from the home and among strangers yet still constitute a parenting practice. Indeed in Seymour's study of bringing up a family while running a hospitality establishment, she found one family who regularly ate away from the hotel/home specifically so they could enjoy uninterrupted family time together, a parenting practice which was appreciated by the children involved (2007a).

Children and Young People's Role in Parenting

It has been said that 'the home is a location where children have little privacy or autonomy relative to adults, being subject to the gaze of parents' (Valentine 2001: 77), but children and young people can employ strategies to elude this gaze, and recent research has recognized children's role in parenting practices and explored the situational strategic dialogue created between children and parents. This research focus is drawn together in Madge and Willmott's (2007) review for the Joseph Rowntree Foundation of research on children's views and experiences of parenting and resulted in the new programme of policy-related research on parenting which the JRF has funded.

Research with this focus recognizes that parent–child interactions are dynamic and negotiated between actors. Solberg (1997) studied children in families in Norway and contended that 'it is the organisation of daily life, the dividing up of tasks between family members and the laying down of rules of conduct that implicitly determines what it means to be a child' (p. 126). Much of this organization, division of tasks and rule-setting will be led by parents but can be amended through parent–child interactions, and Solberg shows the ways in which children can influence the negotiations they have with parents to achieve outcomes which are in their own favour.

Similarly, Kelley et al. state that '[a view of children as social actors means that] we would expect them to participate in constituting the social order of the home and to negotiate control of decision making' (1998: 17). These authors found that children's responses to perceived parental control was resisted by the use of 'sabotage' strategies which allow renegotiation rather than open defiance of parental edicts (p. 22). We provide a detailed example of such a sabotage strategy below using the ESRC time study data. Madge and Willmott (2007) cite Buckingham's (1996) research on how 6–16-year-olds negotiated television viewing. Here children accepted parental authority but felt able to make their own decisions, and in a study of the same topic in Sweden (Eckert 2004), children displayed what Madge and Willmott remind us Mayall (2001: 121) has called 'resentful resistance'. Clearly then, children do not simply passively accept the dictates of their parents, but how can we conceptualize the agency of the former when they are situated in positions of structural and generational disadvantage in relation to the latter?

'Spaces of Betweenness' in Parenting Practices

In considering how children influence parenting practices, we have found the concept of 'spaces of betweenness' useful. Cindi Katz's (1994) concept of 'spaces of betweenness' (although originally used to discuss the subject position of critical scholars) acknowledges that individuals are situated in 'multiply determined fields' (p. 72). Hence, to apply it to the subject position of children and young people, one can both recognize the unequal relations of power between adults and children but acknowledge that, in particular circumstances, they are negotiated and changeable. As Aitken (2001) has noted, the child is neither an autonomous subject nor merely a node in a matrix of power. Instead s/he is conceptualized as a concrete being in a range of material contexts. Using this concept allows a shift of focus (to paraphrase Punch 2004) to go beyond the what to the how of children and young people's engagement with parenting practices.

The concept of 'spaces of betweenness' can be utilized in two ways. First, in an abstract way to illuminate examples of children and young people's resistance or negotiation of parenting practices. Here 'spaces of betweenness' are constructed as metaphorical interstices in power relations. Such examples of children's involvement in parenting practices are shown in the research by Solberg (1997) cited earlier and in Alanen and Mayall's (2001) edited collection on cross-cultural examples of intergenerational relations, particularly in Montandon's (2001) chapter on parental education practices in Geneva. This work demonstrates children engaging in verbal strategies or ignoring their parent's requests, while, as mentioned previously, Kelley et al. (1998) discuss children's 'sabotage strategies'. A detailed example of such a sabotage strategy can be found in McNamee's re-analysis of the time study data from James et al.'s ESRC project. Here we find that while more than 80 per cent of children report being interrupted in their chosen activities by parents, less than 20 per cent of children say that when interrupted they stop what they are doing straight away. Most will stop 'after a few minutes' but some (around 15 per cent) refuse to be interrupted. Hence, while children and young people may not openly defy or disobey their parents, they will resist or renegotiate the terms of their compliance.

A second utilization of the concept of 'spaces of betweenness' can encompass a more literal interpretation of the phrase by focusing on material or physical space. The growth of research on the geographies of childhood has emphasized the role of place and space in the lives of children and young people. The attention paid to 'spatiality' (Keith and Pile 1993), that is the complex interweaving of the social and the spatial, has led to an acknowledgement that researchers must examine the 'use and meaning of the physical environment' (Christensen 2003: 14) in children and young people's lives. This concerns both the micro environment of specific buildings but also the significant differences in experiences arising from childhoods and adolescences which are, for example, located in rural and urban settings (McNamee 1998a, Jones 1997).

Punch's (2001) ethnographic research on the domestic labour of Bolivian children shows how this second material interpretation of 'spaces of betweenness' can be applied. In her examination of the use of space and time by rural children when doing jobs, Punch considers that, in order to do resistance, the children in her study are aided by the fact that many of their chores are conducted in public spaces and during unsurveilled time. She describes how the children in the Bolivian community she studied 'go to the hillsides in search of animals or firewood, fetch water from the river and carry out regular errands for their parents to other households or to the shops in the community square' (Punch 2004: 102). These locations provide the opportunity for the children in the study to combine work with play. While doing their chores they may meet and play with friends, chat or play with siblings, or simply take a long time to do the task in order to delay their return home as they will probably be given another chore to perform. Children minding animals will claim that they are late home because they had to search for a missing animal, when actually they were playing. Similarly, a child may offer to go to the village store, rather than muck out the animals, as he can then stop to play with other children on the way (Punch 2004: 107).

In the UK, there is a significant reduction in the number of children who travel to school unaccompanied, while 'playing out' (in the street or away from the home) has been replaced by playing in the home due to increased fears of the dangers of the strangers who inhabit public spaces (Scott et al. 1998). In her UK study, Valentine (1997) has discussed the ways in which children employ a range of strategies to allay parents' fears about public space. She contends that children and young people have a greater familiarity with their local public spaces than do their parents. Children therefore see themselves as more competent in public space than their parents portray them, and will, for example, simply not tell parents about events which might worry them in order to maintain their freedom out of doors (Valentine 1997). Hence, we can see that spatiality plays a role in children and young people's engagement with parenting practices.

In the Global North context, the availability of public space for children is perceived as increasingly being lost (Mayall 2001: 127). As a result, children's roles and activities in the domestic arena may be affected. As Sibley noted 'The child, the family and domestic space need to be considered together in order to understand the role of boundaries in childhood' (1995: 128). Children may lose the ability to avoid becoming involved in labour at home (Seymour 2005) or may turn to virtual spaces in the form of heterotopias (McNamee 2000). Both potential outcomes will be discussed in turn.

First, in Seymour's study of the construction of family life in hotels, pubs and boarding houses, the contribution of children to the labour of the business is recognized. One dimension of this is the emotional labour required to make guests feel 'at home' and to minimize any indication of family discord (Seymour 2005). Yet the reality of children's labour in the family business is at odds with Global North ideologies of childhood. These notions of an ideal childhood mean that 'childhood is associated with play and education rather than work and economic responsibility' (Scott 2000: 98). These discursive constructions of childhood as consisting of a time of innocence and freedom from the responsibilities and realities of adult life have been labelled as 'romanticized' by James et al. (2004), but they remain influential. Heesterman (2005) and Van der Hoek (2005) also outline further examples of the extent to which children's labour activities contrast with the discourse of Global North childhood as a time of non-work.

Indeed, children in family-run hospitality establishments such as those studied by Seymour (2005) may face the likelihood of a greater call on their labour. It appears that the norms of 'good parenting' have changed to include increased surveillance of one's children. This has combined with a rise in risk aversion in UK parents leading to the requirement that children and young people stay in domestic rather than public spaces. The 'better' the parent, the more watched are their children and the more likely they are to spend their time in the home. Yet a situation in which the child is increasingly surveilled by their parents and required to spend more time in the business premises means they are more likely to be co-opted into the labour of the workplace. As one parent in Seymour's study remarked of her young son who was growing up in a family-run boarding house, 'He's got to learn those social skills' (interview 6, female hotel owner). However, as outlined above, childhood labour, whether physical or emotional, is antithetical to the discourse of the Global North 'ideal' childhood. There appears then, for parents and children living in family-run hotels, pubs and boarding houses, a tension in which the spatial and supervisory dimensions of contemporary models of good parenting place increasing demands on children's contribution to the business and, as a result, directly conflict with notions of an ideal childhood. This means, paradoxically, that the 'better' the parent, the less 'ideal' the experience of the child. However, as Seymour shows (2005), children and young people who are living in such single location home/workplaces do show considerable agency in the extent to which they respond to such demands for emotional labour and in the ways they use the performance of it to their own advantage.

In our second example of the impact of the loss of public space and increasing confinement in domestic space on Global North childhoods, we turn to children's use of virtual space via computers. McNamee (2000) argued that, in the face of increasing parental control over children's space (both in the public and private arena), playing with video games provides an extra dimension in which the child is able to control his or her environment, and in which the child is able to do things which they are unable to do in reality. One interviewee, Carl, for example said:

> … it's like an adventure, isn't it? Like an adventure 'cos you want to see what's on in the game, like you've finished a level, and you want to see the other one, that's what spurs you on, don't it? So in the end you go 'Oh my god, I've finished the game'.

In this way, when Carl plays a game, he is experiencing that game as an adventure – he is in a real place (his bedroom) engaging with a real piece of technology, but the space in which he experiences and enjoys the game is not real. It is a heterotopia – one of Foucault's 'other spaces' – not a real space (McNamee 2000: 484). In this study, McNamee draws on Foucault's (1986: 24) discussion of the notions of 'utopia' and 'heterotopia'. A utopia is a site with no real place, it is an analogy – an inversion of, or a direct representation of, a real space in society. A heterotopia is, he argues, a real place which is like a countersite – 'a kind of effectively enacted utopia in which the real sites are simultaneously represented, contested and inverted'. The study of heterotopias, he contends, could provide 'a sort of mythic and real contestation of the space in which we live' (1986: 24). In the 'spaces of betweenness' now available to them, often the only escape children have from parental control is in imaginary space.

However, children and young people do not only suffer negatively from their parents' 'power over' them. Children and youth are also able to exercise a positive Foucauldian 'power to' in their domestic arenas (McNamee 2000). Hence Christensen (2002) has shown how children see themselves as proactive in family discussions about the use of time and, perhaps even more proactively, Punch (2001) has shown how children exercise autonomy around family practices and take the initiative in doing things for the household. Similarly Seymour's research on children growing up in their family-run hotels, pubs and boarding houses (2007b: 12) shows examples of the children making suggestions to their parents on ways to improve the delivery of the business, as the following quote illustrates:

> That's another thing, the family is contributing to that, they're coming up with ideas, even the kids, 'Mum, why don't we do this? Why don't we do it that way?'. And some of them have been really good ideas, and they've taken off, so they do, we do let them have some sort of input, you know erm, 'cos it's their home. When all's said and done, it is their home and they can look at it from a different point of view sometimes. You know, we're tunnel-visioned and the kids'll come in and say 'Why don't you do it like this?' and 'Oh, we didn't think of that', you know. (Interview 17, female hotel owner)

Yet it is necessary to introduce a note of caution. We would argue that this focus on children as proactive, competent individuals has led to a view, often commented on in the media and in common-sense views, of the over-importance of children in family life, and has represented children as driving family decisions, for example. As this chapter goes on to discuss, a revisiting of the data can show us an alternative interpretation.

Children's Agency in the Domestic Sphere – An Overstatement?

The new paradigm of the social study of childhood (James et al. 1998) established the child as a competent social actor and highlighted the socially constructed nature of childhood. This led to a call for research that would ascertain the child's perspective in everyday life and this call saw a prodigious volume of research in response (see, for example, McNamee 1998a, 1998b, 2000, Hutchby and Moran Ellis 1998, Punch 2004). However, more recent research has had an awareness of the danger of overstating children's agency both around significant family changes such as parental employment and divorce (Jensen and McKee 2003a, Moxnes 2003) and more prosaic everyday life activities (Alanen and Mayall 2001, Mayall 2001). For, as Aitken has stated (2001: 174), 'Parental authority may be abused in ways more insidious than any other form of authority but unless it exists, parenting itself is impossible'.

Hence more recent studies acknowledge the constraints (as well as the liberties) that children may be living within and are producing more nuanced accounts of childhood in relation to structure/agency debates. Rather than presenting the child as a free agent, in this chapter we seek to recognize the power differential which operates in adult–child and indeed child–child relationships by recentring children in the relationships and institutions in which they conduct their everyday life.

Children and young people are aware of adult–child power dynamics and say, very reasonably, that being consulted is more important than having things your own way (Morrow 1998). Children don't feel they make too many decisions for themselves (Madge 2006) but do want a say in matters that concern them. However, as we argue here, the view that children hold of their own centrality in the parent–child relationship is not borne out by research. For example, in a MORI study of the UK carried out in 2000 for the National Family & Parenting Institute, the data showed that almost 75 per cent of young people felt that children being listened to was important whereas only 41 per cent of the adults questioned felt that listening to children was important.

Are Children Listened to? Differences in Public and Private Arenas

There is a rhetoric of listening to the child's voice in UK policy (although little actual involvement of children in the setting up of parenting programmes, as shown by Madge and Willmott 2007). UK government policy has attempted to give a platform to the voice of the child and to intervene in the oppositional construction of children as 'not adult' (Jenks 1996). This is evident in court proceedings relating to divorce, for example (see McNamee et al. 2004). However, the granting of a voice to children and young people in policy assumes the intervening agent of an institution between the basic child–adult relationship. Hence the child has an advocate. Despite this rhetoric of listening to the child's voice in all matters that concern them (Every Child Matters 2004, Children Act 1989, United Nations Convention on the Rights of the Child 1989, Article 12), in practice children and young people's voices are, at best, muted and at worst not heard in many arenas of social life such as education or family law (see, for example, Hill et al. 2004). In the case of family law proceedings, practitioners working with children around representing their voices in court are working within a complex set of tensions, one such being the tension between representing the child's wishes and feelings (as in the Children Act 1989) and the perceived best interests of the child. Children must be seen (by adults) as being able to have a credible voice before practitioners feel they can report their wishes and feelings to the court. One practitioner said:

> All the time, you've got to go with the child's best interest […] okay, we listen to wishes and feelings, but at the end of the day we're adults […] (and) those wishes and feelings don't key into our [perception of] best interest, and we have to work at it from the best interest point of view.

In this way, the child's expressed wish may not be forcefully represented to the court (McNamee et al. 2004) and thus the voice of the child becomes filtered through the production of the court report.

In the private domain of the family, children and young people's voices are often filtered through those of the parent. There is, therefore, a contradiction between the emphasis on child participation in the public sphere – where the views and wishes of children and young people are sought in matters concerning them – and in the invisibility of children and young people in the place where perhaps they are most controlled and where they spend most of their time, that is at home with the family. In everyday 'private' domestic settings, the basic dyadic relationship between adult and child has no intervening agent to facilitate the latter's voice. Children only want to have a say but, as the MORI survey (2000) suggests, many parents are not predisposed to listen.

There is therefore a contradiction between the emphasis on child participation in policy and practice and the lack of voice at home. Indeed, it is not just a lack of voice but the MORI survey suggests a lack of interest in what children say or any conception that children can contribute, so there appears to be an essential difference of opinion between children's and adults' views of negotiations within families. Despite the promotion of children and young people as social actors in academia and social policy, this does not appear to have been accepted by the parents in the MORI study. In the ESRC Time project, while children ascribed to the rhetoric of having a voice, they recognized the reality of their domestic situations as shown in their responses outlined below to a questionnaire on their use and control of time.

Children and Young People's Involvement in the Control of their Time

In this section, we revisit the quantitative data collected by McNamee as part of the ESRC project on 'Children's Understanding of the Social Organisation of Time'. The data are drawn from a questionnaire survey of 11-year-old children who had just made the transition from primary to secondary school. There were 260 children from a rural school, and 232 from an urban school. The sample was almost equally split by gender. The results suggest that children's time is largely controlled by parents and that children experience this control of time as something from which they long to escape. (This may not come as news to researchers into the social study of childhood.)

Interestingly, although most parents would probably feel that their role as income generators is vital to family life, and would assume that this is understood by children, the study showed that while most children reported that their parent(s) worked, around a third of children were unable to say exactly in what kind of work their parent was engaged. Whether this is due to lack of interest or miscommunication is not evident from the data, but suggests that negotiations and decision-making by both parties is made in a context of a partial understanding of the situation.

Looking at the quantitative data, the time children spend on a day-to-day level is composed mainly of schoolwork, homework, housework and brief periods of play. From getting up to going to bed, the children in this study were always subject to the demands of education and family. Earlier we spoke about examples of 'resentful resistance' (Mayall 2001: 121). However, the overall picture revealed is of adult control with very little child decision-making. What we are suggesting is that instances of resistance may be isolated occurrences in a larger picture of adult control. Too much research focused on these instances may have overemphasized the extent of children's resistance.

The ESRC data show that on school days, parents decide what time children get up and go to bed. Teachers decide what children will do during their time at school. Once home, homework needs to be done (and housework fitted in). Half of the children said that their parents make sure that the child's homework is done, i.e. homework is policed by parents. Homework not done is thus punished – sometimes by the school but in addition between a quarter and 41 per cent of children said parents would punish them for not doing homework. Punishment for not doing homework can be violent ('I get the slipper'), but often parents target punishment in gender-specific ways. When parents punish, girls will be punished by restricting their outdoor activities, while boys will be punished by having their games machines or TVs taken from them. Parents accurately target children's free time activities for maximum impact, thus removing some of the 'spaces of betweenness' (and public and virtual spaces) that children can claim for themselves.

When the children surveyed are with their families, their time and activities are clearly controlled and therefore it is unsurprising that they say they enjoy the activities they carry out with friends over those conducted with family – although they did enjoy certain family activities, such as visiting or shopping, over being with friends. There is a need for further research in this area to discover whether children just prefer the activities they share with friends over those they do with families or whether they would enjoy being with family more if they had a greater say over the use of their own time. In the original study it proved impractical to talk to parents but this was seen as unproblematic since 'these interviews were intended only to provide background data on family life' (James et al. 2005). The rereading of the data in this chapter suggests that parents' views provide, not simply the context in which to understand children's perceptions of family life, but an additional data set which allows the research to focus on the differences in views between children and adults and the processes of interaction between them.

So the data from the time questionnaire show examples of small instances of resistance but they don't override the larger context which is one of parental control, and that is why the children in the study say they look forward to being older (to being adult, in fact) as a time when they will have more say over their own time. Some comments include:

It's my life and I can decide what I want to do.

Because my parents won't say what I do in my own time.

In this study, the 'spaces of betweenness' appear to be very small and hence the time of childhood would appear to be a time of anticipation of ridding oneself of the binds of family. While academia, and to some extent UK policy, has a view of the child as a competent social actor, in the reality of everyday life this is not a view subscribed to by parents. Children understand this and feel that it is only once they are adult that they will attain agency. As one child said, 'No-one takes children seriously'.

Conclusion

Part of the critique of the emergent 'new paradigm' of the social study of childhood (James and Prout 1990) was that the sociology of family had neglected to incorporate the child in those studies. The nascent paradigm thus separated the child from the family in order to develop the focus on the child as agent and to privilege children's perspectives and voices. We are arguing here that a focus on children separate from the family leads to a partial view. What is required now is to re-situate the child within the family in order to make visible the differing perceptions around family life held by both parents and children (and other family members). What we are calling for is research that will examine parents' and children's views together as this will elucidate more clearly the realities of everyday family life. Without this, childhood and parenting practices cannot be fully understood.

Within UK social policy and in academia, the child has become acknowledged as a competent social actor. However, within the family, the child's voice is filtered through that of the parent(s). Children's everyday lives are lived in the context of adult control, leaving few 'spaces of betweenness' for agency, resistance or voice, as we have argued here. We are of the view that outside of policy and academia, that is, in the everyday lived practice of being a family, both children and adults seem to recognize structural and generational constraints more than a focus on the child as isolated from the family will reveal.

In the context of UK policy, which increasingly sees children as the outcome of parenting practices, and sees the training of parents as the best approach to prevent anti-social behaviour, perhaps what is required is research which takes a whole family approach, but which still privileges the voice of the child. This would mean continuing the tradition of viewing the child as a competent social actor but also 'zooming out' to get a whole picture of familial relations and interactions.

It appears then that the time has come to widen the focus on the child as agent. What is needed now is to examine everyday life in the context of agency and structure and to bring children back in to the families from which they were conceptually separated. We are aware of course that calls for this were made previously. In 1996, Brannen and O'Brien were clear that they did not wish to 'detach children from their family settings ... but to recontextualize children within their families' (p. 1), although they were keen at this time to 'prioritize' (p. 1) children in families. In the following decade, Jensen and McKee (2003b) questioned the assumed influence of children over societal changes and parental choices, and illustrated the need for more empirical material on the role of parents and other adults in families (pp. 1–2). It appears that the project of establishing the social study of childhood needed to be more firmly in place before such calls for a wider focus could be acted upon. We are of the opinion that the social study of childhood is now ready to move towards this direction.

Of course, the family is only one institution in which children's everyday lives take place and this 'zooming out' should also apply to research on childhood in all of the social institutions within which childhoods take place. This shifts the social study of childhood from a political stance, which was necessary in the early days of the formulation of the new paradigm, to a more nuanced research agenda which represents more closely the reality of children's (and parents') lives.

Notes

1. A total of 1,600 children aged 8–18 completed a questionnaire, completed a blank page with text and drawing, and 60 children aged 5–16 took part in in-depth interviews. The sample was drawn from an urban and a rural secondary school, and a rural primary school. The sample was almost equally split by gender. Some interviews with parents were also carried out.
2. The data for Seymour's study, gathered in 2001, consist of 15 in-depth interviews with parents who were currently bringing up or had recently brought up their families in hotels, pubs or boarding houses (and their children where possible), six interviews with individuals or couples who had raised families or grown up in such establishments in the 1960s and 1970s and secondary data analysis from 50 oral history interviews that were part of the 'Looking Back, Looking Forward' project carried out by the North Yorkshire Museums Department funded by the Millennium Commission.
3. This project, entitled 'Changing Times: Children's Understanding and Perception of the Social Organisation of Time' (L129251025), was part of the Economic and Social Research Council's 'Children 5–16: Growing into the Twenty First Century' programme. It ran from April 1997 to November 1999.

Bibliography

Aitken, S. 2001. *Geographies of Young People: The Morally Contested Spaces of Identity*. London: Routledge.

Alanen, L. 2001. 'Childhood as a Generational Condition: Children's Daily Lives in a Central Finland Town'. In L. Alanen and B. Mayall (eds), *Conceptualizing Child-Adult Relations*. London: RoutledgeFalmer, 129–43.

Alanen, L. and B. Mayall (eds) 2001. *Conceptualizing Child-Adult Relations*. London: RoutledgeFalmer.

Brannen, J. and M. O'Brien 1996. 'Introduction'. In J. Brannen and M. O'Brien (eds), *Children in Families: Research and Policy*. London: Falmer Press, 1–12.

Buckingham, D. 1996. *Moving Images: Understanding Children's Emotional Responses to Television*. Manchester: Manchester University Press.

Christensen, P. 2002. 'Why More "Quality Time" is Not on the Top of Children's Lists', *Children and Society*, 16: 1–12.

———— 2003. 'Place, Space and Knowledge: Children in the Village and the City'. In P. Christensen and M. O'Brien (eds), *Children in the City: Home, Neighbourhood and Community*. London: RoutledgeFalmer.

Commission for Social Care Inspection (CSCI) 2006. *Supporting Parents, Safeguarding Children*. London: Ofsted.

Department of Children, Schools and Families (DCSF) 2008. *Families in Britain: An Evidence Paper*. December (DCSF-01077-2008).

Department of Education and Skills (DfES) 2004. *Every Child Matters*. London: DfES.

———. 2007. *Every Parent Matters*. London: DfES.

Dermott, E. 2008. *Intimate Fatherhoods*. London: Routledge.

Eckert, G. 2004. '"If I Tell Them then I Can": Ways of Relating to Adult Rules', *Childhood*, 11 (1): 9–26.

Foucault, M. 1986. 'Of Other Spaces' (trans. J. Miskowiec), *Diacritics Spring*, 22–7.

Gillies, M. 2005. 'Meeting Parents' Needs? Discourses of "Support" and "Inclusion" in Family Policy', *Critical Social Policy*, 25 (1): 70–90.

Heesterman, W. 2005. 'Child Labour and Children's Rights: Policy Issues in Three Affluent Societies'. In J. Goddard, S. McNamee, A. James and A. James (eds), *The Politics of Childhood: International Perspectives, Contemporary Developments*. London: Routledge.

Henricson, C. and A. Bainham 2005. *The Child and the Family Policy Divide: Tensions, Convergence and Rights*. York: Joseph Rowntree Foundation.

Hill, M., J. Davis, A. Prout and K. Tisdall 2004. 'Moving the Participation Agenda Forward', *Children and Society*, 18: 77–96.

Hutchby, I. and J. Moran Ellis (eds) 1998. *Children and Social Competence: Arenas of Action*. London: Falmer.

James, A. and A. Prout 1990. *Constructing and Reconstructing Childhood: Contemporary Issues in the Sociological Study of Childhood*. London: Falmer Press.

James, A., C. Jenks and A. Prout 1998. *Theorizing Childhood*. Cambridge: Polity.

James, A., A. James and S. McNamee 2004. 'Turn Down the Volume – Not Hearing Children in Family Proceedings', *Child and Family Law Quarterly*, 16 (2): 189–202.

James, A., P. Christensen and C. Jenks 2005. 'Changing Times Project', Full Report of Research Activities and Results. Swindon: Economic and Social Research Council.

Jenks, C. 1996. *Childhood*. London: Routledge.

Jensen, A. and L. McKee (eds) 2003a. *Children and the Changing Family: Between Transformation and Negotiation*. London: RoutledgeFalmer.

——— 2003b. 'Introduction: Theorizing Childhood and Family Change'. In A. Jensen and L. McKee (eds), *Children and the Changing Family. Between Transformation and Negotiation*. London: RoutledgeFalmer, 1–14.

Jones, O. 1997. 'Little Figures, Big Shadows: Country Childhood Stories'. In P. Cloke and J. Little (eds), *Contested Countryside Cultures: Otherness, Marginalisation and Rurality*. London: Routledge.

Katz, C. 1994. 'Playing the Field: Questions of Fieldwork in Geography', *Professional Geographer*, 46: 67–72.

Keith, M. and S. Pile (eds) 1993. *Place and Politics of Identity*. London: Routledge.

Kelley, P., S. Hood and B. Mayall 1998. 'Children, Parents and Risk', *Health and Social Care in the Community*, 6 (1): 16–24.

Madge, N. 2005. *Children's Views and Experiences of Parenting*. York: Joseph Rowntree Foundation.

——— 2006. *Children These Days*. Bristol: The Policy Press.

Madge, N. and N. Willmott 2007. *Children's Views and Experiences of Parenting*. York: NCB/Joseph Rowntree Organisation.

Mayall, B. 2001. 'Understanding Childhood: A London Study'. In L. Alanen and B. Mayall (eds), *Conceptualizing Child-Adult Relations*. London: RoutledgeFalmer, 114–28.

McNamee, S. 1998a. 'Questioning Video Game Use: An Exploration of the Spatial and Gender Aspects of Children's Leisure'. PhD dissertation, University of Hull.

———— 1998b. 'Youth, Gender and Video Games: Power and Control in the Home'. In G. Valentine and T. Skelton (eds), *Cool Places: Geographies of Youth Cultures*. London: Routledge, 195–206.

———— 2000. 'Foucault's Heterotopia and Children's Everyday Lives', *Childhood: A Global Journal of Child Research*, 7 (4): 479–92.

McNamee, S., A.L. James and A. James 2004. 'Talking, Being Listened to and Being Heard: Family Law and the Construction of Childhood in England and Wales', *Representing Children*, 16 (3): 168–78.

Montandon, C. 2001. 'The Negotiation of Influence: Children's Experience of Parental Education Practices in Geneva'. In L. Alanen and B. Mayall (eds), *Conceptualizing Child-Adult Relations*. London: RoutledgeFalmer, 54–69.

Morgan, D.H.J. 1996. *Family Connections. An Introduction to Family Studies*. Cambridge: Polity Press.

Morrow, V. 1998. *Understanding Families: Children's Perspectives*. London: National Children's Bureau/Joseph Rowntree Foundation.

Moxnes, K. 2003. 'Children Coping with Parental Divorce: What Helps, What Hurts?'. In A. Jensen and L. McKee (eds), *Children and the Changing Family: Between Transformation and Negotiation*. London: RoutledgeFalmer, 90–104.

National Family & Parenting Institute/MORI 2000. *Teenagers' Attitudes to Parenting: A Survey of Young People's Experiences of Being Parented, and Their Views on How to Bring Up Children, 2000*. London: National Family & Parenting Institute.

Punch, S. 2001. 'Negotiating Autonomy: Childhoods in Rural Bolivia'. In L. Alanen and B. Mayall (eds), *Conceptualizing Child-Adult Relations*. London: RoutledgeFalmer, 23–36.

———— 2004. 'Negotiating Autonomy: Children's Use of Time and Space in Rural Bolivia'. In V. Lewis, M. Kellett, C. Robinson, S. Fraser and S. Ding (eds), *The Reality of Research with Children and Young People*. London: Sage.

Ribbens McCarthy, J., R. Edwards and V. Gillies 2003. *Making Families: Moral Tales of Parenting and Step-parenting*. Durham: Sociology Press.

Ritchie, C., E. Flouri and A. Buchanan 2005. *Aspirations and Expectations*. London: National Family & Parenting Institute.

Scott, S. 2000. 'Children as Respondents: The Challenge for Quantitative Methods'. In A. James and P. Christensen (eds), *Conducting Research with Children*. London: Falmer Press, 98–119.

Scott, S., S. Jackson and K. Backett-Milburn 1998. 'Swings and Roundabouts: Risk Anxiety and the Everyday Worlds of Children', *Sociology*, 32 (4): 689–705.

Seymour, J. 2005. 'Entertaining Guests or Entertaining the Guests: Children's Emotional Labour in Hotels, Pubs and Boarding Houses'. In J. Goddard, S. McNamee, A. James and A. James (eds), *The Politics of Childhood: International Perspectives, Contemporary Developments*. Basingstoke: Palgrave Macmillan, 90–106.

———— 2007a. 'Treating the Hotel like a Home: The Contribution of Studying the Single Location Home/Workplace', *Sociology*, 41 (6): 1097–114.

———— 2007b. '"It'd Be to Give the Kids a Proper Family Life": Combining Employment and Home Life in One Location', *Working Papers in Social Sciences and Policy*, No. 18. Hull: University of Hull.

Sibley, D. 1995. 'Families and Domestic Routines: Constructing the Boundaries of Childhood'. In S. Pile and N. Thrift (eds), *Mapping the Subject: Geographies of Cultural Transformation*. London: Routledge, 123–37.

Smart, C., B. Neale and A. Wade 2001. *The Changing Experience of Childhood: Families and Divorce*. Cambridge: Polity.

Solberg, A. 1997. 'Negotiating Childhood: Changing Constructions of Age for Norwegian Children'. In A. James and A. Prout (eds), *Constructing and Reconstructing Childhood: Contemporary Issues in the Sociological Study of Childhood*, 3rd edn. London: Falmer Press, 34–62.

Valentine, G. 1997. '"Oh Yes I Can. Oh No You Can't". Children and Parents' Understandings of Kids' Competence to Negotiate Public Space Safely', *Antipode*, 29 (1): 65–89.

——— 2001. 'On-line Dangers?: Geographies of Parents' Fears for Children's Safety in Cyberspace', *Professional Geographer*, 53 (1): 71–83.

Van der Hoek, T. 2005. 'Growing Up in Poverty While Living in an Affluent Society: Personal Experiences and Coping Strategies of Dutch Poor Children'. In J. Goddard, S. McNamee, A. James and A. James (eds), *The Politics of Childhood: International Perspectives, Contemporary Developments*. London: Routledge, 107–24.

Part III

CROSS-CULTURAL MOBILITY

Chapter 7

CHILDREN'S MOVING STORIES:
HOW THE CHILDREN OF BRITISH LIFESTYLE MIGRANTS COPE WITH SUPER-DIVERSITY

Karen O'Reilly

಄ೄ಄ಀ಄ೄ

Introduction: The Day-to-Day Realities of Super-Diversity

In 1993, as a novice ethnographer and PhD student, I moved out to Spain with my family for 15 months to research the British community living on the Costa del Sol. My children were then 9 and 11 years old and I enrolled them in Spanish school for a year, telling myself I would be happy if all they managed was to learn the language. Since then they have both lived in Spain for some time as young adults. One has also lived in Ecuador and Peru and is now married to a Peruvian; the other has helped produce training materials for import clerks in South America. I like to think of this as a success story, but it should also cause me to stop and think about what we can learn from our children as ethnographers. Telling that story in more depth would involve me confessing there was an occasion when, in order to resist handing over my informants as examples for the mass media to use in articles about the Brits abroad, I persuaded my daughter to volunteer her personal story. She got herself into a terrible tangle by pretending to the journalist to be married to her sister's husband (because her own husband was still in Peru!) and then agreeing to photographs for a national newspaper! But, as I say, that is another story.

The focus in this chapter is on the children of those British migrants we lived amongst and how they cope with, and impact on, the day-to-day realities of life as migrants in conditions of what Steve Vertovec (2007) has called super-diversity. Vertovec contends that contemporary societies can often no longer be characterized in terms of multiculturalism, or even diversity; terms which attempted to capture the relationship between a few large ethnic minority, immigrant groups and homogeneous groups of 'locals'. Because the ethnic and mobility mix has become so complex, a new term is required:

> Britain can now be characterized by 'super-diversity', a notion intended to underline a level and kind of complexity surpassing anything the country has previously experienced. Such a condition is distinguished by a dynamic interplay of variables among an increased number of new, small and scattered, multiple-origin, transnationally connected, socio-economically differentiated and legally stratified immigrants who have arrived over the last decade. (Vertovec 2007: 1024)

There are so many different kinds of migrant, with such differing migration trajectories, experiences and expectations, subject to such variant policy and practice responses, constituted of such an array of class, gender and ethnic backgrounds, that we are confronted with an array of challenges not seen before. I think this is also true of Spain, especially in regions such as the Costa del Sol and the Costa Blanca, which are home to and visited by tourists and migrants from diverse parts of the globe, including Morocco, Romania, Colombia, Ecuador, Germany, Britain and Russia (see www.ine.es). The social scientific challenges posed by such diversity, Vertovec argues, include: the demand for more multivariate analyses, that explore the interaction of country of origin, language, immigration status, age and so on; better qualitative studies of super-diversity, that include some analysis of the role of the state; and thorough investigation of the conditions and challenges of super-diversity. This chapter responds to his specific call for a better understanding of new experiences of space and 'contact', and of new patterns of segregation, transnationalism and integration. Vertovec also notes the need for analysis to work outward, to take account of the meanings participants ascribe to actions, but also to explore the structures which impact upon these perceptions and practices. I am attempting to respond to Vertovec's call, by exploring children's experiences and the various factors which help shape their perceptions and their actions, and which in turn impact on the migration experience for the parents.

Strong Structuration Theory

The chapter also draws on strong structuration theory, as advanced by Rob Stones (2005). Strong structuration attempts to advance Giddens' theory (e.g. 1979, 1984) and respond to criticisms of his work. The key strength of strong structuration, for my purposes, is that it provides concepts to apply to empirical work. Crucially, structuration does not give primacy to either structure or agency but sees them as related through the agents' perceptions, practices, meanings and understandings. In other words, structural constraints can be included in qualitative analysis through awareness of the ways in which they impinge on actors' ways of thinking and feeling. It is seen as crucial to understand practices in order to understand structures and structures to understand practices. The key concepts this chapter relies on are habitus (or general dispositional) and conjuncturally-specific internal structures.

Habitus, as used by Stones, is almost interchangeable with habitus as used by Bourdieu. It refers to taken-for-granted ways of acting and thinking, habits of speech, chains of association, a generalized knowledge, embedded in corporeal schemas, and memory traces (see Stones 2005: 88, Bourdieu 1977, 1998, Bourdieu and Wacquant 1992). The main difference is that Stones wishes to make it clear his use of the concept is non-deterministic, and relates to a general set of transposable dispositions which can be distinguished from the more conjuncturally-specific structures. The latter is the agents' understanding and interpretation of the various rules, norms and expectations associated with given roles and positions, and their relation to other roles/positions. Conjuncturally-specific internalized structures also involve an awareness of the wider context of action, which will be acted on to some extent on the basis of habitus. In other words, how a person acts in a given situation at a given time is to some extent a result of their habitus, which has been built slowly over time in relation to their class, gender, experience and so on, and depends to some extent on how they interpret the given set of external (structural) circumstances they are currently faced with, and negotiate the rules and norms associated with their current role or position.

I also rely on Stones' concepts of hard and more malleable external structures. Structuration accepts a duality (interaction) of structure and agency, in which structure is both medium and outcome of practices. But Stones wants to retain the sense of a more firm dualism (separateness) between agents and external structures in which some structures appear to the agent as intractable at least at the point of action. Children are more likely than powerful adults to be faced on a daily basis with intractable or apparently intractable structures in the form of rules, expectations, laws and financial constraints.

Background

Between 2003 and 2005 I returned to Malaga province, in the south of Spain, to do more ethnographic work and conduct a survey of 340 migrants. British migration in this area had grown, spread inland to more rural areas, and now included several younger migrants with families. The British are now possibly the largest minority group in Spain with a recorded 250,000 residents and estimates trebling that (O'Reilly 2007a). Increasing numbers of young families with children are joining the earlier wave of retirement migrants. There are 30,000 children from the UK now living in Spain. Two-thirds of these (at a rough estimate) attend private international schools. And while these figures already appear substantial, it is worth noting the clustering effect of migration. Migrants do not tend to spread themselves evenly across a country, but for historical or geographical, social or cultural reasons, cluster with other migrants. The local effects of British and North European migration to Spain's coastal zones, especially certain towns and villages in Mallorca, the Costa del Sol and the Costa Blanca, are therefore substantial and profound (Aledo 2005, Waldren 1996).

I returned to the west of Malaga because British migration here could now be conceptualized as rural rather than coastal, and I had explained the lack of integration of British in Spain using the theoretical lens of tourism (O'Reilly 2003, 2007b). I returned because ten years had passed and I wondered if children who had grown up in the area might be more settled; if I might find some sort of (even segmented) assimilation, or some of that symbiosis between insider and outsider once witnessed in Mallorca (Waldren 1996). What I found was a few migrants had learned the language sufficiently to call themselves fluent, some had crossed the imaginary, ethnic boundary and become assimilated or integrated, and several were working at the symbolic border (see Barth 1969), translating and interpreting (usually in low paid, low skill jobs). But, in general, the same old patterns were emerging (see O'Reilly 2000, King et al. 2000, Rodríguez et al. 1998). There was, and still is, very little interaction between British and Spanish in the areas where they settle in large numbers. If anything had changed it was the growing feeling of sadness and regret on the part of many migrants, that their move had been so unsuccessful in those terms. Because, counter to many assumptions made about these migrants, many of them do actually hope and endeavour to integrate more fully.

As I have argued elsewhere, lack of integration is not necessarily a problem (Huber and O'Reilly 2004) and, of course, integration is a contested and contentious term (Eriksen 2007). Many North European migrants in Spain are able to creatively play with the borders to their own ultimate advantage. For others, however, lack of integration equals social exclusion: lack of access to pensions, health care, housing, schooling and the vote (O'Reilly 2007a). These are some of the unintentional structural outcomes. My interest has thus turned to trying to explain the continuing marginalization of some groups, and the contradictions between apparent lack of effort to integrate and sincere regret and disappointment at not being able to. The more I spoke to people about these interests and concerns, the more I was told: you should talk to the children. Migrants seem to invest their hopes and dreams in their children; these migrants felt their own marginalization and frustration were vindicated by the feelings and experiences of their children.

During 2003 and 2004 I took the opportunity to spend some time in an International School in the Costa del Sol. The school follows the English curriculum and takes children from reception to A level. The intake includes a mix of nationalities, including Spanish, but has a majority of British children.[1] Over the space of a year and a half I spent time in the school, in the playground chatting to pupils, in the classrooms, in the staffroom and the secretary's office, and after school talking to parents about their own lives and those of their children. I conducted several group interviews in the classroom, individual and small group interviews outside of the classroom, and got two groups of 11–13-year-olds to write short essays about 'living in Spain'. In this chapter I share with readers the children's stories, experiences, feelings, the choices they make and what they are based on. The children's stories reveal the habitus, or dispositions, and the conjuncturally-specific internal structures that shape their perceptions and practices.

Why Spain?

It is important to note that children do not choose to go to Spain; the parents make the choices and then persuade the children. These are hard structures, confronted by the child as barely malleable. One boy did not want to go to Spain until his parents offered to buy him a new bike; another was persuaded by the promise of a trip to the beach every day. The parents moved to Spain, as they explain it, in search of a whole new way of life. They are attracted by the sun, the warm weather, health benefits, food, and their perception of Spanish culture. They are also attracted by cheap property prices, cheap food, drink and cigarettes. But what parents expect from Spain relies heavily on the country's associations with tourism, with leisure and pleasure, and even authenticity (MacCannell 1999). They are seeking a 'real' Spain, which is a bit quaint and backward, slow, relaxed, has a strong sense of community, and a robust morality: 'an idealised setting that satisfies personal needs' (Waldren 1996: xv). They are escaping, on the other hand, the 'rat race', high crime rates, high unemployment, greyness, cold and misery. The children put this all so succinctly:[2]

- I moved here because of my dads family they were always steling (stealing) and doing bad thing and my mum and dad wanted to make a new start by moving to Spain. (Daniel, Year 7, essay)
- Me and my family moved here because my dad had just sold his business and we were either going to move to America or here. Then we chose Spain because we thought that America was to far away. (Justin, Year 8, essay)
- We moved to Spain because in England you can't do anything because its always raining, but over here there is mostly always sun. (Fran, Year 7)
- I moved out here because my dad turned ill he previously had three hartactas (heart attacks) and he suffered another one last Christmas. The doctor said to move out here so we did. Spain is so much better than England for example if you was to watch English news it would just be about people getting killed, raped and kidnapped whereas out here all they say is where the next fiesta is. (Joshua, Year 8, essay)
- My mum and Dad wanted to move here because of the sun. (Sharon, age 15)

Mixed Messages of Spain

The children are clear why they moved but they get very mixed messages from their parents about life in Spain once they are there. British migrants to Spain generally love their new host country and are happy to have moved (Casado-Díaz 2006).

However, once settled they remain politically, economically, socially, culturally and linguistically marginal (O'Reilly 2007a). Almost a third of respondents to my survey *never* meet Spanish friends, family or neighbours to talk to. Only 2 per cent can hold a conversation in Spanish and even fewer call themselves fluent. Half never read a Spanish newspaper, most have never voted in an election in Spain, and over a third are not registered as resident in Spain. These facts are also revealed through the children.

- I don't speak fluent Spanish, but I know enough to get by, but my Mum and Dad don't speak a word and I have to translate all the time. (Ellie, Year 8)
- I have to translate for them when we go to restaurants and things. It's like, 'oh Scott, what did he say then?' 'ask them for this and that'. You get a bit sick of it after a while. (Scott, age 14)

Many of the working age migrants are working in the informal economy or are early-retired. Several children had parents who were still working in the UK, or elsewhere in the world. Their roots therefore are not in Spain. James' father, for example, goes home three weeks each month for work. Susie and Jennifer (aged 15) both have fathers who live in Spain but run estate agencies in the UK. Charlie's father is an entertainer who travels back to the UK for a week whenever he needs to earn some money.

Several parents have lived abroad for most of their lives, chose Spain from a list of options and make it clear they may move elsewhere in the future. Others are more committed to a new life in Spain, but continue to miss home and family in the UK. In many ways these are transnational migrants, retaining strong links across borders. Ties with home are firmly upheld, with visits for work or shopping, to see family, or for weddings and funerals. They keep in touch via email, internet chat, and telephone; they have a constant stream of friends and relatives visiting from the UK (Williams and Hall 2002). Scott's father, for example, has an air-conditioning company in the UK which he visits for a week each month. His Mum stays behind; she likes to go for lunch with her English friends. Neither speaks much Spanish. But, regardless of these strong ties to home, very few ever admit they would go back home permanently. They denigrate Britain as dull, grey, crime-ridden, hectic, pressured and ruined (O'Reilly 2000, 2002). Christine, a 16-year-old who had been sent to Spain to live with her aunt because she had been expelled from boarding school in the UK told me:

> I mean they all say they'll never go back to England (laughs). Most people who live here say they'll never go back to England. But I still … I think they still feel like England is home.

The parents of Louise, age 16, still have a business and their main property in the UK. Louise knows her Mum misses her family back home but she says she will never leave Spain. Louise, on the other hand, does want to go home, but her Mum doesn't want her to. She feels very torn between loyalties, to her Mother and to her friend back home who, at the time of the interview, had been having an affair with her teacher! Louise says: 'It's like I've got a life here and a life in England and there's lots of stuff going on in England that I feel like I should be there for, like now'.

There are also a lot of tourists coming from the UK to these same areas where the migrants live; they share social and living spaces, and so life in Spain for British migrants is always a bit like a holiday. Reminders of home are continuous. Louise says because there are so many visitors from the UK, when you make friends locally you tend to make friends with people from home.

Why International School?

British children know they live in a tourist place and enjoy the lifestyle that provides; they know that few parents ever want to go home; but they are also aware they live on the margins of society. Their conjuncturally-specific internal structures therefore include an awareness that neither they nor their parents are fully settled or integrated. They are also in a school system that is separate from the mainstream. I asked them why they had chosen to go to international school.[3] The responses fall into two categories which reflect the difference between traditional and non-traditional private school intake. The traditional international/private school intake includes the children of middle-class parents and those we might otherwise call expatriates (see Fechter 2007). Middle-class parents want their children to learn the English curriculum because they believe it is better and that it broadens their children's opportunities. Privately funded education is also usually better funded than state education, and has better resources. Children in international school acquire social and cultural capital as well as human (or educational) capital. Middle-class parents expect their children to be able to compete in a global market and therefore they need to be fluent in written and spoken English. International school is seen to offer an exclusive education. Traditional private school children are there for reasons of their parents' aspirations; it is part and parcel of their class habitus. The children express this thus:

- Well, we meet nicer kids here. (Girl, age 14)
- People are more friendly here than in Spanish school. The Spanish kids here are different, if you know what I mean. (Girl, age 15)
- My parents want me to learn English because they want me to be a lawyer. (Spanish boy, age 16)
- I came here because I will go to Uni in America or maybe England, I don't know, but I'm going to need English anyway. (Boy, age 14)

The non-traditional international school intake includes those who in their home country would not normally aspire to private schooling. Working-class children go to international school because they want to continue with the same curriculum or because they failed to settle in Spanish school. Their parents seem to make this rather expensive choice quite readily, accepting their own marginality. This is just another expression of their own deep ambivalence about Spanish society. Note that it is cheaper than in the UK to go to international school in Spain. Laura (aged 17) started in Spanish school, then went to international school, and is now going back to the UK to go to university. I asked her why she went to Spanish school first.

> I wanted to mix. I didn't want to be like these people who don't learn the language and don't have nothing to do with the Spanish. Ha!
> *Interviewer: So, what happened?*
> To be honest they weren't very nice to me. They were at first. At first I was the new little English girl and they were, like 'oh, she's English, we can practise with her', our English, you know. They were like all over me, but that wore off, and, after a time there were more English there and, well, they weren't really very nice to me. I was having trouble coping 'cos I had only had a few lessons of Spanish before I came and I thought I would just pick it up, really, but you don't.

Experiencing Marginalization

One thing the entire group shares is that some had really tough experiences of intimidation and abuse in Spanish school and some get what they called 'racial abuse' out of school. When one child mentioned any of this in a group the rest would join in and the entire conversation would become very animated and heated, as children rushed to tell me about their own experiences or those of someone they know. As an internalized structure, it is becoming part of the new set of dispositions the group shares. Several children described being treated unfairly when they went to Spanish school. They also described being bullied or teased, picked on, or simply treated as different, either in school or in the street when they are out playing. Children are aware they are in a minority.

- (In Spanish school) they wouldn't even give me a chance to communicate so I was forced to hang around with the English. (Sean, age 14)
- They would shout racial abuse you know, bloody foreigners and this and that, get lost, and that. (Boy, age 17)
- In Spanish school, I did like it but I got bullied I had a fight every day. (Ben, Year 8)
- On Sunday I got chased by loads of them and they just don't like the English, I don't think. (Girl, FG5)
- I see a boy once and they just hit him there and then. They didn't do anything to me. I just walked away, but he got his hat tooken (sic) off him and they kicked him in the face twice, and broke his tooth. (Boy, age 15)
- If you're German or English they want to pick on you. (Girl, FG5)
- The Spanish people they always look aggressive and they're always like watching, like they want to kill you (two boys agree) and if you cross, like you

attempt to walk around them, but they just come over and they say, give me your money, or … (Boy, FG3)

Some described the way they have to hide or play down their nationality at times. One told me he is not allowed to wear his football t-shirt when he goes out to play now because it is seen as antagonistic. Some talk about trying to make Spanish friends and failing. They are aware they are seen as tourists who live there, and that if tourists get into trouble they will be tarred with the same brush (see Waldren 1996). They described being picked on, shouted at and called names. They particularly do not like being called *guiri*, an ambivalent colloquialism for foreigner sometimes used as a term of abuse and sometimes as endearment. One boy told me he had received death threats on his mobile phone; others had received threatening notes. Several had things stolen (hats, bikes), were chased or got into fights. These experiences are not reserved for the English. Nic is Danish but speaks good Spanish and English. He is finishing school soon and taking some time out to plan his future. All he knows is he doesn't want to stay in Spain.

> Last year I was attacked by a few Spanish, for absolutely no reason. They just jumped at me from behind and beat me up quite badly. And a few weeks later one of my friends was beaten up by exactly the same bunch of people. For no reason. They just beat you up because you're not Spanish.

A Spanish boy told me that when he is with English friends, and Spanish boys go by, he doesn't want them to know he is Spanish or they will pick on him for being with the English. These various sets of experiences, feelings, shared emotions, and influences gradually become part of the internal structures children draw on when making their own decisions about who to make friends with and what to do in the future.

Experiencing International School

In international school, children feel safer because they are not confronted with their minority status on a daily basis. They experience the security and solidarity of being in a mixed group, yet in some ways they share the status of the excluded, sharing (and consolidating) their experiences of bullying.

- When I moved to St Mary's I found out it was so much easier and I am friends with people who are different nationality. I think its good that I have made friends with people of different nationality. (Sean, Year 8)
- (In St Mary's) I felt more comfortable with my environment and the people here even if they are not all English they still speak it fluently so now I don't feel so different from everybody else. (Georgina, Year 8)

However, they also mix in their own nationality groups there more easily and find this comforting. This is the pull of the habitus, the affirmation of their own set of dispositions, habits, tastes and preferences. They find interesting ways to express their sense of who they are in their own groups, through dress and music, for example. As Christine and Nic told me:

- If you come here on Mufty day you would be able to tell straight away where everyone came from ... like the punks shall we call them, where they all dress in black, so it is music as well, but all the punks are English, so (laughs). The Danish are all in the fashion of Denmark, and it's Danish brands, and um, like here they all wear like baggy clothes, whereas the Danish are much more brand conscious. (Nic, age 17)
- Yeah, and all the English boys have the same hair cut (laughs). (Christine, age 16)

National identity becomes very important in both positive and negative ways, as they identify with and against each other. But nationality is also confronted by them on a daily basis as a hard external structure. They find themselves living in communities constituted of given nationalities; they can converse linguistically with some groups and not others; they share cultural interests with some groups; they meet children of their own nationality through their parents' friends; and those in Spanish school were often placed together with others of their own nationality.

When you're outside school you hang around with everyone who's English, it makes you feel like why do you need Spanish? If you, like, hang around with everyone who's English, and you speak English here you wonder, why do you need Spanish? Well, you really do still need it, but ... (Boy, Year 8)

Though the above is all as much true of class and gender as nationality, in this super-diverse setting nationality takes on a special relevance. As a particular minority group, the northern Europeans also share an identity that incorporates some social distance, some sense of superiority, a sense of economic wealth and cultural distance. We might think of this as a post-colonial trace, an attitude that has seeped into the habitus over generations. It is revealed in the children's discourses in subtle ways. The non-European migrants are nothing to them, not worthy of any mention. The Spanish, on the other hand, are often treated interchangeably with Gypsies, and portrayed at times as envious, and a little backward.

- When they see you have got more than them they just want to steal it. (Boy, FG5)
- because all the rich people have come here and to buy houses and to stay here and then they know that, and they see that, and that everyone has ... And then they just get aggressive and jealous. (Boy, FG3)
- all the Spanish, well typical Spanish girls I call them, they all go around in tight (...) trousers and tight (...) tops and all the English girls go around in sports tops. (Girl, FG5)
- and the Spanish girls wear them massive shoes as well. You know them really clumpy spice girl shoes (Several girls laugh at once). (Girl, FG5)
- they all dress like their mothers don't they? and they wear them earrings. (Girl, FG5)

One boy said, 'Basically the Spanish are just Gypsies aren't they?'. This last was a quite extreme comment, not representative, but important in that it highlights a common theme where Spanish children and Gypsies were sometimes talked about as if they are the same thing. One group would start talking about Spanish picking on them or attacking them and then drift into a discussion about Gypsies without distinguishing one from another.

Learning about Prejudice

On the other hand, the British children I spoke to tend to deny their own prejudices. Children are learning from each other, from the school, and perhaps from home, that bullying is bad, that to mix in your own nationality is not so good, that you should have a good attitude to language, and should try to integrate. So, in interviews children would say things like 'I'm not being racist but' or would modify a statement with 'not all the Spanish are like that'. They would also enjoy describing the few Spanish friends they have managed to make. But they cannot deny their own comfort at being together. They also learn about each other's nationality in school and see this as a good thing; they learn tolerance and some of each others' language. Lots of essays stressed how they have friends of different languages and learn about each other's language and culture.

- I think its quite bad when you move to a different country and you don't speak the language. (Ellie, Year 8)
- that's ignorant if you're gonna live in Spain and not bother learning the language. (Girl, FG2)
- I have got friends of different nationalities, for example Spanish, English, Irish, Norwegian, etc. I love having friends who can speak different languages because you can learn them yourself and you get to blend in with them and they also learn to speak English. (Jade, Year 8)

Futures in Spain

Most children I spoke to did not see a future for themselves in Spain. International school is a structural postcolonial trace, an institution established to preserve the continuity of the western lifestyle and to raise and teach children uncontaminated by local cultures. Here, of course, it is not the western lifestyle but the class habitus that is being preserved. The school does not have the contacts to enable them to stay in Spain. This is not how that kind of system, established for colonials and expatriates, works. The school curriculum and culture and its wider networks, and therefore the children's role expectations, all assume a return to the UK or elsewhere in what they see as the 'modern western' (usually English-speaking) world, so that even those who do want to stay know they are not supposed to feel that way. Traditional private school pupils see the world as their oyster and believe that Spain – at least this part of it – is rather backward and lacking in opportunities. This is not so much about Spain *per se* as it is about denigrating the local and parochial and celebrating an elite marginality and international travel.

- I don't know. I may go to America, or England perhaps, or maybe Denmark for a while. (Nick, 6th form)
- Yeah, well I think that most people who go to private colleges feel they are going to leave sooner or later. This is my last year, and I think I am going to take a gap year and maybe travel for a bit, but then I am going to go to university either in England or I'm going to go to the states. (Peter, age 17)
- I've got a feeling I am going to live in lots of different countries. First I will start in America because there they speak English. (Alex, age 15)
- (talking about staying in Spain) Um, most of the Spanish boys that I know do building. I know loads of Spanish boys who, you know, that's their goal, that 'I'm gonna go and work on a building site'. I think that's what you do when you leave school early as well.
  Karen: *What about the girls?*
  Girls? Work in a shop. (Sharon, 15)

Working-class children want to take part in the UK opportunity society and believe they can only do that if they go back. Because of their own limited linguistic abilities, they believe that locally they would only obtain work in bars or estate agencies. On the other hand, they know their parents are staying behind and they will miss each other. It is a wrench for them and one this class is not used to; it is not part of the habitus. But their own habitus is changing based on their experiences and networks in international school. They do not learn enough about modern, advanced Spain to envisage themselves working in the mainstream economy. Their experience is marginal like their parents. And why would they want to stay somewhere they feel so excluded and where the parents are not really integrated? The school enables them to feel cocooned and to share the status of the excluded and superior.

- Some do leave school at 16. One of my friends stayed here and did her A levels then stayed here and she is just working in a bar. When they stay here it is just because you haven't really thought about what you want to do. (Girl, age 17)
- I'll go back to University and I think I'll stay over there 'cos, like, here, I don't see any like job opportunities. (Girl, age 15)
- I wanna stay here but there's no jobs, unless you wanna work in Tivoli world. (Girl, age 16)
- Every English person that lives here is like a waiter or an estate agent and I don't wanna be a waiter or an estate agent. (Sean, age 14)

To make such choices can be very difficult for those who would not normally go to private school, who are going back against their parents' wishes, or where the parents are ambivalent. Several I spoke to were going to live with grandparents or aunts and uncles. Everything leads to them leaving Spain except the parents who have not thought this through and do not want them to leave, but by putting them in international school they almost made their leaving a certainty. The parents are torn between letting go and thinking of their children's future, and this is even worse when they are going back to a place they said was so awful.

- My Mum is not happy about me going back, my Dad's a bit disappointed too. (Girl, age 16)
- My parents wanted to mix with the Spanish and sort of have a Spanish way of life, but that's not gonna happen is it? It was a bit of a dream. (Girl, age 17)
- My parents are sad, but it's just something I felt I had to do. (Girl, age 16)
- I'm going back now and now Mum and Dad think they might go back as well. (Steven, age 17)
- It's really hard going back to England to study. My parents make me feel guilty every day. (Girl, age 16)

Conclusion

To summarize, British children in Spain are living with and internalizing the contradictions that mark their parents' lives. They are aware the parents love Spain and that most never want to go home, but that they are not really integrated or even settled. They must share some of this pull towards their host country and antipathy towards their home since it is now part of their migrant habitus. They have had some negative experiences of being members of a marginal minority, and they share and exaggerate these between themselves. In international school they share the status of the excluded and, since some of the children have been to Spanish school and left, they can all claim to have vicariously stepped into Spanish culture and life in more depth than they have. Their North European postcolonial habitus demonstrates some antipathy towards the local Spanish but this is mediated by a class habitus that perceives the Spanish in the school as 'different' and better. They are acquiring a taken-for-granted dislike of prejudice but find this directed towards their experiences of it rather than their own attitudes. For middle-class children, who see the world as their oyster, Spain is one experience amongst many, a rather backward and quaint if rather pleasant temporary phase in their lives. For working-class children who experience what they see as racism and marginalization, who receive mixed messages about what Spain is and means, who enjoy the comfort of international school and a liminal space, but who are pushed into a middle-class trajectory, without all the various forms of capital, choices are limited and the implications profound. Choosing to remain in Spain is denigrated by their peers, but returning to the UK often involves having to live with grandparents or aunts, and is sometimes seen as breaking up the family.

Notes

1. I do not identify the school because, although my research was overt, it is difficult to obtain informed consent from every participant in a public setting. The school, like its surrounding area, is a setting of super-diversity. There are children of many nationalities in the school, but the vast majority are North European or wealthy, middle-class Spanish. Outside the school, as well as the North Europeans who are very much in evidence in affluent areas, the area has numerically important Moroccan, Romanian, Russian, Colombian and Gypsy minorities. The British, the largest migrant group, consists of retirees, seasonal visitors, second home owners, small business owners, self-employed of all class backgrounds, and peripatetic migrants who own homes in two or more countries and move regularly between them. The Spanish in the area are, for the main part, Andalusian, but even here there are vast differences, in economic, social and cultural terms. There is both a lot of poverty and a lot of wealth. Finally, the area hosts internal migrants from various autonomous regions in Spain, and second-home owning Spanish who visit the area for long periods. None of these, then (though I treat them as such for the purposes of brevity), are homogeneous groupings.
2. I have not corrected the spelling where I have quoted from children's written essays, but have added the correct word in brackets where I think this helps. FG = focus group.
3. Several children of British and other North European migrants do, of course, go to Spanish school, which leads to a whole different set of trajectories, which demand whole new research projects.

Bibliography

Aledo, A.T. 2005. 'Los Otros Inmigrantes: residents europeos en el sudeste español'. In J. Fernández-Rufete and M. García Jiménez (eds), *Movimientos migratorios contemporáneous*. Murcia: Universidad Católico de San Antonio.

Barth, F. 1969. 'Introduction'. In F. Barth (ed.), *Ethnic Groups and Boundaries*. Boston, MA: Little Brown, 9–38.

Bourdieu, P. 1977. *Outline of a Theory of Practice*. Cambridge: Cambridge University Press.

——— 1998. *On Television and Journalism*. London: Pluto Press.

Bourdieu, P. and L. Wacquant 1992. *An Invitation to Reflexive Sociology*. Cambridge: Polity Press.

Casado-Díaz, M.A. 2006. 'Retiring to Spain: An Analysis of Differences among North European Nationals', *Journal of Ethnic and Migration Studies*, 32 (8): 1321–39.

Eriksen, T.H. 2007. 'Complexity in Social and Cultural Integration: Some Analytical Dimensions', *Ethnic and Racial Studies*, 30 (6): 1055–69.

Fechter, A.M. 2007. *Transnational Lives. Expatriates in Indonesia*. Aldershot: Ashgate.

Giddens, A. 1979. *Central Problems in Social Theory: Action, Structure and Contradiction in Social Analysis*. London: Macmillan.

——— 1984. *The Constitution of Society: Outline of the Theory of Structuration*. Cambridge: Polity Press.

Huber, A. and K. O'Reilly 2004. 'The Construction of *Heimat* under Conditions of Individualised Modernity: Swiss and British Elderly Migrants in Spain', *Ageing and Society*, 24 (3): 327–52.

King, R., A.M. Warnes and A.M. Williams 2000. *Sunset Lives: British Retirement to Southern Europe*. Oxford: Berg.

MacCannell, D. 1999. *The Tourist: A New Theory of the Leisure Class*. Berkeley, CA: University of California Press.

O'Reilly, K. 2000. *The British on the Costa del Sol*. London: Routledge.

——— 2002. 'Britain in Europe/The British in Spain. Exploring Britain's Changing Relationship to the Other', *Nations and Nationalism*, 8 (2): 179–94.

———— 2003. 'When is a Tourist? The Articulation of Tourism and Migration in Spain's Costa del Sol', *Tourist Studies*, 3 (3): 301–17.

———— 2007a. 'Intra-European Migration and the Mobility-Enclosure Dialectic', *Sociology*, 41 (2): 277–93.

———— 2007b. 'Emerging Tourism Futures: Residential Tourism and Its Implications'. In C. Geoffroy and R. Sibley (eds), *Going Abroad: Travel, Tourism, and Migration. Cross-Cultural Perspectives on Mobility*. Cambridge: Cambridge Scholars Publishing.

Rodríguez, V., G. Fernández-Mayoralas and F. Rojo 1998. 'European Retirees on the Costa del Sol: A Cross-national Comparison', *International Journal of Population Geography*, 4: 183–200.

Stones, R. 2005. *Structuration Theory*. Basingstoke: Palgrave Macmillan.

Vertovec, S. 2007. 'Super-Diversity and its Implications', *Ethnic and Racial Studies*, 30 (6): 1024–54.

Waldren, J. 1996. *Insiders and Outsiders: Paradise and Reality in Mallorca*. Oxford: Berghahn Books.

Williams, A.M. and C.M. Hall 2002. 'Tourism, Migration, Circulation and Mobility: The Contingencies of Time and Place'. In A.M. Williams and C.M. Hall (eds), *Tourism and Migration: New Relationships between Production and Consumption*. London: Kluwer Academic Publishers, 1–60.

Chapter 8
CHILDREN NEGOTIATING IDENTITY IN MALLORCA[1]

Jacqueline Waldren

❧❧❧

Changes in the meanings and realities of childhood in the small Mallorcan village of Deia can be traced through the experiences of foreign and local children growing up there during the Franco regime (1936–75) and after Spain became a democratic nation in 1978 until the present. Childhood held different meanings during these political climates and the roles, agency and positions of children in society have altered considerably. Both the transnational and 'local' children are actively influencing cultural transitions and can no longer be treated merely as extensions to adult studies.

Cultural differences in the meanings of childhood become evident as parents and children from varied social, geographical, economic and ethnic backgrounds reveal their perceptions of identity, parenting, family and education. Childhood, youth, adulthood or parenting cannot be considered universal concepts as is often suggested in social policies. Children and parents may be subject to social inclusion or exclusion impacting on their sense of personhood and cultural identities.

Looking Back

Franco's regime promoted strong values, discipline and punishment to form well brought up children. Lucia Graves, daughter of British poet Robert Graves, writes that 'there was no room for unbelievers in the new, ultra Catholic Spain'. She discovered that the Mother Superior in her new school had called a special assembly to tell the girls they 'had a duty as Catholics, as members of their school and as Spaniards … to try to do their utmost to save the soul of this young English girl, who knows no better, from the flames of Hell' (2001: 98).

126

According to the Catholic doctrine of the day, children were conceived only within marriage and considered gifts: a natural and essential addition to 'a family', church and community. *Familia numerosas* (large numbers of children) were encouraged. A couple might live in their own house or flat but their child/children were cared for as much by grandmothers, grandfathers, siblings, unmarried aunts, among others. Family unity was encouraged. Men and women had traditional roles in the family: women were encouraged to remain at home to care for their children, husbands and elders, while the men provided the economic means. However, these gender ideals were not often practised in this mainly agricultural village where women and children were needed for the seasonal harvests of olives, grapes and citrus fruits. This was a period of stultifying fusion of Catholicism and fascist ideology and especially difficult for children of foreign parents who did not follow these ideals.

The post-Franco era identified children as the future of the country and recommended the development of facilities that would lead to change in society. Family planning, the search for economic stability and women working outside the home all limited the number of children born and set higher goals for their futures. Some say this has impacted on children's social standing in society which can be read as greater demands being put on them to achieve more than their parents did (Labanyi and Graham 1995).

Living Abroad

As Caroline Brettell suggests, 'Life histories (or stories) help us to gain access to others experiences' (1993).[2] This text involves a blending of voices and by extension a blurring of the traditional line between academic scholarship and narrative. It is part biography, autobiography and ethnography. Using my own, my children's and my grandchildren's experiences and perceptions of growing up in this Mallorcan village, and comparing them to their peers' and 'local' experience, reveals changing roles and meanings of childhood over time. The achievement of modern identities engendered a set of habits and reflexes which draw from a variety of lived experience that fuse together in different circumstances and allow children to adapt to new environments more readily than their parents. In many ways parents live their lives through their children, structuring their work and home lives around school, homework, sports, planning for their futures, etc.

I have lived in Deia, Mallorca most of the last 40 years and the ethnographic field has become my home, more personal than an anthropology based on just two years of fieldwork. Moreover, this allows me the insight of 'lived social experience' as well as participant observation over an extended period, albeit from a somewhat subjective/objective perspective. Anthropology at home has its shortcomings, but as a long-term expatriate, my role is somewhat ambiguous. Neither 'local' nor totally foreign, insider nor outsider (Waldren 1996), I am 'at home abroad' and reflexivity obliges me to confront the moral and political responsibility of my actions and provokes a questioning stance (Callaway and Okely 1992: 24).

Married to an American artist who was well known in the village (having spent various summer holidays there and being responsible for the arrival of a number of other expat artists from Paris and the United States), I was recognized as *sa dona d'en Bil* (Bill's wife) by locals and included in a small group of about 20 resident expatriates. English was the lingua franca of the foreign colony and we communicated with locals in Spanish. When each of our four daughters was born, the advice and experience of a few local women was indispensable for access to housing, food, pregnancy information, doctors, midwives, domestic knowledge, etc. Few foreign women had children during my first few years there, so my overall orientation to mothering, nurturing and caring was gained from my neighbours.

These were the Franco years when public uses of local languages were prohibited and traditional value systems were upheld. Living in a flat over a Mallorquin family gave my children access to 'local' homes and lives and they learned Mallorquin (a dialectal variant of Catalan) at the same time as our home-spoken English, and soon added Spanish (Castillian[3] was the national language under Franco) at school. By the time they were three years old, they were all tri-lingual.

Young children (1–5-year-olds) were addressed as *Rei* or *Reina* (King or Queen), warmly encircled by extended family members. The affection lavished on them in most local households was indulgent and supportive in contrast to the official disciplined ideals of the era. Starting school was children's first experience of negotiating identity on their own. For my girls and many others, school represented forms and styles of behaviour and meaning that were strange to them and the transformation over time from the experience of strangeness to that of familiarity deeply marked their lives.

There were three schools in Deia, one for girls, one for boys and a nuns' school where one class was of mixed ages and gender and under fives were cared for in a separate room. Children in pink or blue and white smocks were accompanied by their mother, father, older brother or sister to school and home each day until they were about five years old when they were allowed to walk home on their own and accompany younger siblings as well.

I will relate some of the comments the girls made to me over the years to give some idea of what they seemed to be experiencing during their first years at the local nuns' school: 'I think we mostly prayed, learned the catechism and did needlework'. 'Maria called me "*bruta*" today. I didn't like that.' We later learned that *bruta* (dirty) then described our houses and the way our children dressed. Mallorquin children were meticulously turned out in their starched smocks each day, while mine were sent off in clean but not pressed or starched smocks. As they got older, most children began to refuse to wear their smocks and would carry them to school and remove them the minute they left the premises.

Visits to friends' houses in different parts of the village were not common as similar discriminatory comments ensued when local children wanted to play with foreign neighbours and their mothers implied the houses were 'dirty'. These comments confused the children who had not previously seen their homes as different from others and made them reticent to invite local friends to their houses.

Among the foreign families, some houses were regular after-school play places while other foreign parents did not welcome their children's friends. One young Swiss boy and two Latin American siblings were not allowed to return after school to their parental homes until 8pm. This meant that their friends' (local and foreign) families[4] sort of adopted them during those hours, sharing their *meriendas* (afternoon snacks), toys, playtime and parental interaction. However, these children may well have been the first to cross the real and imagined boundaries between the homes of foreigners and locals and opened the way for others.

Mary Douglas's examination of human notions of dirt and impurity in the context of 'matter out of place' (foreigners were certainly out of place) noted that 'creditability depends on consensus of a moral community and the probability of being accused of pollution will fall on paupers and second class citizens who seldom understand the exchanges, gifts, services, hospitality in which villagers participate' (1970). Foreigners fell into this second-class citizen category in different ways and through nicknames villagers had subtle means of transmitting information about them: *Yo quiero* (I want, an Irishman who knew only those words in Spanish) or *El Pavo* (The Turkey, an American who looked like a turkey) (Waldren 1996: 144).

Through the primary years these real and imagined parental and peer pressures led the foreign children to try to conform as much as possible in dress, behaviour and discourse with their local friends. Once children began to enter one another's homes, they often noted the difference between subjects of conversation at home and in their friends' houses, parental affection, gestures, demonstrativeness, etc. While we were very affectionate within our family at home, our children said they felt a bit embarrassed being hugged by multiple relations at their friends' houses. Their friends were given absolute replies with little explanation while open discussion and communication were encouraged at home. When they asked 'why?', they were not content with the local response 'because that has always been the way' or 'because we (parents) say so'. Mary Douglas (1970) drew attention to such differences in socialization patterns suggesting that, whereas autonomy and unique value of the individual is given in some cultures, there is little reflection on the self and more stress on social role categories in other cultures. Our more informal parenting was in contrast to the local customs and impacted on the sense of difference the girls were experiencing. One commented, 'There were too many choices at home. It's easier to be answered yes or no!'.

Lucia Graves was raised on the island in the years following the Spanish Civil War. She describes what it was like to go to the local girls' school, speak Castillian Spanish and Catalan (used among the children when playing) and return each evening to her very British home, 'so different from the homes of my village friends', where her father worked in a room with books, her mother sat by the fire reading a book with a cat on her lap, and at night they would all listen to the BBC (2001: 51).

Perceptions of Childhood: The First Generation

The meanings and expectations of a mother, father, childhood and parenthood are multiple and diverse. Within Deia, especially among the foreigners, parenting practices and childhood experiences are surprisingly varied considering the limited population. The diverse nationalities, backgrounds and lifestyles provided quite distinct models.

Local families or neighbours who were more closely aligned through social and religious practices included some of us into their lives, caring for our children, inviting us to saints' days or other special events. Children were adored and drawn into every aspect of daily life. However, each child responded differently to some encounters. My oldest daughter seemed at ease at three years old when our neighbours took her to see them butcher a rabbit. She described the process of 'skinning the rabbit' to me with fascination. A few years later, her sister came running back home in tears, appalled by a similar experience.

On returning from the city one day, I found the girls at lunch with our neighbours. The plate on the table held cooked lamb in various chunks including parts of the head and jaws. As one of the girls picked up a piece of jaw meat (with the teeth still in it), I took a deep breath and refrained from showing my initial shock. In retrospect, one wonders at my innocence in allowing them to participate in such actions, yet we were living in a rural setting with people who acquired their food and ours through these procedures and it was a learning experience for all of us. Animal care, products and most food was extremely different between local and foreign houses, and the girls often noted their likes and dislikes to me after politely eating whatever they were given in local houses. Through these experiences we parents became aware of cultural differences in rituals, traditions, food, hygiene, education, human/animal relations and many other areas of life in our new home, while our children absorbed these as ordinary everyday experiences, albeit sometimes frightening. Some foreign girls persuaded their non-Catholic parents to allow them to attend mass and take first communion with their local friends when they were eight years old. None continued when moving on to school outside Deia.

Childhood schooling and language come after the child's unconscious learning through experience, observation, taste, sound, smell. These are vital parts of learning culture. Broch-Due and Rudie noted that 'Large parts of the embedded cultural understandings one forms through experiences of the body. Embodiment forms the non-arbitrary link immersed between cognition and experience and hence memory and meaning are understood and stored via real experiences in concrete social contexts in real human bodies' (1994: 76). Body language expresses their adaptation to local norms and values.

The Second Generation – Post Franco

When our grandchildren started school (1999–2006), lessons were taught in Catalan and they would often speak to their mothers and grandparents in Catalan while we replied in English (although we did understand and speak Catalan by that time). Other children, whose parents did not speak the local languages, faced a challenge when they started school. If we imagine ourselves in a new culture, a new place where we are strangers, we do not understand a single word of the language spoken, we can begin to sense a child's unease. Accompanying one's child to her first day at school, a parent observes the teacher greeting the new student: *'Benvingut a l'escola de Deià'* (Welcome to the Deia School). The child looks helplessly at her parent and replies, 'I don't understand'. A non-Catalan speaking parent would share her child's consternation. The teacher would endeavour to make the child comfortable through gestures and smiles, and lead her into the classroom.

It is not easy being a new student who cannot speak the language in a strange school. You can be taunted, bullied, physically or verbally accosted. Most of the children I interviewed and observed were upset by these early experiences but explained how they learned to defend themselves, offer retorts to their taunters and soon overcame both their feelings of strangeness and the harsh treatment from others. They claimed their acquisition of language skills made this possible. In his second year, an eight-year-old American boy admitted that 'in my first year, I cried every day after school from pure frustration and a year later I understood almost everything in both Spanish and Catalan'.

Learning to adapt by participating on others' terms, mimicking, and soon identifying one's place and modus operandi is an ongoing struggle for a new student. As Judith Okely so vividly writes about vicarious and sensory knowledge: 'Knowledge was embodied through site, taste, sound, touch and smell. Bodily movement, its vigour, stillness or unsteadiness was absorbed' (Callaway and Okely 1992: 38). This also applies to how one absorbs and learns culture to the point that it becomes part of one rather than requiring a conscious effort.

Despite differences in age or gender, children learn language and culturally appropriate actions much more easily than their parents do. At school, information is processed from their teacher or other children (it is common for a bi-lingual student to translate between a teacher and a new student in the early days at the Deia School). Children then become the interpreters for one another and their parents. Often stories are transmitted from child to parent adding new dimensions that were not there before. Like a game of Chinese whispers, messages become embellished or distorted along the route from child to child, child to parent. For example, a note from a teacher reading 'homework is meant to be signed by your parents' may be reported as 'you have to come to school to discuss my homework'. As language skills improve, children phone the parents of their friends to arrange visits and parents communicate back and forth through the children. Parents say, 'the children are too independent, they tell us what they want to do, make the arrangements and we just abide'. They begin to feel compromised as though they are losing control.[5]

In an English-speaking household it is fascinating to see and hear the multiple languages in action. A nine-year-old phones his friend's house: '*Hola Senyora, puc venir a jugar amb Jaume?*' (Can I come and play with James?). He turns to his Dad saying: 'Dad, Jaume's mom said I can go to his house to play'. Dad replies: 'Ok. You need to be home by eight'. '*Senyora, di a Jaume que tenc d'estar en casa a les vuit*' (Please tell James I have to be home by eight). Imagine what it is like where the mother is Norwegian, the father German/American, and the children attend a Catalan school. Although strange to us, it actually becomes quite 'natural' for the children to move in and out of the various languages they have learned in childhood. In some instances small children who have learned Catalan at school will not speak it at home, knowing their parents do not understand and wanting to keep their language and social worlds separate. The children absorb culture with their language acquisition: learn to express themselves idiomatically, know what to say when, where and to whom.

Lucia Graves captured the complexities that arise from being multi-lingual: 'I began to see that being trilingual meant I had never been able to focus fully on any one of my languages and that each one covered only particular areas of experience, and as a result I could not express myself fully in any of them' (2001: 115).

The conversation around our dinner table when children, partners, in-laws and grandchildren are together flows somewhat seamlessly through English, Catalan and Spanish. Our daughters may use English to us, to their children and one another, translate into Catalan or Spanish for their partners, while the children speak to me at different intervals in different languages and play or converse in Catalan, Spanish and/or English among themselves. They might tell me a story in Catalan to which I reply in English. My French/Spanish speaking stepdaughter insisted I speak only English (instead of Spanish or halting French) to her when she was eleven. Her fluency developed soon after. However, living in Madrid, she has always spoken Spanish to her husband and two teenage boys who have learned English at school but do not speak French. My nine-year-old granddaughter has recently begun to insist I speak only English to her. I am not sure if this is because she is embarrassed by my strangely accented Catalan or if she is beginning to make clear distinctions between her multicultural families. She loves me telling her stories in English of her mother and aunts growing up and to challenge me to a game of chess on the computer (which she knows more about than I do). When we dine at our daughters' houses, Spanish and Catalan dominate. Especially colourful are telephone conversations between the sisters: 'Hi, how are you', 'Good thanks', '*Mira, te queria preguntar*' (Castillian: look, I wanted to ask you) ...', 'si, si' (yes, yes), '*perque me preguntes?*' (Catalan: why do you ask?). If the subject pertains to local Deia issues, they will use Catalan, they will use Spanish for work and wider issues, joke or argue in Catalan and intersperse English here and there.

The myriad of complex forms of conversation practised is daunting and reveals how 'natural' it is for some to move in and out of various languages in a continuous manner identifying with the different culture and personalities in each context. Language can play a dynamic role in children's adaptation to new cultures and their identity formation in the new setting. Again Lucia Graves vividly reveals her experience:

> As we were foreigners – and looked it – we were addressed automatically in Spanish. Even today people are often surprised to hear me and my brothers speaking Majorcan[6] as one of them; perhaps they feel I have taken something from them that was too intimate to share with strangers. But rightly or wrongly, I did take it, and it is now part of my being that opens up when I speak the language again ... Like all bilingual (trilingual, if I count Spanish) I moved easily between two separate worlds, changing my gestures, my facial expressions and my intonations as required, almost switching identities when I switched languages. (2001: 26)

When my children first went to school, speaking Spanish was anathema to village people, but Castillian speakers were perceived to reflect education, social advancement and prestige. However, after Franco's death (1975), by the 1980s Mallorquin[7] was given precedent on the island as an expression of the new regional autonomy and an important expression of the new democracy after 40 years of dictatorship. Foucault's deconstruction of power-laden discourses, or Derrida's insistence that language composes our consciousness itself place identity, language and power firmly on even ground. However, cultural models cannot be taught exclusively by linguistic means. As we have seen in the previous examples, prior to language acquisition, awareness of differences in behaviour, time and place are embodied.

Re-Interpreting the Past

While my first two daughters feel their multicultural household and village experience taught them to interact with many different people and situations, my third daughter is still sensitive to the feelings she had as a child 'of being different, never quite fitting in'. She developed a feeling of an oppositional and ambiguous identity, a multiple and flexible identity which she could draw on in diverse situations. Each time she returns from studying abroad, the whole scenario is relived and sometimes most painful, yet she uses these experiences to organize and direct a village theatre company which performs at annual village fiestas, and the local cast is made up of her previous schoolmates and other locals. They began with Mallorquin authors and moved on to Spanish, French and English playwrights. If the works are not published in Catalan, they do the translations. The last two years they wrote their own plays. Their cooperative exercise and the works they perform reflect their changing views of their society, the wider world which impinges on it and their relationships with one another over time as well as the issues that arise in their lives today.

Those who grew up with my daughters have all moved in various directions through time and space. One young woman became a nun much to the dismay of her family.[8] She said when she was a girl, she was not allowed to read when she went to bed at night and the convent offered her a chance to pursue higher education. For those who went on to college and careers beyond the horizons of their peers, their parents and the village, 'local' identity is complex. Becoming educated distances them from their school friends and neighbours and some find more in common with foreigners than with some of their local friends who left school to marry, have children and assume age-appropriate responsibilities. However, that distance may expand definitions of 'home and community' to include a wider range of experiences beyond the 'local'.

Today my daughters' local friends laughingly tell me how much they admired our food habits. I would make tuna or egg sandwiches with mayonnaise and lettuce for the girls' snack at school, while their local friends had *p'amb oli* (bread rubbed with olive oil and tomato) or *sobrasada* (paprika sausage) or a piece of chocolate in a bread roll. They say they always tried to trade sandwiches with my girls and often make 'our' kind of sandwiches in their own homes, today.[9] For many, the differences that once cast negative connotations on foreign children are now remembered with nostalgia and part of an ideal past.

So here we have girls and boys growing up together with huge differences being overcome through embodiment, learning and shared experiences. Each child learns to deal with these experiences in different ways. One is strong willed, clearly expressive yet absolutely clear on how she acts with different cultural tools. Another is self-conscious, questioning, comparing cultures; a third is humorous, critical and confrontational, winning some friends for life and shocking others, and the younger one has returned from her schooling and journeys to Britain to her social roots. C. Michalopoulou-Veikou (unpublished paper) suggests that:

> when children experience cultural change and new schools, the process of their forced adaptation to the new dominant sociocultural environment may result in a forced 'subtractive acculturation' assuming the new system will lead to an erosion of their own identity and cultural frame of reference (and thus to be socially isolated) or to eliminate it and adopt behaviour patterns of the host culture and attitudes conducive to the host culture and social success.

The complexity of identity formation was made evident when I was asked to write an article for the book *Cross-Cultural Marriage* (Breger and Hill 1998). I told my eldest daughter how delighted I was to finally be able to discuss my children's multicultural experiences growing up in the village, their integration into local life and their 'mixed marriages'.[10] She replied: 'Mom, my husband and I grew up in the same culture.' She was actually the first of her generation to marry a local. Those who have identified so much with local life that they have formed relationships with Mallorquin or Spanish partners, set up households and found jobs in the village seem to have integrated their various experiences into a comfortable identity. Just as I found with the concepts of insider and outsider (Waldren 1996), identity is circumstantial, calling on that which best suits the situation. Like place and space notions of inside and outside are not mutually exclusive.

There is no doubt that the girls and others of their generation were attracted to those with whom they felt they had most in common while growing up. However, new experiences, becoming parents, employment options, sometimes revealed differences some had not recognized earlier. Unlike that of their older sister, two of the marriages did not survive. The girls said they discovered that their sense of identity as they grew older was quite distinct from others' (their partners, their in-laws, their peers, foreign friends and even their parents).

The Same But Different

Local children also grew up different from one another and often this was due to where they lived in the village. One farming family in the lower village had three daughters around the same age as the three children of two American artists in a nearby house. As they played together on the street, they bantered back and forth in indistinct forms until, without really realizing it, they were conversing first with gestures then with motions and finally in words. The American children learned Mallorquin and the Mallorquins learned English. These local girls were the first to be able to work in a hotel catering to tourists where English was the dominant language spoken. The American boy identified completely with his Mallorquin peers, spoke only Catalan (even to his parents), married a Mallorquin girl and until he was 23 years old barely used his English mother tongue. His complete adherence to local customs and remarkable facility at fishing, hunting and other 'local' activities gained him the respect of his peers and their parents. Only when offered a job with an American celebrity who required a bi-lingual general estate manager did he return to using English.

The above examples reveal various processes of identity formation over time. This process begins in early childhood. The classical anthropological interpretations become more complex in these ambiguous cultural experiences. If every act of identification implies a 'we' as well as a 'they', self-identity is neither given nor innate; the way in which it is generated is always a psychosocial process (Epstein 1978: xiii).

Within many complex societies the loss of certain aspects of ritual leads to confusion in identity and position amongst children and adolescents. Participating in local and home rituals and daily practices, children become accustomed to both. The lack of this clarity is a cause of much confusion amongst the youth in many Western countries (Neville 1984: 158). While some youths will be exposed to their heritage through the use of rituals associated with their home country, this does little to confirm or verify their position within society in the country in which they live. Kimball claims that 'ritual epitomises and represents the processes of everyday life' (Neville 1984: 151). Where these rituals are removed from their context and celebrated in a country where everyday life is very different, it is only natural that confusion about their relevancy should be experienced. However we have found that celebrating Christmas, followed by the local day of Three Kings or the celebration of birthdays in place of saints' days added to the children's sense of dual culture and was soon adopted as well by local children. The village events far outnumbered ours and combined to give not only the children but entire expat families a full calendar of special days. As Timera (2002) notes, parents are not consciously opposing local society or values. They simply transmit who they are and what they believe, in accordance with their own historical and cultural contexts. Thus it is in the family setting that the child first discovers the conflictual nature of otherness and school reinforces their awareness of difference. Socialization and adaptation by the child proceeds from there.

Language and Identity

After Franco's death, the Balearic Islands gained autonomy (along with 16 other regions in Spain) and Deia was one of the first schools where lessons were taught completely in Catalan from nursery[11] to twelve years old. Nursery begins at the age of three and compulsory education begins at five years of age with children attending primary school, which, in most cases, is local. The school had 40 students, 30 per cent of which were foreign students aged three to twelve. This intense introduction of the language allowed foreign children to adapt to local life more quickly than those of the previous years. They were also able to continue advancing in English and Spanish which were taught twice a week.

Foreign children schooled in Deia during 1978–89 remarked on their varied experiences adapting to the local school and their treatment by the other children. They feel their relationship with village friends changed when they went abroad to study. They say there is a certain investment of time, when one learns to conform to local values, that seems to be an essential part of being accepted as a friend. When one alters the status quo, by going away to study, they find on their return that they have to re-negotiate their local role by subtle, constant involvement in local activities with their peers. They also felt the effort was theirs to make and there was little or no interest shown by local or foreign friends in their experiences outside of Deia.[12]

Don Jaume, the first teacher to direct the Catalan programme begun in Deia's school in 1977 and taught by him for 12 years before he moved to a nearby town, returned after he retired from the teaching profession in 2008 to be honoured at the Deia annual village fiesta. Many alumni aged 29–45 from his Deia classes re-united and performed a short skit in his honour. There were many locals and German, British, American, French and Australians joined together to commemorate their school days in Deia. Don Jaume had prepared a slide show of photos from his teaching days there and many of the alumni could be seen as children in these photos. Time had obviously softened the painful memories and the reunion allowed them to look back on the best parts of their years at school together in Deia.

The above examples are of children's experiences within the village, at the local schools and may well be different from those who were schooled in the city. Not all the foreign children went to the local schools. Some were sent to private Spanish, British, French or German schools in Palma, or to the nearby town of Soller. Spain had and has a state-funded school system along with private schools and a range of international/foreign schools. Around 30 per cent of Spain's schoolchildren attend private schools, the majority of which are co-educational.

The line between public, private and church schools can be blurred, with many nominally private or church schools receiving their principal support from the state. Schooling in all but the foreign schools was only in the Spanish language until 1975 when regional languages were introduced once again. No longer forced to speak Spanish, Catalan became the official Balearic language in 1981.

International and foreign schools use English as the main teaching language and some of the British families sent their children to Deia school from nursery to eight or twelve years of age when they changed to the British schools in Palma. Our daughters left the village to study with us in Oxford when 16, 14, 12 and 7. The eldest three found British 'culture', schooling and peer pressure to be quite different from their Spanish experiences. They commented on their difficulties adapting to the climate, school routines, meal times, social interaction and, once again, peer pressure. Fluent in English, they had no language barrier but when asked where they were from and they replied 'Mallorca' (instead of the anticipated America based on their accents), the replies were typically, 'Majorca, that's where you go on holiday, you don't live there!' Despite language similarities, in Britain they were strangers in a strange land. The search for an acceptable social self in Britain meant abandoning parts of their village-formed identities and accepting the unfamiliar American identity imposed by their peers.[13]

From their village life where everyone knew their parents, their history, greeted them on the street, welcomed them into their homes, they felt they had entered a new, strange and formal atmosphere. However, they made friends with other 'visiting students' (mainly Spanish speakers) and were eager to return to the village whenever possible. The youngest adapted more easily to the British system, learning new behaviours, vocabulary and pronunciation in a different way than her older sisters. Her 'best friends' in Oxford were Irish and Spanish and English became her dominant language. Despite spending school and summer holidays in Deia, her Catalan was rusty by the time she returned. Attending art college in Mallorca and social encounters revived her use of Spanish and Catalan.

Some foreign children wanted to study in their parents' home countries,[14] somehow feeling that they lost out on their heritage and only by returning would they fully understand themselves and their parents. 'Returning' to a place they do not remember (or may have never known) often increases the sense of marginality they experienced growing up in Deia. Many young foreigners who were born or brought up in Deia were sent abroad to study and longed to return to Deia during their holidays, but after a month 'back-home' new faces are a welcome change to the all-too-familiar ones they have known all their lives. The more time they spend away from Deia, the more they need new and different people when they return.

Do Children Have Choice?

Expatriates, like myself and many other parents in Deia, take their children abroad or give birth to them in distant places where they may not recognize the differences the children may encounter. Military personnel or diplomatic families relocate every two years; artists or writers with their children seek out 'idyllic places' to explore their creative potential. Some adults see separation of children and parents as a problem for the children; however, British families have been sending their children off to boarding school 'for their benefit' for centuries.[15] In many developing countries, when parents immigrate for work opportunities, grandparents and other family members raise their children; military and diplomatic children may be sent to international schools on location; and Kibbutz children live in peer groups visiting their parents only a few hours each day. Children are adopted across national borders and continents, sent to war, to work in mines or brothels (Howell 2006: 7). The perceptions and meanings of childhood are extremely diverse and affect the way we discuss these issues. The experiences of these children and their parents' practices are different but in all these situations the child has no choice, they follow the routes chosen by their parents. Although they are not active agents in the initial journeys, in time their decisions may alter the future plans of their parents (see chapter by O'Reilly in this volume). We have seen how, even within a single family, marked differences in how children react to these changes differs depending on context, age, gender and social attitudes.

Local or Multicultural?

Between 1950 and 1980 most of the young people in Deia left the village to find work in the burgeoning tourist industry developing in the island's coastal areas. That meant more houses were available for buyers who were usually foreigners as the prices had risen enormously over the decade. By the 1980s, with increased prosperity, young men were unwilling to follow their fathers into construction work, stonemasonry, carpentry or agricultural labour, and young women refused to clean houses as their mothers had. Instead, my children and most of the Mallorquins of their generation were able to find work in the new infrastructures catering to tourism within the village: real estate, hotels, restaurants, boutiques, etc.

The 1980s saw many more foreigners and tourists coming to the village with businesses all catering to the mainly British and German guests. Resident foreign young women who spoke fluent English and European Community members were much in demand. New friendships were formed among both local and foreign employees of the hotel with whom they found much in common. Education, age and new forms of friendships allowed them to be more at ease with their old friends and neighbours and contemporaries shared memories and lived together in the village space. The regular salaries, structured work week and more free time, living near parents and life-long friends of many nationalities offered a new direction and created a much more cosmopolitan life for this generation. This was the beginning of mixed marriages between Mallorquins and German or American or British men and women who met working together in hotels or restaurants or in local cafes and discos.

By the mid-1990s the rapid changes and affluence was such that young men and women had experienced what it was like to be an employee and serve others and were ready to assert their independence as entrepreneurs in the previously rejected trades or businesses of their parents with newfound confidence. They had travelled to exotic destinations, seen how others lived and were ready to move on in Deia. One became a real estate broker, another took over his father's construction company, another who had become one of the island's bike champions combined this with working in his father's carpentry business which would become his on his father's retirement. A woman started an events management business and has recently hired three more women to help her with the enormous number of weddings, christenings and communions that are taking place in the village. These are expensive, sophisticated luxury events (for mostly non-residents) which equal those anywhere in the world.

This mountain village, once the home of an agricultural population spread about in small houses or living and working on large self-contained estates, welcomed the occasional foreigner as a distraction from everyday events when 'local' clearly meant that one had a birthright, a family, a home which gave one a sense of identity and belonging to previous generations, traditions and place. Today the meaning of 'local' is more complex. There are almost 900 registered residents and 40 per cent of the village is owned and inhabited by foreigners, some of whom have resided there for 50 years, whose children have been born and brought up there and whose loved ones are buried there.

Reconnecting with the Past

Today, foreigners and locals share many aspects of local life and are often competitors for the same resources: land, houses, consumer goods, jobs and services. Hotel, bar and restaurant employment offers young people good incomes, extended holiday time, structured working lives unlike their parents' working lives. These new multicultural 'local' families are bi- and tri-lingual, socially diverse, well-off and no longer inhibited by their parents' peasant or expat bohemian pasts. In fact, it was these pasts on which they built the ethos of their village and maintained their identities in what has become one of the most popular island destinations in Europe.

As tourism became more important to the Balearic economy, Deia's once peasant population realized that the pastoral existence they so wanted to leave behind, the terraced landscape, the climate, and stone houses as well as resident foreign artists, were now part of the 'local myth' which had grown through tourism's perceptions and experiences of identifying with and appreciating the village's ethos of 'peasant' life, 'natural' beauty, 'exotic' residents and 'perfect' climate. It is clear that the environment has become not the location of production but the object of consumption, offering a spatial narrative complete with legitimizing myths of famous residents and local conflicts (Hewison 1987).

The cultural production of tourism in Mallorca is evidenced everywhere. In Deia, expatriates have established lifestyles which transcend locality (and temporalities) with their transnational identities and cultural diversities.

Expatriate identity has become located in this experience of 'communitas' with others, not just those in the immediate environment, but anyone around the world who has shared experiences at one time or another in Deia. Foreigners and 'locals' maintain the landscapes, traditions and heritage in the hope of attracting the leisured to experience the location and idyllic setting. The places and spaces become transformed as do the people experiencing them (Waldren 2007: 85).

Return or Rude Awakening?

The transformation from child to youth today is being influenced by the speed of technological change: television, e-mail, internet, cheaper telephone rates, Skype, mobile phones and Facebook familiarize them with activities, spaces, and local and foreign friends around the globe. To the young the café remains the centre of village life and the place where new arrivals and regulars meet up. The children of long-term foreigners become friends and informants for newcomers and the interpreters of their own and their parents' society, past and present. Those over 30 feel they had more difficulty with their peers than the young foreign children that are in school today and think maybe everyone speaking Catalan makes the contact easier. As adults they have discussed their frustrations and experiences and succeeded in re-forming and maintaining friendships with the locals who shared those experiences.

Not all are content with their lives: some young foreign men who grew up in Deia express a sense of loss, a lack of direction. Nothing seems to live up to their youthful experiences freely growing up in the party atmosphere of Deia. They try different jobs, leave Deia for short periods only to return sooner than planned. Often talented (artists, graphic designers, ship engineers, film makers, etc.), well educated and travelled, they seem unable to stick to anything except one another and the fun loving, drug and drink sharing life they have with their contemporaries in Deia. They are forever seeking excitement with little fear of the consequences and even the loss of life or limbs does not deter them from their pleasure seeking.[16] Their parents may not have been the best models and they seem to be following in their footsteps. As children they had no choice in moving to Deia and over time it became their 'home', a safe haven to return to from near and far. Among what some refer to as the 'lost generation', some local and foreign teens to 30-year-olds (and even older) are able to hold off any serious consideration of their futures as café life and activities among their peers offer distraction and shared time, much to the dismay of their parents.

Most local and foreign men over the age of 18 are moving out of their parental homes into shared accommodation or converting small animal huts into rustic liveable homes. The bohemian lifestyles of the expats of the 1950s and 1960s is now much more evident among young Mallorquins who grew up in the new prosperity after the 1980s, and whose lifestyles are condoned by their families as stages along life's winding road. The rapid changes and wealth have had other ramifications: divorce among Mallorquins is occurring more often than ever imagined, people are retiring at 55, grandparents are travelling and not so available for childcare, the cost of living, mortgages, new cars and nursery fees are high, requiring most women and men to work full-time. A few school graduates are going on to college to become teachers and social workers, while others prefer to return to a less professional status job in order to live in the village.

While becoming part of a 'global world', the various groups in Deia have worked together (sometimes unknowingly) to maintain an image of a traditional village, where families carry on communal activities within the ancient walls but in reality family, home, neighbours, village and the landscape all have different meanings today for people who live there. New arrivals enter the village, children attend the school and experience some of the transitions noted for previous generations.

Two Afro-American boys and their parents arrived in June 2007. The boys (five and nine years old, respectively) and their father spoke only English and had not had any experience outside of the United States. Their mother grew up in Deia and spoke Mallorquin but she was often at work when the children were out of school and their dad was at home. One year later, at school[17] in and out of Mallorquin and foreign homes, playing with Mallorquin and English neighbours, the children were acclimatized to the environment, landscape (running up and down hills), language, culture, foods and children's life in Deia. One commented on how 'it was so weird that here I recognize people on the street, we all say hi. I love walking to school with my friends. In America we had to be driven everywhere' (see also Goodman, this volume). Their father became known as 'the brown boys' father'[18] and depended on them for translation in the shops, on the phone and among local parents.

On the first inter-school soccer day they attended, Deia was playing against the neighbouring town of Valldemossa. The local 6–10-year-olds lost by one goal. The coach approached the new boys accompanied by their father and asked if they would like to join the team in Valldemossa for the coming season. He said he saw a potential and commented on their rapid creative footwork. All of this communication was carried on in part Catalan but much more in signs and gestures. Later in the week, the coach phoned and explained to the nine-year-old what he and his brother would need to bring for their training sessions and this was duly translated to his father. Although their father could not understand a word of Catalan, his love of sport and experience with American football, although different, allowed him to give the boys some valuable pointers, show them football matches on the computer and share his cultural knowledge with them. Parents are drawn into the sports activities as they provide transportation to and from games, form car pools with other parents and support their teams at weekend games with other towns. As Dyck notes, 'studying sport can furnish us with important insights into the dynamics of a wide range of fundamental social processes, including for example the dilemmas of contemporary parenting and child and youth peer relations' (2007: 124). So many issues discussed in this chapter emerge in this short example: family dynamics, children as interpreters for their parents, physical and social characteristics as identity markers, sports as a mode of social inclusion and multicultural co-existence, language as a catalyst for adaptation and identity, and school progress.

Conclusions

Childhood continues to be an elusive time span during which identities are formed and re-formed. Cultural values regarding the meaning of children, parenting, families and belonging vary greatly across cultures and even within cultures. I have shown how the foreign children who were born or brought up in Deia had no choice in following the routes chosen by their parents. However, in time, their decisions and choices altered their parents' future plans.

Childhood held different meanings during the political changes occurring in Spain from the 1950s to the present, and the experiences of local and foreign children were distinct during these periods. Social, economic and political changes impacted on perceptions of childhood, gender roles and ideals, parenting, local identity and conceptions of 'the village' (Waldren 1996).[19] The achievement of modern identities engenders a set of habits and reflexes which draw from a variety of lived experiences that have fused together in different ways for foreign children and their parents. Their identity is formed through a number of different associations: through their home language and customs, through the house they live in, its history and myths, through school friends and social and physical characteristics the village imposes on them (Waldren 1996). The variety of parenting practices, identity choices and childhood experiences were surprisingly varied considering the limited population.

The children, through lived experience and everyday interaction with local life, have managed to cross the real and imagined boundaries between foreigners and locals that once seemed impenetrable. They absorb culture with their language acquisition: learning to express themselves idiomatically, knowing what to say when, where and to whom. As J. Butler noted: 'Identities are a performative narrative. You become what you have learned to be' (1990: 163). In the case of the multicultural children in Deia, the myriad of complex forms of interaction practised reveals an automatic flow in and out of various language performances in a continuous dialogue identifying with the different culture and personalities in each context.

The children have opened the way for their parents to become aware of cultural differences in language, behaviour, food, hygiene, education, seasonality, human/ animal relations and many other areas of their shared lives. Learning to adapt by participating on other's terms is a struggle sometimes resented by parents who came to Deia seeking less structured lifestyles and now admit 'We changed for the sake of the children'.

Today, foreign residents and tourists, once curiosities, have become part of everyday existence. The changing nature of identity among locals and foreigners in Deia as they moved through life's stages from child to youth to adult has been influenced by prosperity, travel, tourism and modern communications.

Connotations of identity, the village, home and community fluctuate. This process of identity formation over time becomes more complex in these ambiguous multicultural experiences.

This picturesque village in the mountains of Mallorca, which has been depicted by artists and writers and was home to an agricultural populace now oriented to the service industry, seems to be inhabited today by groups of people with diverse goals and appreciation for the 'new forms' of life opened to them all. The adults may speak different languages, the local and foreign children still taunt each other while settling into the school, but language acquisition and daily interaction offer children the opportunity to gain social skills and education needed for their sense of 'fitting in' and youth growing up together have more in common than ever before. Integration or assimilation are not one-sided, each child unknowingly brings new elements into the complex negotiations of identity.

While becoming part of a global world, the various groups in Deia have somehow worked together to create a myth of the rural peasant and bohemian artist that melds the multicultural inhabitants into an 'imagined community'. The childhood experiences of those who are now adults and new generations that followed them have made this transition possible. One hopes that the children's contradictions and confrontations of difference and similarity will continue to be the agents of change in the future.

Notes

1. The different spellings of the island's name carry diverse connotations and I use the Spanish spelling Mallorca except in direct quotes where the English Majorca, which is so often associated with mass tourism, is used.
2. Brettell writes about her mother.
3. In the 1978 Constitution, it stated that 'Castillian is the official Spanish language'. The use of 'Castillian' and not 'Spanish' makes an important statement acknowledging the existence of various Spanish languages. This was to make sure that the future role of regional languages will always hold second place to Castillian.
4. A fundamental problem of discussing family is that one is dealing with many forms, not just between foreigners and locals but within those categories as well (Waldren 1996: 58).
5. Jo Boyden (2006: 6) notes that young people's involvement in political violence or crime invokes emotions in adults that run deep, in some cases parents even expressing doubts about their own children. These fears are not focused on the loss of childhood innocence but on loss of family socialization. I think both apply in my example.
6. Majorcan is the English spelling and Mallorquin is the Castillian spelling.
7. Mallorquin is a dialectal variant of Catalan spoken throughout the island, and many people refuse to acknowledge its Catalan roots. However, Catalan is the official taught and written language.
8. Although a religious calling had once been encouraged for young men and women, and even seen to be prestigious for the family, a nun's life since the 1980s was seen to deprive a young woman of her independence and future prospects.
9. A wide body of literature emphasizes memory structured through relationships to food providing access to history and memories not found in other types of accounts.
10. Three of the girls married Mallorquin men.

11. Nursery included babies to four-year-olds, allowing women to help in the agricultural cycles.
12. This has changed radically since an entire generation now uses Facebook to instantly share news of the village and friends around the world.
13. See chapter by O'Reilly in this volume.
14. Jaffee notes that Corsicans schooled in France felt 'the achievement of an acceptable social self on the continent required, at some level, an abandonment of the self valued on the island' (1997: 161).
15. The role of boarding schools in separating children from parents – e.g. 'even little boys were sent to English boarding school at the early age of five, before he was even able to tie his shoelaces' (Bryceson and Vuorela 2002: 66) – also uprooted children from the traditions of their parents.
16. One of their crowd died of an overdose while working and playing in London in 2008. All his friends from Deia attended the funeral vowing to alter their wild ways. However, even after they brought some of his ashes back to Deia, they celebrated with heavy drinking that 'helped them forget the tragedy', and little changed.
17. Keeping new students up with their age group in a new second language is quite challenging for a teacher and requires excessive parental supported homework that foreign parents again feel unable to complete.
18. Referred to as the 'brown boys' for their Afro-American heritage and colour.
19. Of course age, changing economic situations, social and political perspectives and conditions as well as success or not in their chosen careers in the arts they came to pursue in Deia, also impacted on their lives.

Bibliography

Boyden, J. 2006. 'Children, War and World Disorder in the 21st Century: A Review of the Theories and the Literature on Children's Contributions to Armed Violence'. QEHWPS138, Oxford: Oxford Department of International Development.

Breger, R. and R. Hill (eds) 1998. *Cross-Cultural Marriage: Identity and Choice*. Oxford: Berg.

Brettell, C. and D. Kertzer (eds) 1993. 'Advances in Italian and Iberian Family History', *Journal of Family History*, 12 (1): 87–120.

Broch-Due, V. and I. Rudie (eds) 1994. 'An Introduction'. In *Carved Flesh and Cast Selves*. Oxford: Berg.

Bryceson, D. and U. Vuorela (eds) 2002. *The Transnational Family and Migration: Past and Present*. Oxford: Berg.

Butler, J. 1990. *Gender Trouble: Feminism and the Subversion of Identity*. London: Routledge.

Callaway, H. and J. Okely (eds) 1992. *Anthropology and Autobiography*. London: Routledge.

Douglas, M. 1970. *Natural Symbols*. New York: Pantheon.

Dyck, N. 2007. 'Playing like Canadians: Improvising Nation and Identity Through Sport'. In S. Coleman and T. Kohn (eds), *The Discipline of Leisure: Embodying Cultures of 'Recreation'*. Oxford: Berghahn Books.

Epstein, A.L. 1978. *Ethos and Identity: Three Studies in Ethnicity*. London: Tavistock.

Graves, L. 2001. *A Woman Unknown*. London: Counterpoint.

Hewison, D. 1987. *The Heritage Industry: Britain in a Climate of Decline*. London: Methuen.

Howell, S. 2006. *The Kinning of Foreigners: Transnational Adoption in a Global Perspective*. Oxford: Berghahn Books.

Jaffee, D. 1997. 'Asynchronus Learning: Technology and Pedagogical Strategy in a Distance Learning Course', *Teaching Sociology*, 25: 262–77.

Labanyi, J. and H. Graham (eds) 1995. *Spanish Cultural Studies*. Oxford: Oxford University Press.

Michalopoulou-Veikou, C. 1999. 'The Evil Eye: The Dynamics of Seeing in a Community of Macedonia'. PhD thesis, Athens: Pantheon University.

Montgomery, H., R. Burr and M. Woodhead (eds). 2004. *Changing Childhoods: Local and Global*. Chichester: John Wiley & Sons.

Neville, G.K. 1984. 'Learning Culture through Ritual', *Anthropological and Educational Quarterly*, 15 (2): 151–66.

Timera, M. 2002. 'Righteous or Rebellious? Social Trajectory of Sahelian Youth in France'. In D. Bryceson and U. Vuorela (eds), *The Transnational Family and Migration: Past and Present*. Oxford: Berg.

Waldren, J. 1996. *Insiders and Outsiders: Paradise and Reality in Mallorca*. Oxford: Berghahn Books.

——— 1997. 'We Are Not Tourists, We Live Here'. In S. Abram, J. Waldren and D. MacLeod (eds), *Tourists and Tourism: Identifying with People and Places*. Oxford: Berg.

——— 2007. 'Reframing Place, Time and Experience: Leisure and Illusion in Mallorca'. In S. Coleman and T. Kohn (eds), *The Discipline of Leisure: Embodying Cultures of 'Recreation'*. Oxford: Berghahn Books.

Chapter 9
IDENTITY WITHOUT BIRTHRIGHT:
NEGOTIATING CHILDREN'S CITIZENSHIP AND IDENTITY IN CROSS-CULTURAL BUREAUCRACY

Ignacy-Marek Kaminski

Introduction

Anthropologists define parenting as the behaviour of adults nurturing their children – ideally a two-way relationship of positive feedback between the parent and child that can be achieved in a panoply of different culturally specific ways. This perspective is international but not transnational.[1] It overlooks the possibility of children's statelessness, a grey zone of cross-cultural bureaucracy that can impact profoundly on children's identities.

It is generally taken for granted that a child at birth will be accepted as a member of the nation within which s/he is born (*jus soli* – right of the soil) and/or of the nation of the child's parents (*jus sanguinis* – right of blood).[2] This chapter reflects on the plight of parents with children who are not availed of either of these forms of citizenship. This dilemma surfaces *before* the child is born. With rapidly accelerating globalization, cross-cultural marriages are becoming commonplace. The legal and cultural dilemmas that transnational children and their parents have to deal with at the early and later stages of family life are essential to the child's identity and are often too complex to afford anticipation of the future consequences for the child and civil society at large. These issues are explored by relating my family's personal experiences, beginning with my marriage in Sweden (1977) and move to Japan (1980). My wife and I had particularly varied cultural backgrounds, so the transnationalism of our children was especially intricate, but their quagmires and ultimately opportunities in principle and practice reflect those of many other transnational children in our global age (Bauman 1998).

Autoethnography:
Research by Unifying the Personal and the Professional

I am writing this retrospectively with the hindsight of over 30 years. My children are independent adults with international professional careers now. For the last four decades, I have been involved in field research with minority and aboriginal groups divided across national and cultural boundaries: Gypsy-Roma, Inuit, Ainu, Okinawans (Kaminski 1979, 1985, 1988, 2004, 2009a). What these culturally and geographically distant people had in common were their experiences of statelessness, frequently changing citizenship of their offspring, and their struggles to accommodate their family life to accelerating geo-political transitions taking place around them. I witnessed legal and sometimes physical abuse that adults and children encountered in their daily interaction with state and bureaucracies (Horne and Kaminski 1981, Kaminski and Westin 1985: 9–11, 35–46, 105–37, 145–7). It is not coincidental that I chose this area of field studies. I myself was originally a refugee. I left Poland in 1972 to pursue my doctoral research in Sweden and was not to return for 18 years. In Poland, I had been in opposition to the system and detained, but I had left Poland with the intention of returning after my PhD. This was thwarted by the conditionality imposed on me by the Polish state when I asked for an extension of my Polish passport to finish my doctoral dissertation. My refusal to become a collaborator with the communist state left me without a valid Polish passport and effectively stateless.[3] I therefore had no option but to apply for Swedish citizenship which was granted on the basis of my ongoing work as an anthropologist in Sweden.

The complexity of my Polish-Swedish nationality background was to become far more intricate when I met and married a Japanese national. My wife, however, was a Japanese national of mixed origin, Japanese-Korean.[4] My own traumatic experiences as a refugee and later as an anthropologist gave me direct experience of the vulnerability of statelessness and later as expectant parents we experienced the complexities involved in the legal acknowledgement of a child born into such a multicultural union.

It was both life and these field research experiences that affected my research methodology (Bruner 1986, 1993, Ellis and Bochner 1996, Ellis and Berger 2002) and focused my interest on the child–parent relationship vis-à-vis the state's role in the child's identity formation (Lange and Westin 1981, 1984, Kaminski and Gripman 1985, Goodman 2000).

Familial and National Identity and Symbolism: Akane-Liv's Birth

Like so many young parents awaiting the birth of our first child, we chose names well before the birth: 'Akane Liv' for a daughter, and 'Ken' for a son. As expectant parents, the symbols behind the chosen names were anticipated to be key to the child's acceptance in the countries of his or her birth and ancestry. The names had to encompass the various facets of family and nationality in the child's transnational context. What kind of identity might a Eurasian offspring with a Japanese mother and a Polish father born in Sweden develop in the future? It was going to depend on many socio-cultural and legal factors that we could neither foresee, nor had full control over at that time. What we did influence, however, was the child's early identity formation by incorporating symbolic meanings into its given names. As our first-born daughter was going to inherit my Slavic family surname at birth, I wanted her first given name to reflect her mother's home country of Japan, though the ancient Japanese name 'Akane' written in Latin alphabet would mean nothing to her European relatives, 'Akane' written in the Chinese pictograph (茜) meant 'The red colour of a morning sky'. Akane's second name 'Liv', an old Scandinavian name (meaning 'Life'), was chosen to honour the country she was going to be born in at the end of summer 1978. Though Akane's mother was a Japanese citizen at birth, and I was a refugee from communist Poland who had been granted provisional Swedish citizenship after completing a required five years of residency, we were informed in early 1978 that our child was going to be born stateless.

How Was This Possible?

To understand how the then citizenship legislations of Sweden, Poland and Japan respectively inadvertently created a stateless trap for our unborn child, I need to briefly explore the legal background of the three nation-states.

Sweden

According to Swedish Immigration and Naturalization Board (SIV) guidelines (Statens Invandrarverk 1976), a foreigner granted Swedish citizenship must fulfil a condition of being released from his previous citizenship before his/her new citizenship is confirmed.

After the communist Polish government refused to extend validity of my Polish passport during my research work in Sweden, I was issued a Swedish stateless passport. This meant that though *de facto* I was not a bearer of a Polish passport, I was still categorized *de jure* by the SIV as a 'stateless Polish citizen'. I was subsequently required by the SIV to request a document officially confirming I was not a Polish citizen from a Polish Consulate in Sweden. I was also reassured by a SIV officer that it was just a legal technicality and even if I were denied such a document, I would still receive Swedish citizenship after an additional two years.

When I informed the SIV officer that my wife was already in early pregnancy and I needed to secure my legal status before the birth of our offspring, I was told to explain these circumstances to the Polish General Consulate. According to the SIV's expert who was a lawyer by training, the consular officials of the countries accredited in Sweden were expected to provide the necessary documents long before the expected birth.

As will be explained in the following sections, the official bureaucrat described a straightforward solution unconcerned with the social and cultural implications of his interpretation (Chan-Tiberghien 2004, Westin 1998). He neither took into account my and the other refugees' previous experience with communist bureaucracies, nor did he consider it important to explore these socio-political and cultural issues further.

Polish Consular Agendas: Abortion or Collaboration

I had been denied extension of my Polish passport which resulted in a subsequent exile that lasted 18 years, because of my consistent refusal to collaborate with the communist regime (and not sharing my field interviews with the consular officers). Then, in early 1978, I had no choice but to follow the advice of the SIV legal expert and deal again with the same Polish consular services who had tried

Figure 9.1. Akane-Liv Okamoto-Kaminski wearing her Polish National Dress in the family Tokyo home, 1982.

to blackmail me several years earlier (Kaminski 1980: 6–11). They told me that they would offer me 'a deal' due to my new family circumstances: my request would be dealt with as a priority as long as I would be willing to now undergo questioning (about my contacts among the Polish émigrés in Sweden) that I had declined earlier. When I refused to collaborate, I was advised that a non-priority handling of consular documents may take a year or more. My argument that our child was expected within a half year was met with the consular officer's comment that 'abortion is still legal in Poland'.[5]

Japanese Embassy: No Passport

After the two failed attempts (SIV, Polish Consulate) to find a legal solution, we contacted the Japanese Embassy. We were told that the Embassy could not issue a Japanese passport for the child, as according to Japanese legislation, a Japanese woman married to a foreign national could not pass over her citizenship to her offspring. My Japanese wife was advised that the child born of a Japanese mother would have to inherit her foreign husband's nationality. The Japanese consular official established that the child was fathered by the bearer of a Swedish stateless passport. Then he concluded that the expectant Japanese mother would, after the birth of her child, have to apply for a Japanese visitor visa for her stateless child. Then, based on this initial entrance status, the child will be registered by the Japanese local authorities into the family register (*koseki*) as a stateless offspring (Debito 2004, 2008, Wetherall 2008).

As an anthropologist and prospective father of a Eurasian child, I had to consider several issues at the personal, socio-cultural and legal levels at the same time. What were the legal and social standing of the stateless people and other minorities in 1978 Japan? And what were the potential social and cultural implications for my Japanese in-laws having a stateless child incorporated into their *koseki* (family register)?[6] And finally, I had to recognize that these broader social issues added to my Japanese in-laws' initial consternation when their daughter married a bearer of a stateless passport.

On reflection, I still wonder to what extent the stigma attached to members of ethnic and social minorities results from historically determined prejudices caused by the Japanese imperial expansion or are ongoing cultural processes (determined by the concepts of purity/pollution) most influential in the stigma attached to social and ethnic minorities in Japan (e.g. Burakumin, Ainu, Okinawans) and offspring of cross-cultural marriages?

A Political and Legal Grey Zone: Stateless Offspring of 'Transitive Citizens'

Japan, in contrast to a multiculturally oriented Sweden, is generally regarded by scholars as a distinctly homogeneous society (Horne and Kaminski 1981). While the image of cultural homogeneity and social equality is being promoted by Japanese politicians and mainstream think-tanks (Kaminski 1994), the country's ethnic and social minorities were demanding changes to discriminatory laws and respect for their basic human rights (Goodman 2008, Wetherall 2008, Willis and Murphy-Shigematsu 2008).

In 1978 Japan, the third generation Japan-born former colonial citizens of Korean and Chinese ancestry who remained in Japan after World War II were still denied equal employment and residence rights. Although their parents were born in Japan and they paid the same taxes as Japanese citizens, they could neither vote in municipal elections nor be employed by the municipal authorities, as office clerks, firemen or teachers. The offspring of Korean and Chinese labourers were divided along ethnic and political lines. It was not uncommon to find four different passports in a three-generational Korean family permanently residing in Japan: the oldest generation had either stateless ID or North Korean passports. Some of their children changed their North Korean passports to South Korean ones in the late 1960s, while their grandchildren, wanting to escape ethnic stigmatization or marry Japanese nationals, often opted for the lengthy naturalization process that included Japanization of their names. All these legal changes had to be incorporated to the family register (*koseki*) that was stored in the municipal offices. This meant that even in the fourth generation a family's past could be traced by the families of potential marriage partners, employers or any other parties interested in checking the 'blood purity' of its members (Kaminski 1979).

Koseki was a useful administrative tool for the local Japanese authorities to record the population flow and household changes under their jurisdiction as much as it could be abused if used to stigmatize those considered to be impure. Not only the descendants of the former colonial subjects (Koreans, Chinese) but also the ethnic Japanese known as Burakumin frequently had their *koseki* screened by private investigators. Burakumin, who were historically viewed as polluted due to occupations related to blood (leather and animal food processing, butchering, or graveyard work), still remain the largest socially segregated group in contemporary Japan (Willis and Murphy-Shigematsu 2008). Although discrimination against Burakumin was abolished as long ago as 1868,[7] their ancestors are still being traced through the *koseki*. In Japan of the late 1970s, there were frequent reports of family suicides caused by their social or ethnic 'birth-stigma' being revealed through the abuse of *koseki* records.

All of the above impacted on my auto-ethnography and follow-up to the case of our Eurasian child that was going to be born stateless in a few months.

Anthropologist as Agent of Change

My attempts with both the Polish Consulate and Japanese Embassy failed. Though they failed for different reasons, the outcome was the same: Akane-Liv was going to be stigmatized at birth. I once again contacted the Swedish Immigration and

Naturalization Board (SIV) and explained the legal and social background of the case, but the officer's response was that he had to follow the law. And the SIV regulations clearly stated that I either had to convince the Polish Consulate to provide the necessary document and get my Swedish citizenship at once, or I would have to wait the mandatory two years for my Swedish passport. I was also instructed that the child can be naturalized as a Swedish citizen within five years. My follow-up attempts to explain the stigma attached to statelessness in the child's mother's country were rebuffed by the SIV officer's superior who claimed that he was not in a position to change the Swedish rules because of circumstances involving the Japanese Embassy and the Polish Consulate. While the official acknowledged that the legal issues may concern cross-cultural parentage among other ethnic groups in Sweden as well, he also said that the reinterpretation of the nationality regulations could only be done by the Swedish government.

Thus the only option remaining to me was to use my anthropological expertise to have the case of an unborn child proven at a Cabinet meeting of the Swedish government and I had only a few months left to do it.

There were several time-consuming problems I had to deal with simultaneously. Firstly, I had to gather impartial expertise by international academics specializing in Asian and minority studies. That was the easiest part. There was an extensive body of legal, psychological and anthropological research published by internationally noted scholars, including Swedish and Japanese academics (Corlin 1975, Trankell 1972, Westin 1977, Maruyama 1978).

Secondly, I could not be an expert witness in my own case (Kaminski 1978). I had to find a Swedish Asian expert willing to go through the extensive data I had gathered and write a brief for the SIV. The senior Asian expert on social and ethnic minorities (my PhD supervisor at the time) at the Department of Social Anthropology of the University of Gothenburg was willing to analyse the field data I had gathered on the socio-cultural implications of pollution. He not only provided the SIV with an extensive analysis, but also followed the case up through all the levels of decision-making until it reached the Cabinet Office.[8]

The result was that a few weeks before 'The red colour of a morning sky' (Akane) was born, the Swedish minister responsible for immigration and naturalization affairs signed a document making me a Swedish national and exempting me from waiting the additional two years, thus allowing our Eurasian child to be born as a Swedish citizen.

Our family case set a legal precedent to be used in determining similar cases involving offspring of cross-cultural marriages. Furthermore, the fact that the case involved the scholarly documented insights of an anthropologist-and-a-father had generated a debate among both academics and policy-makers regarding the necessity of introducing dual citizenship.[9] So subsequently this field anthropologist had indirectly become an active agent of social changes that two decades later resulted in the Swedish legislation granting dual citizenship to children born of immigrant parents.[10]

Case Study 1: Fieldwork, Parenting and Officialdom

I was in the middle of my field research on Japanese minorities in Tokyo neighbourhoods when my son Ken was born in Tokyo (1982). I subsequently combined my parental and research roles by caring for our four-year-old daughter Akane and our newly born son while my wife attended college. Part of my comparative field research focused on methodology and my double role as a parent/researcher was already published (Horne and Kaminski 1981), when my son (who was a few months old) and I were detained by an immigration officer at our family home in Tokyo. The officer who arrived by train from Osaka 500 km away identified us as 'illegal aliens' under arrest, then he ordered a van with reinforcements from the Tokyo Shinagawa Regional Immigration Bureau. The arrest van with three additional officers arrived at the time when I was scheduled to pick up my daughter from kindergarten. One of the neighbourhood women had in the meantime contacted my wife. When my wife arrived she refused to hand our son – the 'illegal alien' – voluntarily to the immigration officers without an official arrest warrant. So I was the only one put under arrest.

During the interrogation in the Shinagawa Immigration Bureau, though I had provided a valid Swedish passport, a letter from the Japanese Embassy in Stockholm confirming my field research status as a grantee of the Japanese Governmental Mombusho Fellowship associated with Tokyo Metropolitan University, I was nevertheless addressed as an 'illegal Polish alien'. My requests to contact the Swedish Consul and access an attorney were refused. Instead, I was pressured to admit that I and my son had resided in Japan without a valid residence permit. Furthermore, I was informed that I would remain in detention until my deportation from Japan. The fact that I was married to a Japanese citizen, was a legal guardian of our two children, and financially providing for a family of four through the post-doctoral grant provided by the Japanese Ministry of Education, had no impact whatsoever. According to the immigration records, I had entered Japan for the first time to do field research among the Ainu minority in Hokkaido in 1976 as a stateless Polish citizen on the refugee passport issued by Sweden. Despite the fact that my nationality and marital status had altered since the time of my Ainu research, my initial identification as a 'stateless Pole' continued to serve as a reference for my interrogators. What I was able to reconstruct several days later was that my arrest was caused by a bureaucratic registration error in my local Tokyo ward office and by the neighbourhood community police (*koban*). This in turn generated a chain effect that mobilized different levels of the immigration system and caused, what was later confirmed, unwarranted use of force by the Japanese law enforcement (Parker 2001, Chan-Tiberghien 2004, Debito 2004, 2008).

Case Study 2: A Detainee Becomes a Researcher

A few days after my release from the Tokyo-Shinagawa Regional Immigration Bureau, I 'activated' the Japanese contacts I was entrusted with by my PhD thesis external adviser, Arne Trankell, Professor of Psychology at Stockholm University. Trankell, an internationally published authority on Witness Psychology and court expertise in Japan (1972), introduced me to his Japanese academic colleague who was a retired high official of the Japanese Ministry of Justice.

As a follow-up to these recommendations I was invited by the Justice Ministry to conduct extensive interviews with the Counsellor to the Minister, the State Prosecutor and the Head of the Japanese Immigration Authority. I was treated courteously by all the officials and received all statistical references I had requested regarding the immigration procedures, community policing of resident aliens and ethnic minorities. I presented my field case without disclosing that these were my own transnational family's real-life experiences with the Japanese law enforcement at the local level. I was assured no officer could have been sent from a distant prefecture to detain a foreign father with an infant in Tokyo. And certainly could not ask for the arrest van with reinforcement from the Tokyo Immigration Bureau. My request to spend a working day at the Immigration Bureau was also granted. I chose the same Regional Immigration Bureau in Tokyo Shinagawa that had detained me. I presented the field case to the Head of the Bureau, who like his superiors assured me that such a case could not have happened. I followed this up by interviewing the head of a section responsible for detention of illegal aliens. I was assured again that it could not have happened. But it had!

Investigating the Investigators

After my experience, I was able to relate my personal and professional insights to the experiences of my informants (Ellis 1997, 2004). In contrast to Parker, an American legal scholar who followed the traditional Japanese model of vertical introduction from the highest ministerial officials to the lowest police officers (Parker 2001: xx) while conducting an eight month long participant field research with the Japanese neighbourhood police (*koban*) and Neighbourhood Associations (in 1980 and 1999), but who was not able to penetrate the ethnic undercurrents in Japan, I had used a reverse method. I also conducted extensive interviews with the highest levels of the Japanese immigration and law enforcement authorities at the Ministry of Justice but only *after* my detention, when I could ask the government officials the questions the members of the minorities residing in Japan put to me but were prevented from asking the authorities, and thus verify my findings during the progress of my field research (Kaminski 1982, 1983, Westin 1998).

Multi-lingual Parenting and Cross-cultural Schooling

The transnationalization of societies and cultures that was often described in abstract terms as a part of globalization by post-modernists had touched our family life early. Since the births of our children (1978, 1982), both my wife and

I used our native languages to communicate with them (Japanese and Polish, respectively). At the same time, our children were, due to my long-term field research, exposed to schooling and studies in three other languages: Swedish, English and Japanese (Kaminski 1994). Their language experiences had varied as much in length as in their exposure to such different socio-cultural and educational models as Swedish, Japanese, American, Australian and British. While both Akane and Ken were quatri-lingual at various periods of their childhood, the Japanese and English have gradually become more instrumental languages in their adult lives than the Swedish and Polish they used to speak fluently at kindergarten and primary school. The impact of these four languages on the early formation of their transnational identity and the choices of their professional careers across state and cultural boundaries seems clearly positive (Okely 1992).

An Early Multi-lingual Schooling in Sweden

Akane and Ken mastered Swedish language (like the natives) while simultaneously cultivating their ethnic languages through the Multi-lingual Swedish Kindergarten Program (MSKP), and in the case of Akane, by attending the Ethnic School Program (ESP). In 1980s Sweden, children with parent(s) other than Swedish were provided with a free two-hour weekly instruction in their mother tongue in kindergarten and pre-school (Kaminski and Westin 1985). At the age of seven, we enrolled Akane into a Swedish private school in Stockholm that offered the choice of English and French as foreign languages in the first grade. Simultaneously, Akane attended the Weekend Japanese School (WJS) where she socialized with both children of mixed Japanese parentage or Japanese expats.

Transfer to Mono-lingual Japanese Public Education

After completing her first grade in multicultural Sweden, Akane re-entered the Japanese public school, while Ken re-entered Japanese kindergarten. Although both my children had prior experiences of Japanese kindergarten and pre-school education (in mainland Japan and Okinawa), their re-entrance to the mono-cultural educational system had not progressed smoothly. Akane, who could not get used to the uniform Japanese educational system that required the change of her name from Kaminski to Okamoto, had particular difficulties in adjustment to the group pressures. Both children continued to speak Swedish to each other during times of distress for the first several months. When, one day, unable to handle the group pressure and bullying, Akane escaped the classroom wearing her school uniform, she was spotted on her way home by a neighbourhood housewife. The woman, concerned about her welfare, invited her home for tea. Then she promptly telephoned the neighbourhood police (*koban*), who in turn contacted the school. Akane was returned in tears to school. She was both humiliated and confused by the chain of events her attempt to return home had caused in the neighbourhood.

Stephen Murphy-Shigematsu, a Japanese-American psychologist with extensive schooling and professional experience in both the USA and Japan, re-examined his own childhood trauma and naturalization process in his auto-psychological works (e.g. Murphy-Shigematsu 2008). Murphy-Shigematsu's dilemmas were the same my own children had to deal with many years later. Although they were born 10,000 kilometres apart, belonged to different generations, and were classified as 'Amerasian' and 'Eurasian' respectively, the questions Murphy-Shigematsu had posed concerned them and other 'mixed children' equally:

Why hadn't I been given Japanese nationality at birth? Simply due to a discrimination against Japanese women who had not the right at that time to pass a nationality to their children. Or was it discrimination against multi-ethnic people whose fathers were not Japanese? Was it sexual discrimination based on the lingering influence of Confucianism? Or was it racial ideology embedded in the state's ideology of ethnic homogeneity? Did it spring from a pervasive mythology of divine origins and a long history of oneness? (Murphy-Shigematsu 2008: 282)

Furthermore, to understand why Akane was confused by the chain reaction she had caused in the neighbourhood by leaving her classroom group without authorization, we have to outline how the Japanese neighbourhood policing, Parents and Teachers Association (PTA) and Voluntary Neighbourhood Association collaborate together to secure the group cohesion (Parker 2001: 126–71).

While the children were undergoing their gradual adjustment to the Japanese educational system and I continued my field research among the Japanese minority groups, I decided to enrol Ken and Akane to the afternoon Swedish classes run by the Swedish Community and the Swedish Embassy in Tokyo. I expected that this double educational model would provide the continuity of their earlier education and links with multicultural Sweden. It worked for a short time, but gradually both children rebelled. The reasons for their refusal to attend the extramural Swedish education in Tokyo were both practical and emotional. The four hours commuting in the overcrowded trains for two hours of Swedish lessons after a long day in the Japanese school were physically demanding. However, the more important factor I realized was that what I had considered an advantage for them in the future, they experienced as an immediate burden and *de facto* stigmatization. In contrast to Sweden, speaking foreign languages was not considered by the children's Japanese classmates an advantage and often invited an ethnic bullying that was also frequently experienced by Japan-born Korean and Chinese minorities (Wetherall 2008). As a result my children refused to speak Swedish with each other first, then refused to reply to me in Polish in Japanese public spaces.

The only time I was able to reactivate these two languages was at bedtime. We slept in the traditional Japanese way by sharing closely placed family futons on the *tatami* (bamboo mat). Every evening, I continued to tell my children the same Polish-Swedish fables I used to share with them during our life in Sweden. The fables that I invented were about magic animals flying across the world and meeting different kinds of people. The stories followed the same routines: the fables that started in Polish gradually turned into Swedish but the plot remained the same. It always incorporated our ancestors and the family members living in different parts of the world and interacting with the forest and sea creatures.

Many years later, when both these languages were dominated by Japanese and English, both children still remember their childhood stories in detail. What is even more important, the challenging Polish and Swedish sounds that are difficult to master by adults have remained dormant in their memory. When Ken, after graduating from the Japanese University in Tokyo, enrolled in the Summer School of Polish Culture and Language at my previous university in Krakow, he was able to reactivate effortlessly these tongue-twisting Polish sounds (*'czesc, prosze bardzo'*, etc). It was also the language he had begun to use again to communicate with the Polish branch of our multicultural family. Furthermore, after graduating from Oxford University and realizing he could use his unusual combination of languages and dual Swedish-Japanese citizenship to gain employment in a major multinational corporation in London, he continued studying Polish in evening courses at London University.

I frequently used traditional festivities to reactivate these early childhood memories by serving the festive food the children used to love during the Polish and Swedish celebrations of religious and folk rituals, like Christmas, Easter, Midsummer, *Santa Lucia*. When Akane returned to Sweden as an adult, the first words she had recovered were the words related to the food served during these celebrations. Similarly, she remembers the Polish words for festive food and the words of songs. The seemingly insignificant bedtime fables with a clearly designed linguistic and cross-cultural plot structure had imprinted an identity foundation that was solid though dormant and often operated on a subconscious level (Webber 2007: 73).[11]

Learning from Children

The children were the first ones to find inconsistencies in our transnational life patterns and the contradictory demands of their teachers and peers. As will be detailed below, gradually our traditional family roles had evolved, and our increasingly trans-cultural children had become our teachers in cross-cultural parenting, cultural compromises and social readjustments. Through their experiences we, as their parents, were entering the diverse and often highly chaotic world inhabited by a growing group of transnational/trans-cultural nomads. We had no choice but to venture as a family through the borderlands of cultures, bureaucracy and personal emotions.

In retrospect, I can see how much my anthropological training had helped me in overcoming the practical problems of multi-lingual parenting and cross-cultural schooling of my Eurasian children. It doesn't mean that our transnational family life was free of false cultural assumptions or errors in our parental judgements. On the contrary, we had no choice but to learn through our unintentional mistakes rather than adjusting our lives to preconceived social categories like Polish, Japanese or Swedish.

Reviewing our child-parenting experience, I have no doubt that the major impacts on building their multicultural identity were not only the educational institutions they had to attend, but the interaction of the children's experiences and feelings and our readjustment of long-held values from our own pasts and the various cultural groups we lived among. We let our children influence the mode of our cross-cultural parenting at home and in public space. As recently discussed by Murphy-Shigematsu:

> Perhaps more than any other minorities in Japan, multiethnic individuals may challenge notions of cultural nationalism if they choose to act out cultural differences. They cannot be easily dismissed simply as foreigners, for they are also Japanese citizens and of 'Japanese' ancestry. They are both insiders and outsiders. Recognition of their existence may help break down the mental walls erected by the fiction of Japanese uniqueness between 'Japanese' and others. (2008: 301)

Japanese Society and Changing Models of Parenting

One of the reasons social anthropologists have been frequently focusing their field research on the margins of society is, as Goodman pointed out, that these findings could help the researchers to grasp what is happening in its core (2008). Japanese society, with its rapidly emerging hybrid forms of multicultural identities and changing models of parenting may serve as an indicator of both the forthcoming global changes as well as the profound local transformations. According to the Japanese Ministry of Justice, over two million foreign nationals from 188 countries reside in Japan (1.6 per cent of Japan's population) in 2004. This is an almost 50 per cent increase during the last ten years. Some 40 per cent of those non-Japanese living in Japan are now permanent residents. The number of inter-cultural marriages (and divorces) is increasing steadily, and so is the number of children growing up in the non-mainstream 'Japanese' households. These progressing ethno-demographic changes require new social and educational policies, as well as adjustment of the immigration and citizenship laws.

Chan-Tiberghien (2004) and Wetherall (2008) argue that the comparative studies of minorities in Japan may help to predict the future course of socio-political changes in Japan as a whole. Goodman, who has carried out extensive field research among minority groups and children in Japan, suggests that, while studying the societal transformations,

> at the same time we need to understand the changing legal context in which minority status is played out in Japan. Are legal revisions designed to increase or control the flow of immigrant groups? To help them assimilate or to encourage them to move on? … How should Japan cope with immigration and deal with its sense of nationhood? … As I and colleagues (Goodman et al. 2003: 4–5) have argued elsewhere, the answer may lie not in curtailing immigration in the name of homogeneity, but in recognizing that migration, both into and out of Japanese territorial boundaries, has shaped and will continue to shape, the notion of Japanese homogeneity. (Goodman 2008: 331)

One of the early indications of the future changes in the Japanese political culture and state-controlled education was the *Prime Minister's Report on Japan's Goals in the 21st Century*. The report had not only acknowledged the lack of tolerance in the group-oriented and mono-ethnic Japanese educational system, but also advocated a need for a more individualized parenting model that would in turn foster a new generation of 'empowered' individuals:

> The other essential change is to redefine and rebuild the relationship between private and public space in civil society. This means first and foremost promoting individuality and individual initiatives: unleashing sturdy individuals who are free, self-reliant, and responsible, individuals whose ability to empathize with others makes them inclusive.

My research continued to confront these issues in the field. I became increasingly aware that translation of the central government's policies into social interaction among multicultural grassroots communities was obstructed by the local authorities and law enforcement officials.

Chan-Tiberghien, in her *Gender and Human Rights Politics in Japan*, pointed out both socio-cultural and legal obstacles to implement the report's objectives. She listed the Japanese nationality issues and continuing regeneration of Japan-born 'resident aliens' among the major matters that needed to be resolved by the Japanese lawmakers (2004: 111). The majority of those individuals born and raised in Japan were offspring of former Japanese colonial subjects (mostly Koreans and Chinese) who were stripped of their Japanese nationality by the San Francisco Peace Treaty in 1952. Among 951,000 Koreans living in Japan in 2001, more than 90 per cent were second-, third-, fourth- and fifth-generation Koreans and Korean-Japanese. Although they were born and raised in Japan and in many cases did not speak Korean at all, more than 61 per cent did not possess Japanese nationality. As my field research confirmed (Kaminski 1982, 2004), it was not uncommon to find four different legal categories in a three-generational 'Japanese household' (the Japan-born grandparents either possessed the stateless ID or North Korean citizenship, their children had South Korean passports, and some of their grandchildren either possessed Korean passports and Korean names, or had opted to undergo the Japanese naturalization that frequently resulted in Japanization of their Korean names on their Japanese passports). To deal with these complex family and passport issues, in 1991 the Japanese government passed the Special Law on the Immigration Control of Those Who Have Lost Japanese Nationality and Others on the Basis of the Treaty of Peace with Japan. Subsequently the Korean 'aliens' in Japan had become 'special permanent residents' who require re-entry permits and were reminded they could be subjected to deportation under certain conditions. The most common arguments against naturalization among the Japan-born ethnic Koreans I had interviewed in Kanto and Kansai regions (of main Honshu Island) were their wishes to keep their Korean family names as well as to be granted the rights to dual citizenship.[12]

There is well-documented international research proving that, despite the formal revision of the state policy forcing resident Koreans to adopt Japanese family names (Debito 2008, Willis and Murphy-Shigematsu 2008), the ethnic Koreans wishing to become naturalized Japanese citizens have continued to be pressured by the Japanese immigration officials to change their names. Although the pressure is disguised as administrative guidance, it still remains, according to the international human rights experts, an illegal practice (Chan-Tiberghien 2004).

The second obstacle to accelerate the integration of ethnic minorities and offspring with cross-cultural parentage into Japanese society is the legal interpretation of dual citizenship as well as the frequent abuses of power by the Japanese law enforcement officials exemplified in case study 2. Wetherall (anthropologist, permanent resident of Japan and a father of two Japanese-American children) argues that 'not only does the Nationality Law nowhere categorically prohibit dual or multiple nationality, but it actually gives the Minister of Justice the discretionary power to mitigate provisions for loss of nationality' (2008). In the course of my fieldwork among Japanese social and ethnic minorities that have spanned over two decades, I encountered numerous examples of the absence of discretionary power of the Justice Ministry in such cases and flagrant abuses of human rights committed against members of minorities that went unreported.

There are several historical and social reasons why victims are hesitant to identify law enforcement officials as legal abusers. Parker (2001) had confirmed that a reported suspect can be kept for 23 days in police custody. 'The court must approve detention beyond seventy two hours, and then again after thirteen days, but these extensions are almost pro forma. Court approval is granted in 99.9 percent of cases' (2001: 204). He suggests that, although the Neighbourhood Associations ('*tonari-gumi*') that were semi-official arms of police were disbanded after the war, the reformed post-war Neighbourhood Associations ('*chonaikai*') had structurally remained the same instrument of community control (2001: 25–6), that particularly affected the members of minority groups and their families. As my own research had confirmed the Neighbourhood Associations, in addition to collaborating with the local police officers and PTA, were traditionally involved in integrating the community by performing social and civic duties, e.g. organizing and collecting money for the local celebrations of birth, marriage and the local religious and school festivals. Parker concludes in the revised edition of his 1981–82 research report that 'the Japanese allow police to penetrate far more deeply into the community' (2001: 245).

Both Parker and I conducted parts of our separate field research as official grantees (Fulbright and Mombusho Programs, respectively) in the same area (Tokyo and Osaka). Our perception of the reality experienced by our informants was determined by our differing methodological and scholarly approaches: overt and covert participant observation. Subsequently, the knowledge we gained from our interaction in the field differed in many aspects. Nevertheless, it generated complementary dynamics.

Case 3: Coming Full Circle: Akane-Liv and Ken-Stanislaw as Transnational Professionals

My grown children frequently visit their two European Union countries, Poland and Sweden, and feel as comfortable in their mother country of Japan as their father's European Union. They chose to link their Polish and Japanese names Okamoto-Kaminski to reflect their comfort with their multicultural parentage. Their past viewed from the present has enriched them. They both have become harmonious transnationals.[13]

Akane has become a singer and actress. Her debut in the famous Japanese all women *Takarazuka* musical theatre[14] as the first European-born actress (*Akane Kami-tsuki*) was covered by Japanese TV mainstream channels. Six years later, after becoming an independent singer, her solo concert in Poland included Japanese and Polish songs which were reported by the largest Polish daily *Gazeta Wyborcza*, and in 2009 the Swedish Embassy's official Tokyo web page endorsed her latest concert with extensive references to her ethnic heritage and international musical accomplishments.

Ken, between graduation in Economics from Tokyo Meiji University and a Masters Program in Sociology at Oxford University, had studied Polish Language and Culture at my Alma Mater, Jagiellonian University of Krakow. Then, after graduation and specialization in the sociology of the internet, he joined a leading international finance institution's headquarters in London where he worked with the major Japanese corporate clients investing in the European Union. After promotion to assistant manager, he was seconded as an expat to the Tokyo office as an EU expert. Subsequently, after two years in Japan, he was offered two professional options in 2009: either to continue working at the Tokyo Office or return to London HQ and use his newly gained Japanese financial knowledge. He opted for a management position in London.

Conclusions

In this chapter, I have reviewed the socio-cultural and legal mechanisms affecting Eurasian offspring born from an international marriage where national bureaucracies contrived to deny their existence before and after birth. By reporting my personal case from the perspective of a father of multicultural adult children and as a cultural anthropologist specializing in studies of global migrations and transnational identity, I have illustrated the broader dilemmas our civil societies are facing.[15] Due to my increasingly personal and professional involvement in immigration and naturalization procedures that directly concerned the welfare of my own offspring, my research methodology melded with my changing family role as a husband and a father.

Edward Bruner points out (1993: 6) that 'in the traditional mode the ethnographer had to suppress, segment, and disguise part of the self, whereas now the ethnographer may reclaim all parts of the self, can unify the personal and the professional, can be both literary and scientific, or can use one in the service of the Other'. Similarly, Carolyn Ellis's concept of autoethnography describes the 'research, writing, story, and method that connect the autobiographical and personal to the cultural, social and political' (2004: xix).

When the future welfare of my multicultural offspring was at stake, it was not enough to combine the traditional ethnographic data gathering methods with an overt participant observation (Goodman 2000, 2005, 2006). I had to become an actual agent of change.[16] The subsequent use of a covert research technique (being an object and a subject of research) while dealing with the governmental agencies in three different states was not determined by theoretical choices (Kaminski 2004, 2008, 2009b), but caused by the contradictory legislations that I, and the other transnational families living in a legal grey zone, had to cope with (Hannerz 1983, 1994).

Global changes over the past three decades (Bauman 1998) are reflected in the lives of my two Eurasian children.[17] The fall of Communism, the introduction of matrilineal citizenship by the Japanese parliament, and dual citizenship by the Swedish government impacted on Akane and Ken's lives for the better in the end.[18]

Figure 9.2. Akane-Liv and Ken-Stanislaw preparing for their first Swedish Midsummer celebrations, Stockholm 1986.

Acknowledgements

This chapter is dedicated with my humble gratitude to the living and deceased members of the Rosvall-Engelbrektsson clan who 'adopted' me in Sweden in 1972, and have continued to support my growing transnational family along with my anthropological field research for almost four decades. Thank you, Nanne and Jan, for being my life-long mentors in the art of transnational kinning and my closest family-in-exile.

Notes

1. The concept of transnationalism is not obviously limited to migration-related phenomena, but refers to a wider class of actions, processes and institutions that cross the boundaries of states or national communities. See Bauman's classic study on globalization (1998) and compare with the range of topics on multi-ethnicity and transnational families covered by Westin et al. (2009), Bryceson and Vuorela (2002: 3–30), Bryceson (2002: 31–59, 265–7), as well as kinning and identity formation of transnational adoptees in Scandinavia (Howell 2006: 3–5, 12–14, 121–5).

2. Two common ways of recognizing citizenship are '*jus sanguinis*' (right of blood) and '*jus soli*' (right of the soil). *Jus sanguinis* means that if your parents are citizens, you acquire citizenship. *Jus soli* means that you acquire citizenship if you are born within the country. Japan is basically *jus sanguinis*. Until 1985, Japan ignored any other nationality that a Japanese citizen happened to be born with. The Japanese nationality law requires anyone born in 1985 or later to choose citizenship by their 22nd birthday. Until then dual citizenship is allowed. After that, many people take a 'don't ask don't tell' position, which reportedly can work unless you try to get a government-related job. Compare <www.debito.org>, <www.wetherall.org> and Japanese Ministry of Justice <www.moj.go.jp/english/information/tcon-01.html>

3. The documents from the Polish State Security's Archives (UB) now being progressively declassified by the *Instytut Pamieci Narodowej (IPN)* show how widespread illegal recruitment activities were conducted by the Polish Foreign Ministry's officials stationed abroad. These activities targeting Polish immigrants were not only limited to the Sweden-based ethnic Poles, but also affected their foreign spouses' social identity, and as my case proves, the future welfare of their cross-cultural offspring. While my case is only one of many, it also gives insights into the complexity of field experiences of an anthropologist working among his fellow Eastern European refugees (Kaminski 1980: 3–25, 109–12, 281–96, 304–53). See also Mach (2007: 54–72).

4. Koreans were former colonial subjects who became stateless as a group in post-World War II Japan (Kaminski 1982b).

5. In Poland (and other communist-controlled countries), abortion was legalized, while the Catholic Church, to which 90% of Poles officially belonged, had continued to be strongly against it (interview with Cardinal Stanislaw Dziwisz, Vatican, 16 January 2005). See also Dziwisz (2007).

6. Although my father-in-law was ethnic Japanese, my mother-in-law was of Korean ancestry (born in a Japan-occupied Korea), which was already considered a stigma in their *koseki* (Kaminski 1982a).

7. Discrimination against Burakumin was abolished by the 1868 Meji Restoration Act that brought about the modernization of Japan (Kaminski 1979).

8. Various coincidental linkages were revealed that allowed this approach to be accepted: the then Head of SIV was the former Swedish Envoy to China with both personal and professional links to the international community of anthropologists specializing in Asian Studies. See also Corlin (1994: 347).

9. On 1 July 2001, a new Citizenship Act came into effect in Sweden. The new law makes it possible to have dual citizenship. The law also gives children further opportunity to become Swedish citizens independent of their parents (see the Swedish Migration Board website: http://www.migrationsverket.se/info/start_en.html. Similar legal changes are currently being considered by

163

Japanese law makers: The Japanese Nationality Law (Law No. 147 of 1950, as amended by Law No. 268 of 1952, Law No. 45 of 1984, Law No. 89 of 1993 and Law No. 147 of 2004, Law No. 88 of 2008) Article 2. A child shall, in any of the following cases, be a Japanese national: (1) when, at the time of its birth, the father or the mother is a Japanese national; (2) when the father who died prior to the birth of the child was a Japanese national at the time of his death; (3) when both parents are unknown or have no nationality in a case where the child is born in Japan. See <www.debito.org> and <www.wetherall.org>.

10. In Sweden, the interests and rights of children (up to the age of 18) are protected by their own Ombudsman (Legal Adviser). The Children Ombudsman (BO) office monitors implementation of the United Nations Convention on the Rights of the Child (the CRC) by Swedish government agencies, municipalities, county councils and other administrative bodies. Though the Ombudsman office cannot legally supervise the state or municipal authorities or interfere in individual cases (like naturalization), the office can influence the attitudes of decision-makers by submitting bills for legislative changes to the Swedish government and parliament, e.g. dual citizenship for children with immigrant background. This development was followed up by the establishment of the European Network of Ombudspersons for Children (ENOC) in 1997. The ENOC structures are already established in 24 countries of the 47 member states of the Council of Europe and are particularly active in protecting the rights of children with immigrant backgrounds <barnombudsmannen@bo.se>. The European Commission's multicultural project on the use of internet and new media by immigrant children in six EU countries <www.chicam.org> promoted integration of innovative methodological approaches using the latest IT developments (see Note 15).

11. Webber (2007) addresses the question of language and culture in a broader philosophical context: 'The human capacity to make sense of the past, and to do so in accordance with present perceived needs, would seem to be an intellectual universal, similar, for example, to the ability of a child to learn a native language, and to do so in such a way as to be eventually able to understand the utterances it has never heard before. But, as we know, the totality of grammar of a language is an abstraction, for it cannot be altogether brought to consciousness' (2007: 73).

12. Waldren discusses the importance of names as metaphors for social relations past and present in her work *Insiders and Outsiders* (1996: 78–89). See also Westin et al. (2009).

13. Transitions of Akane's identity can be traced in her choice of stage names 1998–2009. She performed in Takarazuka's *Yuki Gumi* (Snow Group) under the stage name *Akane God Moon* <http://takarazuka-revue.info/tiki-index.php?page=Kamizuki+Akane>. Although she used *Kami-tsuki/Kamizuki* as a variation of her Polish surname, it was written in Chinese characters and thus read as *Kami* = God, *Tsuki* = Moon. After leaving Takarazuka, she performs as Okamoto Akane in Nissay Theatre, Tokyo, while she continues using the stage name Akane Okamoto-Kaminski as a soloist in the EU. In 2009 the circle was completed: she returned to her birth name *Akane-Liv* in her album for Tokyo Victor Records <http://www.jvcmusic.co.jp/-/Artist/A022867.html> and decided to use her Polish baptism name *Jadwiga* in her blog and contacts with her Polish kin and media. Her brother, after relocating to the EU, has added to his Japanese first name Ken (meaning 'healthy'), a Polish name of his paternal grandfather, *Stanislaw*. The name Stanislaw (he received through baptism at birth) was recorded on the paternal side of my family for several hundred years and was always given to the first-born son of Ignacy. He became *Ken-Stanislaw Kaminski of Kamionki* and his lengthy and often emotionally loaded transnational kinning process was finally completed in the eyes of his Polish relatives. Howell (2006) suggests 'that the "power of kinship", the fact of being emotionally and socially (and permanently) related to others – not the handling of the autonomous self – may largely account for how people experience their personhood, be they adopted or not' (2006: 134).

14. Although there is a large body of international anthropological literature on gender and sociocultural aspects of Takarazuka Theatre (including a PhD thesis published by Jennifer Robertson in 1998, and a recent paper by Powell in 2005), most of the field research was limited to the structured interviews with the actresses arranged and supervised by the Takarazuka management and/or the compilation of historical data with media reports and personal interviews with the members of Takarazuka fun clubs. Robertson (1998) addresses some of the methodological problems she had encountered during her Japanese fieldwork and her own difficulties to venture beyond the 'arranged interviews' and the 'official story' (1998: xiv, 41–6). Powell, who refers to Robertson's work (2005: 143–4) is less concerned about the ethnographic relevance of the field data, and more with the theoretical and historical aspects of Takarazuka as a social and cultural phenomenon. The question remains as to what extent the application of social theories to fragmented ethnographic data (and second-hand sources) may bring us as researchers closer to understanding the frequently changing socio-cultural realities of our informants (Hannerz 1983, 1994, Bauman 1998, Robertson 2005, Goodman 2006, 2008, Kaminski 1979, 1984, 2009b, Westin 1989).

15. Choice of field methodology and then choice of reporting style of one's research are among dilemmas frequently encountered by academics (see bibliography and website references, Ellis 2000, http://www.youtube.com/watch?v=hvhsdqyRyww). Our methodological choices can vary as much as our shifting personal attachment to the people we encounter during our fieldwork, and so may our need to share our research experience with civil society at large. Lindisfarne (2000), who transformed her field research into a literary text, addresses these dilemmas in the postscript (pp. 123–59) to her collection of the reality-based short stories. 'Academics tend to write books with other academics in mind. While preaching to the converted may guarantee professional recognition and security, it is also likely to be a circular process, tedious to the insiders and dismissed by others for its utter irrelevance to their lives' (2000: 149–50). See also <www.youtube.com/watch?v=bcnY_kF62Ww> and compare with the EU-financed new media mega project EUR 23113 *Children in Communication about Migration – CHICAM* <www.chicam.org> and Stephen Murphy-Shigematsu <http://www.multiculturalleadership.com/index.htm>.

16. The methodological and ethical dilemmas are not only limited to researchers involved in Asian studies and their/our human sources of information. The earlier studies of social, cultural and emotional borderlands that our informants have to continue living in (long after we had left the field and published our academic findings) are continuously being re-examined by both the researchers themselves and/or the subjects of their/our research. See Brzezinski (1972), Corlin (1975), Maruyama (1978), Hannerz (1983), Kaminski and Gripman (1985), Okely (1992), Robertson (1998), Bryceson and Vuorela (2002) and Goodman (2002), and compare with Arhem (1994), Hannerz (1994), Ellis (2004), Robertson (2005), Hendry and Wong (2006), Howell (2006), Bryceson et al. (2007), Mach (2007), Goodman (2008), Morton (2008), Brzostowski (2009) and Garrett (2009).

17. Ms. Keiko Chiba, Justice Minister in the Japanese Government of PM Yukio Hatoyama (formed 16 September 2009) and a member of a legislators' group supporting Amnesty International, has officially declared the need for 'coexistence with foreign national residents, and an independent organization in each prefecture to protect human rights' <http://www.japantimes.co.jp/cabinet/cabinet.html>.

18. Akane and Ken (who frequently volunteered in my field data gathering) were always given working versions of my publications, films and new media projects in advance. However, respecting my Japanese wife and her parents' increasing concerns about the legal and social implications of my field research for the family privacy, I have (since becoming a single parent) deliberately confined this ethnographic account to our cross-cultural children and my side alone.

Bibliography

Arhem, K. (ed.) 1994. *Den antropologiska erfarenheten.* Stockholm: Carlssons Bokforlag.

Bauman, Z. 1998. *Globalization: The Human Consequences.* New York: Columbia University Press.

Bruner, E. 1986. 'Experience and its Expressions'. In V. Turner and E. Bruner (eds), *The Anthropology of Experience.* Urbana, IL: University of Illinois Press, 3–30.

—— 1993. 'Introduction: The Ethnographic Self and Personal Self'. In P. Benson (ed.), *Anthropology and Literature.* Urbana, IL: University of Illinois Press, 1–26.

Bryceson, D. 2002. 'Europe's Transnational Families and Migration: Past and Present'. In D. Bryceson and U. Vuorela (eds), *The Transnational Family: New European Frontiers and Global Networks.* Oxford: Berg, 31–59.

Bryceson, D. and U. Vuorela 2002. 'Transnational Families in the Twenty-first Century'. In D. Bryceson and U. Vuorela (eds), *The Transnational Family: New European Frontiers and Global Networks.* Oxford: Berg, 3–30.

Bryceson, D., J. Okely and J. Webber (eds) 2007. *Identity and Networks: Fashioning Gender and Ethnicity across Cultures.* Oxford: Berghahn Books.

Brzezinski, Z. 1972. *The Fragile Blossom: Crisis and Changes in Japan.* New York: Harper & Row.

Brzostowski, E. 2009. *Evangelization in Japan?* Delhi: ISPCK Press.

Chan-Tiberghien, J. 2004. *Gender and Human Rights Politics in Japan: Global Norms and Domestic Networks.* Stanford, CA: Stanford University Press.

Corlin, C. 1975. *The Nation in Your Mind.* Goteborg: Department of Social Anthropology, University of Gothenburg.

—— 1994. 'Antropologiska farvatten'. In K. Arhem (ed.), *Den antropologiska erfarenheten.* Stockholm: Carlssons Bokforlag, 345–50.

Debito, A. 2004. *Japanese Only.* Tokyo: Akashi Shoten.

—— 2008. 'Language and Propaganda in Japanese Newspapers on Minority Speakers'. Paper presented at the 5th International Symposium on Language and Propaganda. Linguapax Asia, Tokyo University, 26 October 2008.

Debito, A. and A. Higuchi 2008. *Handbook for Newcomers and Immigrants to Japan.* Tokyo: Akashi Shoten.

Dziwisz, S. 2007. *Swiadectwo.* W rozmowie z Gian Franco Svidercoschi (Una vita con Carol), Poznan: TBA and P. Hauser.

Ellis, C. 1997. 'Evocative Autoethnography: Writing Emotionally about our Lives'. In W. Tierney and Y. Lincoln (eds), *Representation and the Text: Reframing the Narrative Voice.* Albany, NY: SUNY Press, 116–39.

—— 2004. *The Ethnographic I: A Methodological Novel about Autoethnography.* Walnut Creek, CA: Alta Mira Press.

Ellis, C. and L. Berger 2002. 'Their Story/My Story: Including the Researcher's Experience in Interviews'. In J. Gubrium and J. Holstein (eds), *Handbook of Interview Research: Context and Method.* Thousand Oaks, CA: Sage.

Ellis, C. and A.P. Bochner (eds) 1996. *Composing Ethnography: Alternative Forms of Qualitative Writing.* Walnut Creek, CA: Alta Mira Press.

—— 2000. 'Autoethnography, Personal Narrative, Reflexivity: Research as Subject'. In N. Denzin and P. Lincoln (eds), *Handbook of Qualitative Research,* 2nd edn. Thousand Oaks, CA: Sage, 733–68.

European Commission 2007. *Children in Communication about Migration – CHICAM. EUR 23113 — EU Research on Social Sciences and Humanities.* Luxembourg: Office for Official Publications of the European Communities, <www.chicam.org>.

Garrett, D.H. 2009. 'An Introduction to TIP (Trafficking in Persons): Scales, Types, and Definitions'. Paper presented at the 6th International Symposium on Language and Human Trafficking. Linguapax Asia, Tokyo University, 14 June 2009.

Goodman, R. 2000. 'Fieldwork and Reflexivity: Thoughts from the Anthropology of Japan'. In P. Dresch, W. James and D. Parkin (eds), *Anthropologists in a Wider World: Essays on Field Research*. Oxford: Berghahn Books, 151–65.

——— (ed.) 2002. *Family and Social Policy in Japan. Anthropological Approaches*. Cambridge: Cambridge University Press.

——— 2005. 'Making Majority Culture'. In J. Robertson (ed.), *A Companion to the Anthropology of Japan*. Oxford: Blackwell Publishing, 59–72.

——— 2006. 'Thoughts on the Relationship between Anthropological Theory, Methods and the Study of Japanese Society'. In J. Hendry and D. Wong (eds), *Dismantling the East-West Dichotomy: Views from Japanese Anthropology*. London: Routledge, 22–30.

——— 2008. 'Afterword: Marginals, Minorities, and Migrants – Studying the Japanese Borderlands in Contemporary Japan'. In D.B. Willis and S. Murphy-Shigematsu (eds), *Transcultural Japan: At the Borderlands of Race, Gender, and Identity*. New York: Routledge, 325–33.

Goodman, G., Peach, C., Takenaka, A., and White, P. 2003. 'The Experience of Japan's New Migrants and Overseas Communities in Anthropological, Geographical, Historical and Sociological Perspective'. In R. Goodman, C. Peach, A. Takenaka and P. White (eds), *Global Japan: The Experience of Japan's New Minorities and Overseas Communities*. London: Routledge Curzon, 1–20.

Hannerz, U. 1983. *Över gränser: studier i dagens socialantropologi*. Lund: Liber.

——— 1994. 'Mångfalden och världsvimlet'. In K. Arhem (ed.), *Den antropologiska erfarenheten*. Stockholm: Carlssons Bokforlag, 149–67.

Hendry, J. and D. Wong (eds) 2006. *Dismantling the East-West Dichotomy: Views from Japanese Anthropology*. London: Routledge.

Horne, M. and I.-M. Kaminski 1981. 'Guest Scholars: Insiders or Outsiders? A Polyocular Approach', *Japanese Studies Center News*, 6 (3): 2–5. The Japan Foundation.

Howell, S. 2006. *The Kinning of Foreigners: Transnational Adoption in a Global Perspective*. Oxford: Berghahn Books.

Kaminski, I-M. 1978. 'Uniformerad minoritetsforsking'. *Invandrare och minoriteter – Scandinavian Migration and Minority Review*, 3 (4).

——— 1979. 'There is No Escape from Passing: Burakumin and Gypsy-Roma', *Antropologiska Studier*, 28: 52–68.

——— 1980. *The State of Ambiguity: Studies of Gypsy Refugees*. Göteborg: University of Gothenburg.

——— 1982a. 'Application of Ethnography of Law and Political Anthropology'. In J. Suzuki et al. (eds), *Shakai jinruigaku nempo* 8. Tokyo: Tokyo Metropolitan University and Kobundo Press, 1–29.

——— 1982b. 'Japan: från yttre till inre internationalisering', *Invandrare och minoriteter – Scandinavian Migration and Minority Review*, 5: 1–9.

——— 1983. 'Ethnic Groups: From Minority to Global Community'. In T. Koyama (ed.), *Gendai hansabetsu no shisoo to undo (Current Thoughts and Movements against Discrimination)*. Tokyo: Shinsensha Press, 306–21.

——— 1984. *Academy in Search for the 'Real Life': Thoughts on Migration and Minority Research*. Tokyo: International Center, Hosei University.

——— 1985. 'Bledne kolo relacji etnicznych' (The vicious circle of ethnic relations), *Contact Dialogue – Review of Polish Jewish Community in Scandinavia*. Göteborg/Copenhagen.

——— 1988. 'Les Ainous. Le peuple d'Okinawa'. In J.F. Sabouret (ed.), *L'Etat du Japon et de ses habitants*. Paris: Editions la Decouverte.

——— 1994. 'A Non-Japanese View on Japanese Family: Examining Future of Family', *NIRA Seisaku Kenkyu (NIRA Policy Research)*, 7 (12): 36–39.

—— 2004. 'Applied Anthropology and Diplomacy: Renegotiating Conflicts in the Eurasian Diplomatic Gray Zone by Using Cultural Symbols'. In H.J. Langholtz and C.E. Stout (eds), *The Psychology of Diplomacy, Psychological Dimensions to War and Peace Series*. Westport, CT: Greenwood Press, 175–206.

—— 2005 [1995]. *Yasashi porando go*. Tokyo: Naundo Phoenix Press.

—— 2008. 'The Changing Language of Japanese Broadcasting: Asahi TV vs. YouTube'. Paper presented at the 5th International Symposium on Language and Propaganda. Linguapax Asia, Tokyo University, 26 October 2008.

—— 2009a. 'A Man of Many Lives', *Transactions of the Asiatic Society of Japan*, ASJ Fourth Series 22: 247–56.

—— 2009b. 'The Language of Human Experience: Human Trafficking and Diplomacy'. Paper presented at the 6th International Symposium on Language and Human Trafficking. Linguapax Asia, Tokyo University, 14 June 2009.

Kaminski, I-M. and M. Gripman 1985. 'Jakten på den fyrkantiga grisen'. *Socialdialog*, 11 (5).

Kaminski, I-M. and C. Westin 1985. *Samverkan: om utbildning, folkbildning och etniska relationer i Sverige*. Stockholm: CEIFO Press Centrum for invandringsforskning, Stockholm University.

Lange, A. and C. Westin 1981. *Etnisk diskriminering och social identitet: forskningsoversikt och teoretisk analys*. Stockholm: Liber/Publica.

—— 1984. 'Social Psychological Aspects of Race and Ethnic Relations'. Paper presented at the International Conference on Theories of Race and Ethnic Relations. St. Catherine's College, Oxford University.

Lindisfarne, N. 2000. *Dancing in Damascus*. Albany, NY: SUNY Press.

Mach, Z. 2007. 'Constructing Identities in a Post-Communist Society: Ethnic, National, and European'. In D. Bryceson, J. Okely and J. Webber (eds), *Identity and Networks: Fashioning Gender and Ethnicity Across Cultures*. Oxford: Berghahn Books, 54–72.

Maruyama, M. 1978. 'Psychotopology and its Application to Cross Disciplinary, Cross Professional and Cross Cultural Communication'. In R-E. Holloman and S. Arutiuvnov (eds), *Perspectives in Ethnicity: World Anthropology*. The Hague: Mouton.

Morton, R. 2008. 'The Six Lives of Father Neal Lawrence'. *Transactions of the Asiatic Society of Japan*. Fourth Series 7, Supplement.

Murphy-Shigematsu, S. 2008. '"The Invisible Man" and Other Narratives of Living in the Borderlands of Race and Nation'. In D.B. Willis and S. Murphy-Shigematsu (eds), *Transcultural Japan: At the Borderlands of Race, Gender, and Identity*. New York: Routledge, 282–304.

Okely, J. 1992. 'Anthropology and Autobiography: Participatory Experience and Embodied Knowledge'. In J. Okely and H. Callaway (eds), *Anthropology and Autobiography*. London: Routledge, 1–28.

Parker, C. 2001. *The Japanese Police System Today: A Comparative Study*. Berlin: Springer.

Powell, B. 2005. 'Cross-Dressing on the Japanese Stage'. In A. Shaw and S. Ardener (eds), *Changing Sex and Bending Gender*. Oxford: Berghahn Books, 138–49.

Prime Minister's Report on Japan's Goals in the 21st Century. Tokyo: Prime Minister's Office, 2000.

Robertson, J. 1998. *Takarazuka: Sexual Politics and Popular Culture in Modern Japan*. Berkeley, CA: University of California Press.

—— (ed.) 2005. *A Companion to the Anthropology of Japan*. Oxford: Blackwell Publishing.

Statens Invandrarverk 1976. *Immigrant in Sweden*. Norrköping: SIV.

Trankell, A. 1972. *Reliability of Evidence: Methods for Analyzing and Assessing Witness Statements*. Stockholm: Beckman. (republished in Japanese)

Waldren, J. 1996. *Insiders and Outsiders: Paradise and Reality in Mallorca*. New Directions in Anthropology Series. Oxford: Berghahn Books.

Webber, J. 2007. 'Making Sense of the Past: Reflections on Jewish Historical Consciousness'. In D. Bryceson, J. Okely and J. Webber (eds), *Identity and Networks: Fashioning Gender and Ethnicity Across Cultures*. Oxford: Berghahn Books, 73–90.

Westin, C. 1977. *Ankomsten: asiater fran Uganda kommer till Sverige*. Stockholm: Socialstyr. [Liber distribution]. National government publication.

—— 1989. 'Swedish Attitudes Towards Migrants and Immigration Policies'. Paper presented at the 1st European Congress of Psychology. Amsterdam, 2–7 July 1989.

—— 1998. 'On Migration and Criminal Offence. Report on a Study from Sweden'. In *IMIS Beitrage Heft 8/1998*. Osnabruck: Universität Osnabruck, Institut für Migrationsforschung und kulturelle Studien (IMIS), 7–30.

Westin, C., J. Bastos, J. Dahinden and P. Gois (eds) 2009. 'Identity Processes and Dynamics in Multi-ethnic Europe', Series – Imiscoe Reports. Amsterdam: Amsterdam University Press.

Wetherall, W. 2008. 'The Racialization of Japan'. In D.B. Willis and S. Murphy-Shigematsu (eds), *Transcultural Japan: At the Borderlands of Race, Gender, and Identity*. New York: Routledge, 264–81.

Willis, D.B. and S. Murphy-Shigematsu (eds) 2008. *Transcultural Japan: At the Borderlands of Race, Gender, and Identity*. New York: Routledge.

Chapter 10
DOING FIELDWORK WITH CHILDREN IN JAPAN

Roger Goodman[1]

Mary Bateson, the daughter of possibly the most famous anthropologists to study child socialization, Margaret Mead and Gregory Bateson, is often said to be the most highly anthropologized child of all time and, when a student, was told by her mother that she could not discard her childhood paintings because she 'had probably had the best-documented childhood in the United States' (Bateson 1984: 30). The psychologist, R.D. Laing (1978), recorded his conversations with his children over a six-year period and presented them as material for others to analyse how children develop their cognitive universes. My children have suffered similarly from having a father who is an anthropologist of education and child welfare. During my last two periods of sabbatical leave, I have dragged my expanding family to Japan and placed the children in the local schools and nurseries for a year. My oldest son has had the unusual experience of both participating in the entrance ceremony of one elementary school in Osaka and receiving a graduation certificate from another one in Kyoto exactly six years later.

Although I have been teaching and researching at all levels of Japan's educational and child welfare system for the past 20 years, seeing the system through the eyes of a parent has significantly altered my perception of it. At the same time, I am happy to say that none of my three children seem to have suffered from the experience. What are some of the main points that struck us all that differentiated the experience of small children in Japanese and UK schools? The first is the amount of freedom and autonomy enjoyed by young Japanese children. While in England I not only have to deliver my children to school up until they reach about the age of ten, but I have to do so within about a ten minute window between 8.45 and 8.55. Arriving too early is as heinous a crime (the school is not insured to look after the children before 8.45) as arriving too late. In Japan, in Osaka and Kyoto all the children walk to school themselves, in small neighbourhood groups generally under the care of the oldest child in the group. They arrive at least 30 minutes before school starts and burn off huge amounts of energy in the school playground before the beginning of lessons. Much more to our surprise, they come home completely independently at varying times between 1.30 pm and 5.00 pm depending on their schedules and personal whim. In Osaka (one of the world's largest cities), the local parks play a tune at 5.00 pm, which all school age children know means it is time to return home. It is a common sight to see first grade children as young as six travelling by themselves on buses and changing trains at major termini all by themselves; in England any six-year-old regularly seen doing this would probably be reported to the local social services.

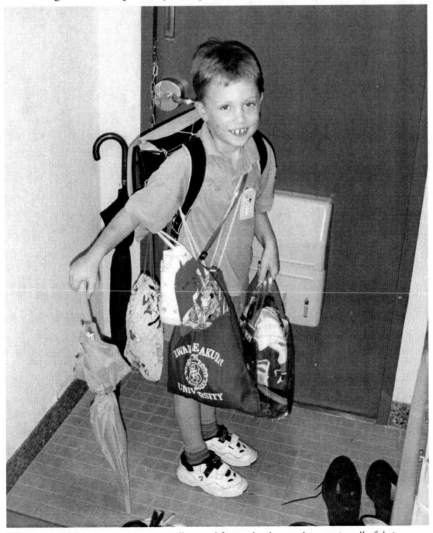

Figure 10.1. Children as young as six walk to and from school every day carrying all of their equipment for the day with them.

That such a system still pertains in Japan is due, of course, to the belief that people are still basically good and that society is still basically safe. While in the UK, responsible parenting is based on the assumption that behind every tree

Figure 10.2. Parents regularly attend classes to watch what their children are doing and how they are taught.

lurks a potential child abuser, in Japan the chances of a child being attacked are still considered negligible. In Osaka, my six-year-old brought back a piece of paper one day saying that a strange man had been trying to coax young children into his car in the neighbourhood – and parents should warn their children of the dangers of accepting such an offer. There was no suggestion that parents should either take their children to school or come and pick them up from it.

If the responsibility of the British teacher extends only to the school gate during regular school hours in the UK, then in Japan it goes right up to – and into – the house of the children who attend their classes. All elementary school teachers must visit the homes of their children at least once a year and in practice they often do so more often. In Kyoto, my children's classroom teachers regularly rang to say they would be over in ten minutes. The children never quite got used to this, and one of them once hid in a cupboard in order to protect his privacy during one such visit. They also take a didactic position in relation to the parents of their children. We were constantly told off (chided might be a better word) by the twenty-something classroom teacher of my second son in Kyoto for having forgotten to send something with him to school or for not having responded to the mountain of paperwork he brought back almost every day.

At the same time, we as parents were constantly invited to invade the 'privacy' of the teachers' domain. Every month, the school held an open class day when any parent could sit in and observe the class in action and this was often followed by a meeting with the classroom teacher for all the parents of the children in each class to feed back comments from their children. Since these occurred on a weekday, once a year there was a special day of Sunday schooling which allowed fathers to come and watch classes and there was a further period of two days when the school was open to anyone in the local community to wander in and watch any class they wanted. On such occasions, audiences in classes often far outnumbered children in them and the discussions afterwards belied the image of conflict avoidance often ascribed to Japanese. Indeed, I was struck by the difference between those meetings arranged with school inspectors for parents in England (when parents close ranks and rush to the defence of 'their' teachers) and the demands of Japanese parents for better performance from the teachers who teach their children.

Parents want two things from elementary schools in Japan. They want their children to be socialized to be responsible and co-operative individuals and they want them to be given the basic skills so that they can do themselves justice in an examination system, which is still largely perceived to determine social success in Japan. Although there are the universal inter-generational panics about the badly behaved problem youth of today which are continuously played on by the Japanese media, from an English perspective the Japanese system is still stunningly successful at the former of these. At one level this is attested to by what happens outside the classroom. Japan enjoys by far the lowest use of illicit drugs, number of teenage mothers and rates of recorded juvenile crime among the OECD countries.

Indeed, between 1985 and 1995, the official juvenile crime rate declined significantly despite the fact that this period saw the country plunge into recession. Much has been made of rises since 1995, but these are actually only to pre-1985 levels. One of the main social panics has been about what is known in Japanese as *gakkyū hōkai* (classroom collapse) where teachers have been unable to exert any control over their charges. Over the past 15 years, I have met a number of people in Japan who know someone who knows someone whose class has collapsed in such a fashion, but have yet to meet such a teacher or see such a class myself. If sociologists in Japan are correct, then the school my sons attended in Kyoto might have been one which was expected to see such a problem: it was based in a downtown working class area of the city with not only a large Japanese-Korean ethnic minority but also what is euphemistically known as a community of *burakumin* (literally 'hamlet people', but referring to the presence of what some comparativists have called Japan's 'outcaste' or 'untouchable' group, a left-over from Japan's feudal past who continue to be discriminated against). The school also integrated – to a much higher degree and for much longer than in the UK – children with severe learning as well as physical disabilities. Yet, my children saw no signs of bullying or disobedience throughout their time in the school. It was true that one teacher left on long-term sick leave during the course of the year, but this was put down to him being unable to cope with the pressure from the parents rather than from the children.

How do Japanese schools get their children to behave so well? There are a number of interesting techniques at play here. The first is that children are taught to make a clear distinction between study and play from as soon as they start school. Indeed, the first three years of school in Japan (and children do not start until the first of April after their sixth birthday, so some of them are almost seven while, in England, children start as 'Rising Fives', i.e. two or more years earlier) are largely devoted to learning how to learn rather than learning itself. Only in the fourth grade (age ten) does the famed emphasis on learning itself in Japan begin, and then the learning curve – based on the foundation of the previous three years – is very steep indeed. As I discovered in an earlier research project on Japanese children who had lived overseas and returned to Japan (Goodman 1990), miss a year in the system after the age of ten and you are going to have trouble catching up. (As far as we – or more importantly they – can tell, neither of my children aged nine and twelve at the time missed out on any significantly new area of study in the year they were away from the British system, as much of the curriculum at this stage is simply an incremental development of material covered the year before.) Learning the difference between play and work means that when children play they are allowed to do so virtually without regulation or restrictions. Enter a school during playtime and one would have thought the whole place was completely out of control. Once the bell goes for class, though, children settle down (according to sociologists who have taken the trouble to measure such things) an astounding *ten* times faster than their peers in the UK and US (Cummings 2003: 184). In most cases the responsibility for getting the class to settle down rests with their peers and not the teacher. And since children take it in turns to be class monitors, they can see that it is in their interest to follow instructions if they want others to follow their instructions when they are monitors.

The use of children to monitor and support other children in Japanese schools is well documented, but it is still fascinating to watch in process. Every class that I have ever seen in Japan is divided into groups, either by lot or by the teacher but never by self-selection as is often the case in English schools. Groups are encouraged to compete with each other and to take responsibility for the actions of each of their members. If someone in any group does something wrong, then they are seen as letting down the whole group and need to apologize and make up for this. On the other hand, in order to compete with other groups, stronger group members need to help weaker ones. My children have been huge beneficiaries of this as other children in their group have taken it upon themselves to both explain what work they have to do and how to do it.

Groups (as one can see later in companies, although one must be careful of extrapolating directly from one type of group to another) have a sense of inclusivity, which is broader than that of friendship. The Japanese indeed have a word for this obligation that they feel to fellow groups members, '*tsukiai*'. While *tsukiai* transcends both relations of kin and friendship, these categories, of course, are not mutually incompatible and it was doubtless through a combination of *tsukiai* and friendship that other children in their classes would insist on incorporating my children (even when, as at the beginning, they spoke absolutely no Japanese) into their activities. One curious by-product of this was my 12-year-old son's reintroduction to girls; in British school, the gender division is almost complete by the age of nine. In Japan, because of the fact that all groups throughout the system are mixed-sex, boys and girls interact on a much more co-operative basis throughout their school careers.

If the socializing functions of the school system are so impressive, what about the academic ones? In the 1980s, when the Japanese economy looked set to become the strongest in the world, Japan became the first port-of-call for all new North American and European Education Ministers. The development of the core curriculum in the UK, for example, can be seen (to some degree) as influenced by the Japanese model of that period. Curiously, as western policy-makers were rushing to Japan to find answers (in most cases actually confirmation or support for already-formed plans) for their educational problems, Japanese policy-makers were rushing to the UK and US to look for solutions to what they saw as their overheated and over-centralized system. The development of what is known as *yutori kyōiku* (relaxed education) in Japan, for example, can be seen (to some degree) as influenced by the UK model of that period. There remains a great deal, I believe, that UK schools can learn from the Japanese model. The most important of these is high expectations for all children. Japanese teachers do not avoid 'labelling' because it is politically incorrect; they avoid it because it is simply not part of their world-view. They seem to genuinely believe that everyone has the (basically equal) potential to learn everything if they are properly taught and put in the effort. There was a statue outside my children's elementary school in Kyoto of Ninomiya Sontoku, a feudal period agronomist. He is caught carrying firewood on his back and reading by the light of the moon since he was brought up by an uncle who gave him no time to study and forced him to work for him. He symbolizes what can be achieved if one works hard enough.

In Japanese educational philosophy, everything can be taught, everything can be learned and everything can be examined. I one day flicked through 120 still-life pictures drawn by 12-year-olds of a flower vase, flowers and some fruit. I could recognize what each depicted as all the children had been taught the basic principles of angle, perspective and proportion. In Japan, all children learn also to read music. Japan has the highest literacy rate in the world despite also having the most difficult writing system. People in all echelons of society in Japan are as embarrassed to be innumerate as British people would be to be illiterate. As English schools cut back on art and music (in the belief that those with natural ability will find other means to develop these?), they deprive not only individuals, but society at large of important means of common communication. (As one goes around a Japanese factory or office one notices that people draw the messages they want all to imbibe more often than they write them.)

It is indeed difficult to exaggerate the importance given to the common performance and enjoyment of sports and arts in Japanese schools. Almost a month is set aside each year to prepare for the annual sports and cultural festivals. Every child must participate in both. On Sports Day in Kyoto, the whole school clapped as a severely physically disabled girl completed the 100 meters with her walking frame and her point was scored for the Reds, one of the three teams into which the whole school of 1,100 had been divided. My older son – who had assiduously managed to avoid performing on stage in the UK since the age of six – was forced to debut speaking in Japanese in front of an audience of a thousand children, who, unbeknownst to him, had been told by their teachers not to laugh at his accent. The sense of achievement that both children felt on not letting down their teammates and classmates was palpable.

Figure 10.3. All children, whatever their musical or theatrical talents or instincts, must participate in regular public performances in front of parents and other children.

In the end, the politicians always tell us, the quality of education that children receive all comes down to money. The Japanese case, though, suggests that it is not just about how much money is spent on education, but about how that money is used. The single thing that most convinced me that those British and American politicians who visited Japanese schools in the 1980s only saw what they wanted to see was the complete absence of descriptions in their accounts of the physical layout of Japanese schools. On an initial viewing, Japanese schools, apart from a few private ones, are uniformly grim. They have neither air conditioners (much of Japan is sub-tropical in summer) nor central heating (much of Japan is covered by snow for months of the year). Buildings are generally old, run-down and poorly lit with a dusty playground squeezed between them. They are also dirty. As is well known, children do the cleaning themselves in Japanese schools and, however well-organized they might be, six-, seven- and eight-year-olds are not the most effective of cleaners.

So, if Japanese spending on primary and secondary education is, as the figures suggest, higher than in the UK, where does the money get spent? The answer is on textbooks and teachers rather than on buildings and brooms. Every child has a copy of every book for every course they study. While much has been made of the fact that the state controls the contents of these textbooks (which to some is tantamount to censorship), the fact that they are provided free to every child means that they (and their parents) know what they will be covering and that children always have work which they can both revise and prepare. Teachers in Japan are also well paid not only by global but also by local standards (see Cummings 2003: 72). Teaching is a highly competitive field to enter and teachers still enjoy high status. Even the staff at the nursery and kindergarten my children have attended have all been graduates of higher education institutions.

Once, while doing research in Japan, I found a book deep in the bowels of the university library where I was based entitled *Children and Anthropological Research* (Butler and Turner 1982). While most authors were able to find positives in the experience of taking their children overseas for a year or more, the book also contained a worrying catalogue of short- and long-term damage that the experience had caused their children. I put it quickly back on the shelf. In retrospect, though, I am confident that my children's experiences overall were positive: they picked up Japanese quickly; they learned to cross communication boundaries; they became accustomed to a different cuisine and culture; they became tolerant of other peoples' ways of doing things.

Notes

This chapter is a revised version of an article previously published in the *St Antony's College Record*, 2004, pp. 27–36, Oxford University.

1. This essay gives me an opportunity to thank those who facilitated my children being able to enter local schools in Japan. In 1997–8, Hirochika Nakamaki organized for my son Sam (then aged six) to attend Toyokawa Minamai Shōgakkō and Joe aged three to attend Onohara Gakuen in Osaka. In 2003–4, Makoto and Kyoko Kosaka introduced us to Saiin Shōgakkō and Kasuga Yochien in Kyoto.

Bibliography

Bateson, M.C. 1984. *With a Daughter's Eye: A Memoir of Margaret Mead and Gregory Bateson.* New York: W. Morrow.

Butler, B. and D.M. Turner 1982. *Children and Anthropological Research.* New York: Plenum Press.

Cummings, W.K. 2003. *The Institutions of Education: A Comparative Study of Educational Development in the Six Core Nations.* Oxford: Symposium Books.

Goodman, R. 1990. *Japan's 'International Youth': The Emergence of a New Class of Schoolchildren.* Oxford: Oxford University Press.

Laing, R.D. 1978. *Conversations with Children.* Harmondsworth: Penguin Books.

Notes on Contributors

Louisa Darian

Louisa Darian is a Research and Policy Officer at the National Council for Voluntary Organisations working on funding policy. Before that she worked at YWCA England and Wales specializing in young women's poverty. She has a Masters in Comparative Social Policy where she looked at support for lone mothers from an international perspective.

Elsa Dawson

Elsa Dawson is a Diversity and Gender Consultant, providing training and evaluation services to development agencies. She has worked for Save the Children UK and Oxfam GB in South America, Albania and the UK. She is the mother of Elisa, her 13-year-old daughter with severe learning difficulties, diagnosed with Angelman Syndrome.

Roger Goodman

Roger Goodman is Nissan Professor of Modern Japanese Studies and Head of the Social Sciences Division at the University of Oxford. His research concentrates mainly on the areas of Japanese education and social policy. His many publications include *Japan's International Youth* (Oxford University Press, 1990) and *Children of the Japanese State* (Oxford University Press, 2000), and he is currently completing a monograph on the reforms taking place in Japanese higher education.

Ignacy-Marek Kaminski

Ignacy-Marek Kaminski received his PhD in Social Anthropology from the University of Gothenburg in 1980. He is Lecturer in Social Anthropology, Mejiro University, Tokyo, and concurrently Associate Senior Research Fellow in the Department of Social Anthropology, School of Global Studies, Göteborg University and Visiting Senior Fellow at Linacre College, Oxford University. His research focuses on transitive identity, conflict resolution, and leadership. He has conducted fieldwork and filmmaking among Roma, Inuit, Ainu and Okinawans. He was elected to the Swedish Writers' Union in 1984. His works are published in twelve languages.

Anna Lærke

Anna Lærke received her PhD in Social Anthropology from SOAS, University of London. She teaches at The Open University, Child and Youth Study Group, Faculty of Education and Language Studies and works for the charity Home-Star Oxford. Her latest book (co-edited by Heidi Armbruster) is *Taking Sides: Ethics, Politics, and Fieldwork in Anthropology* (Berghahn Books, 2008).

Sally McNamee

Sally McNamee is Assistant Professor in the Childhood and Social Institutions Program at King's University College, University of Western Ontario, Canada. She has been researching and teaching in the area of childhood since 1993. Her research interests include constructions of childhood, children and leisure and children in families.

Karen O'Reilly

Karen O'Reilly is Reader in Sociology at Loughborough University. She has a background in sociology and social anthropology and a keen interest in ethnographic methods. She is author of *The British on the Costa del Sol*, *Ethnographic Methods* and *Key Concepts in Ethnography*, and numerous journal articles in the fields of tourism and migration. Her research in Spain has spanned nearly 15 years and includes long-term ethnographic fieldwork, qualitative interviews with groups and individuals, as well as survey methods.

Sarab Abu-Rabia Quedar

Sarab Abu-Rabia Quedar has a PhD in Social Anthropology. She was the first Bedouin woman to be awarded a PhD. She is a Lecturer on Bedouin Girls' Education, Tradition and Modernization in the Department of Man in Desert, Blaustein Institute for Desert Research, Ben Gurion University, Israel. In 2008 she was Visiting Fellow in International Gender Studies at Oxford University. She is the author of various books, articles and reviews.

Lucy Russell

Lucy Russell has a degree in Anthropology and Gender from Hull University. She was previously Policy Development Officer at YWCA England and Wales. She has worked with Gypsy travellers and young women in poverty programmes, designing policy and practice.

Julie Seymour

Julie Seymour is Senior Lecturer in Social Research at the University of Hull. Her research focuses on how adults and children 'do' and negotiate family life and discusses domestic labour, adult chronic illness and disability and children's roles in parenting practices. She is completing a book on family-run hotels which examines spatiality, work-life balance and children's emotional labour.

Nafisa Shah

Nafisa Shah completed her doctoral research at the Institute of Social and Cultural Anthropology and Wolfson College, Oxford in 2010. Her field research is on honour-based violence in Upper Sindh, Pakistan. She served a term as a Mayor in her rural home district in Sindh and is presently a member of the National Assembly of Pakistan. Nafisa has worked with development of local communities and is an active member of rights-based movements in Pakistan. She was one of the 1,000 Peace Women of the world nominated for the Nobel Peace award, and was on the roll of Young Global Leaders of the World Economic Forum. She heads the National Commission for Human Development, a social sector organization working on literacy and universal primary education in Pakistan.

Jacqueline Waldren

Jacqueline Waldren, D.Phil (Oxon), is Research Associate, Lecturer and Tutor in the Department of Social and Cultural Anthropology, the Centre for International Gender Studies and a member of Linacre College, University of Oxford. Her research on Europe includes identity, gender, migration, tourism and lifestyle changes. Her publications include *Insiders and Outsiders, Tourists and Tourism, Anthropological Perspectives on Local Development* and many articles. She edits the series New Directions in Anthroplology for Berghahn Books and is Director of DAMARC, Deia Archaeological and Anthropological Museum and Research Centre, Mallorca, Spain.

Index

abortion, 149–50, 163
Abu-Lughod, L., 36, 39, 40
Abu Rabia Quedar, 5, 6
abuse, 54
adolescence, 96
adoption, 3, 12, 14
adult-child dynamics, 4, 5, 9, 13
adultery, 32n9
advocacy, 35
Afghanistan, 20
Afro-American, 141, 144n18
age, 2, 31
agency, 19, 26, 31, 35, 80, 92, 95, 98, 99, 103
Ainu, 147, 150, 153
Aitken, S., 96, 99
Alanen, L., 93, 99
Aledo, A.T., 114
Amnesty International, 165n17
ancestry, 147
  Chinese, 151
  Japanese, 158
  Korean, 163n6
Angelman Syndrome, 84–86, 88
Ann Sullivan School, 87
apprenticeships, 60, 62
Archer, L., 65, 68
Arhem, K., 10, 165n16
Arnstein, A., 61

Arutiuvnov, S., 168
authenticity, 115
autoethnography, 12, 147, 151, 162
autonomy, 99
Awlad Ali Bedouin tribe, 40

Backhans, M., 68
Bainham, A., 94
Balearic Islands, 136
Barth, F., 32n8, 114
Bastos, J., 15, 169
Bateson, M.C., 170, 178
Bauman, Z., 146, 162, 163n1, 165n14
Bedouins, 6
  ethnic minority in Israel, 48
Beck, V., 61, 62
Belen, E., 38
Bellamy, K., 60
Ben-David, J., 37
Berg, B.L., 41
Berger, L., 147, 166
Berkovitch, N., 40
birth, 137, 139, 146, 149
  birthright, 153, 157, 159
  stigma, 83, 151
Bochner, A.P., 147
body language, 130
Bonanni, P., 90
Bose, C., 38

boundaries
  child-adult, 31n2
  role of, 97
  within deprived communities, 80
Bourdieu, P., 13n7, 70, 75, 113, (see also
  habitus)
Boyden, J., 12
Bradley, K., 40
Bradshaw, J., 54
Brannen, J., 103
Breger, R., 134
Brettell, C., 127, 143n2
bride price, 25
British administrators, 32n6
British migrants,
  in Japan, 170–78
  in Spain, 111, 115, 117
Broch-Due, V., 130
brothels, 138
Bruner, E., 147, 161
Brunton, G., 68
Bryceson, D., 13n8, 144n15, 145, 163n1,
  165n16, 168, 169
Brzezinski, Z., 165n16
Brzostowski, E., 165n16
Buckner, L., 58–61
bullying, 57, 118, 119, 121, 131, 155, 156,
  174
Burakumin, 150–51, 163n7, 174
Burchett, H., 68
bureaucracy, 146
Burr, R., 15, 145
Butler, B., 177

Calciano, M.A., 85
Callaway,H., 12, 127, 131, 168
Cameron, S., 60
carework, 55
Carrozzo, R., 90
Casado-Diaz, M.A., 115
Cassen, R., 54
Castilian, 128-29, 132-33, 143n2
Catholic Church, 126–27, 130, 163n5
  Vatican, 163n5
censorship, 177

Chan-Tiberghien, J., 149, 153, 158–60
Chiba, K., 165n17
children, 1
  adult representations, 2
  agents of social change, 80, 92
  autonomy, 7
  citizenship, 10
  cross-cultural understandings, 2
  definitions, 1, 3
  disadvantaged, 95
  empowered, 10
  ethnographic descriptions, 2, 42
  male, 22
  nuanced accounts, 92, 99, 104
  pediatric and pedagogical terms, 2
  rhetoric of, 101
  rural Bolivian, 96
  silence, 70
  social inclusion, 4
  stateless, 10
  structural and generational constraints,
    101
  television viewing, 95
  'us' and 'them' divisions, 70, 76, 78
  use of computer games, 93
  voices, 4, 9, 100–1
Children's Act 1989, 100
Children's Fund Partnerships, 70
Chinese, 131, 148, 151, 156, 173–74
choices, 1, 19, 27, 28, 30, 63
  freedom of, 65
Christensen, P., 93, 96, 99
citizenship, 10, 15, 146–48, 150, 152,
  157–60, 159, 160, 163n2, 163–64n9,
  164n10
  dual citizenship, 159
  Japanese, 157
  matrilineal, 162
  patrilineal, 162
  rights, 10, 146, 163n2
  Swedish, 147–48, 152
civil society, 146, 159, 165n15
classroom, 11, 41, 45, 87, 114, 131, 155,
  173–74
co-education, 6, 136

Cohen, G., 7
cognitive universe, 170
Costa del Sol, 111–14, 180
Coleman, S., 144, 145
colonialism, 1, 21
communism, 162
conflict, 173
Corker, M., 8
Corlin, C., 152, 163n8, 165n16
Cornwall, A., 6
Cummings, W.K., 174, 177
curriculum, 87, 114, 117, 121, 155–58,
    174–75

Dahinden, J., 15, 169
Dalgety, J., 65, 68
Dan, B., 84
Darian, L., 7
Davis, J., 100, 105
Davis, J.M., 8, 14
Dawson, E., 7, 8
Dayan, M., 37
Deakin, U., 62
Debito, A., 150, 153, 160, 163n2,
    163–64n9
deconstruction, 133
Department for Education and Skills, 59
Department for Innovation, Universities and
    Skills, 61
deportation, 153, 159
diplomats, 137–38, 168
disability, 7, 8, 32n3
discrimination, xi, 3, 10, 13, 48–49, 53, 60,
    71, 151, 156, 163n7
discourse, 21
    disposable income, 67
    dominant, 7
    government, 80
    lay discourse, 94
    moral, 94
    political, 35
disempowerment, 39
divorce, 9, 25, 28–29, 32, 140
    inter-cultural, 158
    reciprocal caring, 8

Dogodogo project, 4, 13n5
Douglas, M., 129
Dresch, P., 32, 167
Dyck, N., 141
Dziwisz, S., 163n5

Eckert, G., 95
economy
    market driven, 79
education, 2, 41
    co-education, 35, 46
    female only, 36, 46
    low achievement, 54
    opportunities, 47
    pluralism, 36
    separate facilities, 47
    yutori kyōiku (relaxed education), 175
Ellis, C., 147, 154, 162, 165n16
embodied knowledge, 12
empowerment, 73, 77, 93
Engelbrektsson, N., 163
entryism, 48
environmental justice movement, 38
Epstein, A.L., 135
Equal Opportunities Commission, 65
Eriksen, T.H., 114
Escott, K., 58–61
ethnicity, 9, 60
ethno-demographic changes, 158
Eurasian, 148–49, 161–64
    surnames, 149, 162, 164n13
European Network of Ombudspersons for
    Children (ENOC), 164n10
European Union (EU), 161, 164n10,
    164n13, 165n15
Every Child Matters, 72, 78, 100
exchange, 24
    marriages, 25
expatriates, 11, 117, 121, 128, 137, 139,
    161
exploitation, xi, 3, 7

family, 1–2, 6, 9, 20, 23–24, 27, 29,
    30, 39, 41–43, 46, 73, 77, 80n3, 86,
    93–105, 115–17, 123, 126–29, 135–41,

143nn4–5, 146–63, 164n13, 165n18, 170, 181
business, 97
court reports, 100
honour, 37
hospitality, 97
law, 32n12
perceptions of, 101
Family Resources Survey, 54–58, 71
farming, 21, 24
Fechter, A.M., 117
Feldman, E.J., 41
Fenster, T., 36, 39, 40, 48
Fernández-Mayoralas, G., 125
Fernandez-Rufete, J., 124
fieldwork, 1, 5, 8, 12, 20, 25, 31n1, 70, 124n1, 127, 153, 160, 162, 164–65n14, 170–78
Fletcher, A., 68
Floro, M.S., 56
Flowers, B., 32n4
Foucault, M., 98, 133
discourse, 133
heterotopia, 98
utopia, 98
Francis, B. et al., 65
Franco regime, 126–28, 130, 133, 136
Fuller, A. et al., 62

Gamarudi, S., 3
Gammeltoft, T.M., 8
Garcia Jimenez, M., 124
Garret, D.H., 165n16
gender, xi, 4, 10, 19, 21, 22, 30, 32n3, 35–38, 40, 48, 57–67, 101, 103
division of labour, 58
Human Rights, 159
pay gap, 58, 60, 62
sensitivity, 40, 48
separation, 37
specific punishment, 101
stereotypes, 59, 64
violence, 6
Geoffroy, C., 125
geographies of childhood, 96

Giddens, A., 36, 112
Giedroyc, M.T., 13n5
Gillies, M., 92
Ginsburg, F., 8, 84
globalization, 1, 4, 13, 146, 154, 163n1
Gois, P., 15, 169
Goodman, R., ix, 10–11, 141, 147, 151, 158, 162, 165nn14,16, 174
gossip, 42–43, 46
Graham, H., 127
Graves, L., 126, 129, 132–34
Graves, R., 126
Gripman, M., 147, 165
Guerrini, R., 84
Guiri, 119
Gypsies (Roma), 120–21, 147, 167, 181

habitus, 12, 80, 113–14, 117–23
Hall, C.M., 32n3, 116, 125
Hannerz, U., 162, 165nn14,16
Harden, A., 65
Harriss-White, B., ix
Hatoyama, Y., 165n17
headscarf, 41
Heesterman, W., 97
Helie-Lucas, M., 48
Hendry, J., 165n16, 167
Heinonen, P., ix
Henricson, C., 94
Hill, M., 100
Hill, R., 134
hypermotoric behavior, 84
Hockey, J., 9
Hokkaido, 153
Holloman, R.E., 168
honour, xi, 5–6, 11, 18–23, 28–35, 40–41, 43–46, 49, 52, 54–60, 89, 101, 136, 148, 160, 181, 193
anthropology of, 32n7
Bedouin, 35–44
Israel, 6
killings, 6
Pakistan, 6
Pukhtunwali, 32n8
Hood, S., 95, 105

Horne, M., 147, 150, 153
Hos, R., 37
Howell, S., xii, 12, 138, 163n1, 164n13, 165n16
Huber, A., 114
Hughes, B., 93
Human Development Report, 36, 50
Hutchby, I., 99

identity, xi, 2, 7, 10, 11, 14, 19–21, 94, 120,
    126–28, 133–44, 146–48, 153, 155,
    157–58, 161–63, 180, 194
Ilkkaracan, P., 36
illegal aliens, 153–54
immigrant, 10, 112, 124, 152–54, 158,
    163n3, 164n10
income support, 54
inequalities, 7, 10, 65
integration, 87, 112, 114, 124, 134, 143,
    160, 164n10
Internet, 4–5, 13n5, 116, 140, 161, 164n10
Iran, 32n4
Islam, 21

Jaffee, D., 144n14
Jakubowska, L., 39
James, A., 3, 4, 9, 12, 93, 97
Japanese
    educational philosophy, 176
    Embassy, 150–53
    examination system, 173
    Immigration Authority, 154
    Japanese-Koreans, 147, 174
    Ministry of Education, 153
    Ministry of Justice, 154, 158, 163n2
    Nationality Laws, 163–64n9
    Neighbourhood Associations, 160
    Parliament (Diet), 162
    Prime Minister's Report, 159
Jenks, C., 93, 100
Jensen, A., 99, 103
Johnson, V., 64
Jones, O., 96
Joseph Rowntree Foundation, 94, 95
Joshi, H., 59

Kaminski, I.M., 10, 11
Kandiyoti, D., 36
Katz, C., 9, 92, 93, 95
Katz, Y., 37
Keith, M., 96
Kelley, P., 95, 96
Kenan, A., 37
Kertzer, D., 144
Kibbutz, 138
kindergarten, 153, 155, 177
King, R., 114
Kingdon, G., 54
Knutsson, J., 13n6
Kohn, T., 144, 145
Komulainen, S., 3
Kosaka, M., 177
koseki register, 150–51, 163n6
Kressel, G.M., 37
Kyoto, 170, 173–76, 177n1
Kurian, P., 38

Labanyi, J., 127
Laerke, A., 7, 8, 31–32n2
Lalande, M., 85
Landsman, G., 85
Lange, A., 147
Langholtz, H.J., 168
languages, 3, 11, 20, 36, 41, 84–85,
    111–12, 114, 118, 121, 128, 131–37,
    141–44, 155, 157, 161, 164
    Castillian, 128–29, 132–33, 143nn2,6
    Catalan, 128–29, 131–33, 135–37, 140
    multi-lingual, 132, 154–55, 157
    bi-lingual, 131, 135
LeVine, R.A., 31n2
Levison, D., xi
Levitas, R., 71, 79
lifepaths, 30, 32n4
lifestyles, 1, 11, 130, 139–40, 192
liminal space, 123
Lindisfarne, N., 165n15
Lucas, R., 60

MacCannell, D., 115
MacClancy, J., 12

Mach, Z., 163n3, 165n16
MacLeod, D., 145
McNamee, S., 7, 9
Madge, N., 94, 95, 100
Mallorca, 11, 113–14, 127, 137, 139, 143n1
marginalization, 38, 47, 114, 118, 123
marriage, xi, 3, 5, 19, 21–26, 28–32, 38, 41, 46, 94, 127, 146, 151, 160, 161
    as protection, 46
    civil, 32n12
    cross-cultural, 146, 150, 152, 158
    disputes, 20
    divorce, 92, 99
    intermarriage, 21
    mixed, 134, 138
    of love, 22
    partnership, 94
    puberty and, 38
    separation, 92
    sex before, 32n9
    transactions, 23
Maruyama, M., 152, 165n16
Mayall, B., 93, 95, 99
Mayhew, E., 13n1, 54
Mead, M., 1, 2, 31n2, 170, 178
mediation, 21, 27
McDonough, C., 12
McKee, L., 99, 103
Meir, A., 38, 39
Meji Restoration Act, 163n7
men, 5–7, 19, 23–32, 38, 41, 43, 47, 54–56, 58–61, 89, 127, 138, 140–41, 143
    careers and occupations, 59
    permission to interview wives and daughters, 40
methodology, 31, 40, 147, 153, 161, 165
    focus groups, 70, 76
    interviews, 40–41
    participant observation, 70
    qualitative research, 41
    research agenda, 93
Michalopoulou-Veikou, C., 134
Millennium Cohort survey, 54

Milton Keynes Children's Fund, 70
Mitterauer, M., xii, 2, 3
mobile phones, 119, 140
mobility, vi, 4, 10–11, 19–20, 26, 40, 109, 112
modernization, 6, 35–41, 43, 45, 47, 49, 163, 181
    of space, planning and employment, 38
    Western impact, 36
Moghadam, V., 35
Moloney, J., 55, 67n9
Montandon, C., 96
Montgomery, H., 1, 3, 4, 9, 10, 32n3
Moran Ellis, J., 99
'More Choices, More Chances', 67n11
Morgan, D.H.J., 94
Morton, R., 165n16
mothers, 5, 7, 11, 22–25, 27, 31, 40–46, 54, 56, 65, 69, 74, 79, 90, 120, 128, 131, 138, 173, 179
    mothers in-law, 22
    single, 7, 79
    teenage, 54
    working, 8
multiculturalism, 1, 111, 132–34, 138–39, 142–43, 147, 150, 155–59, 161–64, 164n10, 165n15
Munson, E., 38, 48
Murphy-Shigematsu, S., 151, 156, 158, 160, 165n15
muted groups, 32n3, 100

Nakamaki, H., 177n1
nationality, 147–49, 148, 150, 152–53, 159, 160, 163n2, 163–64n9
Neale, J., 80n2
Nelson, J., 69
neurogenetic disorder, 84
Neville, G.K., 135
nomadic pastoralists, 24

Oakley, A., 32n3, 68
O'Brien, M., 103
O'Donnell, L., 69
OECD, 173

Okely, J., 12, 127, 131, 155, 165n16, 168
Okinawa, 147, 150, 155, 167, 180
Oliver, M., 8, 83, 85, 88, 90
oppression
   institutionalized, 39
   sentimental, 74
O'Reilly, K., 10–12, 138, 144n13
Osaka, 153, 160, 170–73, 177n1
Osgood, J., 65, 68
overseas students, 154–58, 174
Ozbay, F., 38

Pahl, J., 55, 58
Paidar, P., 36
Pakistan Muslim Family Law Ordinance
   1961, 32n12
Pantazis, C.D., 54
parenting, vi, xi, 4, 8–9, 11, 92, 126,
   129–30, 141–42, 146, 153–54, 157–59,
   172, 181
   children's role in, 95
   gone wrong, 92
   income generators, 101
   practices, 9, 92–100
Parham, K., 13n5
Parkin, D., 14, 167
Peach, C., 167
Percy-Smith, B., 64
personhood, 8, 84, 89, 126, 164n13
Peru, 86–88, 111
physical disabilities, 174
Pile, S., 96
Platt, L., 60
Poland
   Foreign Ministry, 163n3
   national dress, 149
police, 20–21, 26, 28–29, 80, 153–55, 160
policies, 3, 4, 7, 9, 13
policy intervention, 9, 92
political violence, 143n5
pollution, 129, 150, 152
postmodern, 35–36, 48
poverty, 7, 8, 53, 56, 75–77, 79–82, 107,
   124, 179, 181
   as activity or process, 80

   as collective problem, 80
   notions of, 71
   trap, 53
Poverty and Social Exclusion Survey, 54
Powel, B., 164–65n14
power, 2, 4, 6–7, 9–10, 12–14, 20–21, 23,
   27, 31–32, 36, 50, 60, 79–82, 92–93,
   96, 106, 133, 160, 164
   differentials, 92
   dynamics, 93, 99
   feeling powerless, 53
   indirect, 21
   social, 3, 9
   state, 21
pregnancy, 77
prejudice, 66, 73, 121, 123, 150
purity, 23, 129, 150, 163
Prout, A., 12, 31n2, 103
Punch, S., 96, 97, 99

quality of life, 53
Quran, 21

racial abuse, 118
Rahat, Israel, 37
Rapp, R., 8, 84
reflexivity, 12
relationships, xii, 6, 9, 11, 22, 27, 40, 68,
   92, 99, 125, 133–34, 143
   forbidden, 6, 47
   hierarchal, 40
   intergenerational, 96
   non-western, 6
   political, 12
   romantic, 6, 43–47
religion, ii, 3–4, 9, 21
reports, 27, 69, 70, 73, 80n1, 92, 94, 151,
   165, 169
   Every Parent Matters, 92
   Joseph Rowntree, 94
   Supporting Parents, 92
Ridge, T., 56, 57, 73
rights, 3–4, 7, 9–10, 13, 13n3, 22–23, 28–
   30, 37–38, 49, 88, 105, 151, 159–60,
   164–65, 181

civil, 38
education, 88
human, 3, 9, 13n3, 29
inheritance, 38
international, 38
residence, 151
UNCRC, 3
Rinaldi, R., 90
rituals, 130, 135, 157
Robertson, J., 164–65n14, 165n16
Rodriguez, V.G., 114
Rojo, F., 125
roles, xii, 1–6, 9, 11, 19, 22–23, 26, 31–32,
    39, 49, 94, 97, 113, 126–27, 142, 153,
    157
    gender, 142
    models, 65
    parental, 5
    redefined, 1
    social, 2
Ritchie, C., 94
Rosen, L., 21
Rosvall, J., 162
Rudie, I., 130
rumour, 42–45
runaway girls, 19, 27, 29–30, 32n4
Russell, L., 7

safety, 67, 94, 107, 172
Sardar Sarovar Project, 39
Scheper-Hughes, N., 2, 8, 84
school, vii, 2–3, 6, 11–12, 35, 37–38,
    40–49, 56–57, 64–65, 69, 75–77,
    87–88, 157, 161, 173
    as a dangerous place, 45
    attitudes toward, 37
    boarding, 116, 138, 144
    dropout rates, 37, 42
    homework, 11, 44,101–02, 127,
        131,144n17
    international, 12, 113, 138
    nurseries, 170
    rural and urban, 101, 104
Scott, S., 97
segregation, 59, 63–64, 112

gender, 64
    occupational, 59, 63
    educational, 112
Sekharen, S., 60
settlements,
    Bedouin, 37, 40, 48
    Egypt, 48
    Jordan, 48
    Saudi Arabia, 48
sex-separation, 35
sexual transgression, 32n9
sexuality, 38, 50, 57
Seymour, J., 7, 9
shame, 33, 34, 37, 42, 50, 57, 74
Shah, N., 5, 6
Shweder, R.A., 1, 3
Sibley, R., 125
Sims, D., 69
social
    actors, 19, 30, 95
    change, 35
    control, 77
    dynamics, 3, 9
    exclusion, 54, 70–89, 91–103, 114
    family breakdown, 77
    networks, 65
    policy rhetoric, 72
socialization, 170
Solberg, A., 95, 96
Son-rise Autism Treatment Centre, 85
space, xi, 6, 20, 27, 31, 38–39, 44, 47–50,
    72–73, 83, 96–98, 112, 114, 123,
    133–34, 138, 158–59
    cultural construction of, 39
    forbidden and permitted, 40
    imaginary, 98
    modern, 44
    of betweenness, 9, 92,95–96, 98, 102–03
    public, 22, 97
    separate but equal, 48
    virtual via computers, 98
Spain, 4, 10–13, 38, 111–18, 120–24, 126,
    136, 142, 180
Spanish Civil War, 129
Spielhofer, T. et al., 62, 63

statelessness,146–47, 152
Staudt, K., 47
Steedman, C., 74
Stones, R., 112–13
Stout, C.E., 168
strategies, 4–6, 9, 56–57, 67n11, 92, 95–97, 107
  verbal, 96
street survivors, 13n5
structuration theory, 112
superdiversity, 111–12, 124–25

Takarazuka Music Theatre, 161, 164n13, 164–65n14
Takenaka, A., 167
targeted universalism, 72, 78
time, xi, 3, 10, 22, 24–25, 28, 30–31, 37, 39, 45, 56, 59–60, 67, 70, 72, 74, 76–77, 79–80, 83, 88–89, 93, 95–103, 111, 113–14, 116, 118, 131, 133, 135–43, 148, 150, 152–53, 155, 156, 164, 170–71, 173–74, 176
  controlled by parents, 101
Timera, M., 135
Tisdall, K., 100, 105
Towersey Folk Festival, vii, 83, 85, 89
technology, xii, 1, 4, 98
Thompson, E.P., 74
Toren, C., 3, 31n2
tradition, 5–6, 26, 35, 38, 41, 47–48, 94, 103
trafficking of girls, 24
transnational,
  children, 11, 146
  families, 162, 163n1
  identity, 155, 161
  migrants, 116
transnationalism, 1, 14n8, 112, 146, 163n1
tsukiai (group exclusivity), 175
Turner, V., 14, 166

Ullman, A., 62
United Nations Convention on the Rights of the Child, 3, 100, 164n10
United Nations Development Program, 36

Unwin, L., 67, 68
urban proletariat, 37
Valentine, G., 95, 97
vengeance, 32n8
Vertovec, S., 111, 112
victims, 3, 6, 22, 40, 47, 54, 75, 160
violence, 3, 6, 9–10, 20, 22, 29, 31, 143, 181
Vuorela, U., 13n8, 144n15, 145, 163n1, 165n16, 166

Wacquant, L., 113
Waldren, J., 1, 10–11, 113–15, 119, 164n12
Warnes, A.M., 124
Webber, J., 157, 164n11, 166, 168
welfare, 11, 71, 170
Westin, C., 1, 147, 149, 152, 154–55, 163n1, 164n12, 165n14
White, P., 167
Williams, A.M., 116, 124–25
Williams, H., 74
Williams, J., 68
Willis, D.B., 151, 160, 167–69
Willis, P.E., 74
Willmott, N., 95
Wolfenstein, M., 1
WOMAD festival, vii, 84
women, 22–23
  and careers, 59
  as carers, 56, 58
  as passive victims, 47
  community groups, 56
  dependent, 55
  disadvantaged, 58, 71
  domestic sphere, 37
  emancipation, 36
  from ethnic minorities, 55
  local feminine codes, 40
  managing debt, 55
  modesty, 48
  problems, 56
  status, 35
Women and Work Commission, 59
Women's Budget Group, 56

Wong, D., 165n16, 167
Woodhead, M., 15, 145

youth, 1, 4, 32, 53, 92, 173
    anti-social behaviour, 77
    Black and minority ethnic, 61
    careers advice and guidance, 63
    crime, 77, 92, 141

employment, 79
mentors, 66
occupational segregation, 63
sexism, 66
Western perspectives, 3
work experience, 65
voices, 66–67